THE RUSSIAN EMPIRE
AND GRAND DUCHY OF MUSCOVY

ESTAT
DE L'EMPIRE
DE RVSSIE ET GRAN-
de Duché de Moscouie.

AVEC

*Ce qui s'y est passé de plus memorable & Tragi-
que, pendant le regne de quatre Empereurs : à
sçauoir depuis l'an 1590. iusques en l'an 1606.
en Septembre.*

Par le Capitaine MARGERET.

A PARIS,

Chez MATHIEV GVILLEMOT, marchant
Libraire au Palais, à la gallerie par où on va
à la Chancellerie.

M. D. C. VII.

Auec priuilege du Roy.

JACQUES MARGERET

THE

RUSSIAN EMPIRE

AND

Grand Duchy of Muscovy

A 17th-Century French Account

Translated and Edited by
Chester S. L. Dunning

UNIVERSITY OF PITTSBURGH PRESS

SERIES IN RUSSIAN AND EAST EUROPEAN STUDIES NO. 5

Published by the University of Pittsburgh Press, Pittsburgh, Pa. 15260
Copyright © 1983, University of Pittsburgh Press
All rights reserved
Feffer and Simons, Inc., London
Manufactured in the United States of America

Library of Congress Cataloging in Publication Data
Margeret, Jacques, ca. 1565
The Russian Empire and Grand Duchy of Muscovy.
Translation of: Estat de l'Empire de Russie et Grande Duche de Muscovie.
1. Soviet Union — History — 1533-1613. 2 Soviet
Union — Social life and customs — 1533-1917. 3 Margeret,
Jacques, ca. 1565. I. Dunning, Chester S.L.,
1949- . II. Title.
DK111.M313   1983   947'.04   82-20126
ISBN 0-8229-3805-7

Frontispiece: Title page from the original edition. Courtesy of the University
Libraries, University of Minnesota.

The preparation of this volume was made possible in part by a grant from the Translations Program of the National Endowment for the Humanities, an independent federal agency.

CONTENTS

ACKNOWLEDGMENTS

IN the eight years since I started this translation project as a doctoral dissertation at Boston College, I have received help from many friends and colleagues. I am especially indebted to L. Scott Van Doren for his assistance in producing an accurate and readable translation. Edward L. Keenan and Robert O. Crummey read early versions of the manuscript and offered valuable suggestions about the introduction and annotation. Catherine Marshall, Managing Editor of University of Pittsburgh Press, also suggested many useful changes in the final draft. Other individuals who offered valuable assistance in one way or another include Raymond T. McNally, Samuel J. Miller, Eric H. Deudon, Michal Barszap, Carol Castelou, Helen Mills, Harold Larson, J. G. Bell, and Zoltan Kosztolnyik.

Completion of this project was made possible in part by a grant from the Division of Research Programs of the National Endowment for the Humanities. Small grants from Texas A&M University and Pembroke State University (North Carolina) facilitated my research at crucial points. I am also indebted to the helpful staff of Houghton Library, Harvard University; Wilson Graduate Library, University of North Carolina, Chapel Hill; the British Library; Bibliothèque Nationale; M. E. Saltykov-Shchedrin State Public Library, Leningrad; and the Interlibrary Services Division at Texas A&M University.

The University of Wisconsin Press kindly granted permission to adapt the map of sixteenth-century Russia originally published in *Rude and Barbarous Kingdom,* ed. Lloyd E. Berry and Robert O. Crummey.

Carole Knapp, Mary Watson, and Donna Chase typed various versions of the manuscript for me. Rosa Richardson typed dozens of letters related to the project. Finally, Elsie Kersten proofread various sections of the manuscript, offered useful suggestions on readability, and graciously put up with Jacques and me for several years.

INTRODUCTION

MUSCOVITE Russia by the end of the sixteenth century had become one of the most extensive realms in Christendom, governed by one of Europe's few absolute monarchs. Yet for all the power and ambition of its rulers, that vast state was still relatively isolated from and unknown to most Europeans. Even though Tsar Ivan IV (r. 1547–84) had established significant commercial contacts with Western Europe, his unsuccessful Livonian War (1558–83), fought against Poland-Lithuania and Sweden, ended with Muscovy temporarily excluded from playing a major role in European affairs. Suffering from the cumulative effects of the "terrible" tsar's foreign and domestic policies, Russia itself was also exhausted by the time of Ivan's death. The state recovered somewhat during the reign of his simple-minded son Fedor, when the new tsar's brother-in-law, Boris Godunov, governed capably as regent. However, when Fedor died without an heir in 1598, the seven-hundred-year-old ruling dynasty of Russia came to an end. Boris became tsar and ruled wisely for several more years, but the combined shock waves of the extinction of the dynasty, the almost simultaneous enserfment of the Russian peasants, and the continuing conflicts among the Muscovite lords left over from the period of Ivan's reign ushered in a catastrophic decade for Russia known to history as the Time of Troubles. This period was characterized by political unrest, famine, social upheaval, economic disruption, and foreign intervention. For a time many doubted that Russia would even survive as an independent state. The Time of Troubles finally ended with the founding of a new ruling dynasty by Mikhail Romanov in 1613, but for several years the tragic events occurring in Muscovy were widely and colorfully reported throughout Europe, stimulating an already awakening interest in that strange and distant land.

When the first printed French account of Russia, Jacques Margeret's *Estat de l'Empire de Russie et Grand Duché de Moscovie*, was published by command of King Henri IV in 1607, it became an immediate success. In Europe's Age of Discovery, Captain Margeret's carefully prepared little book greatly helped the French to "rediscover" Russia.[1] In many ways Margeret was uniquely qualified for this task. He was one of the first of his countrymen ever to travel to Russia and to learn to speak and read Russian. He lived in Muscovy for over six years, held high positions in the Muscovite military, and came to know the country and its leaders very well. Although not a professional writer, he produced a fascinating and readable account of what he saw and heard while in Russian service. His book became a minor classic and was unsurpassed by any other French study of Russia until the era of Peter the Great.[2] It later became one of the very first foreign accounts to be translated into Russian and to be used extensively by Russian historians.[3] For the past two centuries scholars have generally acknowledged Margeret's book to be an extremely valuable and accurate source for early modern Russian history.[4]

The earliest recorded contact between France and Russia dates from the mid-eleventh century, when Henri I married the daughter of Iaroslav the Wise, Grand Prince of Kiev. Although there were some indirect commercial contacts as well, and numerous references to Russia and the Russians in French literature, medieval Franco-Russian relations failed to develop any further.[5]

For many reasons, contact with and knowledge about Russia declined in Western Europe so precipitously that by the fourteenth century, if a Frenchman thought at all about that part of the world, he thought about legendary "Tartary," or Scythia, a land filled with savage horsemen and fabulous beasts. It was not until the Russians freed themselves from Mongol domination in the fifteenth century that significant contact between Russia and much of Europe was restored. Toward the end of the fifteenth century, Grand Prince Ivan III of Moscow tried to reopen direct communications with Western European merchants and governments, but in this he was only partially successful. Russia's isolation from Western Europe was finally and decisively shattered only in the 1550s — first, by the English discovery of the White Sea trade route, and second, by the Russian capture of the East Baltic port of Narva during the Livonian War. By the 1560s many Western Europeans knew about Muscovy, and a large number were engaged in direct trade with that country.

French interest in Russia developed quickly. The adventurer Hans Schlitte, seeking to supply Ivan IV with European artisans and technicians, was welcomed to Paris by Henri II in 1555.[6] Livonian nobles sought an alliance with the French king in 1558, hoping for a French military expedition to preserve Livonia from the advancing Russians.[7] French merchants, on the other hand, took advantage of the invasion of Livonia, and during the 1560s they carried on a vigorous trade directly with the Russians at Narva. The Baltic port offered a good outlet for French merchandise, but imported Russian products were never considered vital to the French nation.[8] The French government was therefore free to engage in Baltic politics. The dream of a French protectorate over Livonia, and presumably French dominance in the lucrative Russian market, was one of the motivations for the successful French proposal that the brother of Charles IX of France be elected

RUSSIA AT THE END OF THE SIXTEENTH CENTURY

king of Poland in 1574.[9] Almost immediately, however, the new king left Poland to ascend the French throne as Henri III. He did not lose interest in Russia, though, even after French designs on Livonia were decisively checked by Swedish and Polish victories over the Russians, including the Swedish capture of Narva in 1581. Searching for an alternate trade route, Henri asked Tsar Fedor about the possibility of the French joining in the White Sea trade. Fedor responded by sending an envoy to France in 1585 to discuss commercial relations.[10] A French embassy went to Moscow in 1586, and in that same year French vessels sailed for the first time to the White Sea.[11] A French company was granted a guarantee of privileges by the Russians in 1587.[12] By the end of the sixteenth century a few French merchants had settled in Moscow where, though they never seriously rivaled their Dutch and English competitors, they made a good profit and had a chance to learn some Russian.[13]

Russia offered adventure as well as trade; along with the merchants came many French mercenary soldiers who served in Russia during its Time of Troubles.[14] The greatest of these French soldiers, as well as one of the first to enter Muscovite service, was Captain Jacques Margeret. Margeret, who came from the county of Auxonne (on the border between Burgundy and Franche-Comté), was a scion of a successful bourgeois family. The first known reference to the Margerets is found in Burgundian records of 1478.[15] By the 1560s the merchant Pierre Margeret was prospering;[16] and by 1571 Chrétien Margeret, who may have been Jacques' older brother or his cousin, was appointed counselor to the *Chambre des Comptes* of Dijon (the sovereign court of accounts for Burgundy), a position which gave him noble status for life. Within several years the Margerets also intermarried with the Bossuets, another respectable Burgundian family which later acquired great fame.[17]

Jacques was probably born in the 1560s.[18] He may have been trained in finance and trade as a youth, but he also learned something of the profession of arms, which was to be his main occupation for more than twenty years. He spoke, read, and wrote French and German fluently and may also have studied some Latin. His awareness of classical literature, the Bible, and the ideas of such giants of the French Renaissance as Montaigne and Jean Bodin suggests that he was a fairly well educated man.[19] The several positions of authority and trust which he held during his life also testify to his intelligence, initiative, and leadership.

Although Russian and Soviet historians have always assumed that Margeret was a Catholic, he was in fact almost certainly a Huguenot, and this undoubtedly influenced his interpretation of Russia.[20] In the later stages of the French Wars of Religion, Margeret and his family fought valiantly for the Protestant King Henri IV. The Catholic League sought revenge against the Margerets by arresting some members of the family and by confiscating Chrétien Margeret's house in Dijon.[21] For his part, Chrétien became deeply involved in successful efforts to obtain loans from the Swiss to support Henri's military operations.[22] In the meantime, royalist headquarters in Burgundy were set up in the strategically located town of Saint-Jean-de-Losne. One of the fifty men of arms chosen to form the mainstay of the town's defense was Jacques Margeret.[23] Despite repeated efforts to capture the town, the heroic defense by the royalists proved to be too difficult for the Catholic League to overcome. Jacques fought for the king elsewhere in Burgundy, and Chrétien Margeret continued to receive more and more responsibility from the king. For example, he was given authority to collect the salt tax (*gabelle*) over a wide area of the country, a task he performed successfully.[24]

When Henri converted to Catholicism in 1593, resistance to royal authority began to break down. The king's troops invaded

Burgundy in May 1595, and by July royalist officials were back in control in Dijon. There Chrétien Margeret resumed his official position which he retained until his death in 1617. By the end of 1595 the king was in control of most of France, and Jacques Margeret, finding no more use for his military skills in Henri's service, set out for employment abroad. It is important to remember that foreign military service was considered an honorable profession in the sixteenth century. In this Margeret fits a common pattern, and his story provides a good example of the transition from the condottiere of the sixteenth century to the leader of mercenary forces in the period of the Thirty Years' War.[25] Along with many French soldiers, Margeret joined the crusade against the Ottoman Turks then being waged in southeastern Europe.[26] He served first Prince Sigismund Bathory of Transylvania (r. 1581-1601) and then the Holy Roman Emperor Rudolph II (r. 1576-1612) in Hungary.[27] Next, Margeret appeared in Poland, where he was given command of a company of foot soldiers. The king of Poland at this time was Sigismund III Vasa (r. 1587-1632), a fanatic Catholic who was more interested in trying to regain the Swedish throne than in fighting the Turks. When Sigismund launched his unsuccessful invasion of Lutheran Sweden in 1598, Margeret was understandably not interested in participating. He soon left Poland for Germany— possibly even returning to Austrian territory, but apparently without reentering imperial service.[28]

In June 1599 the Russian ambassador Afanasii Vlas'ev was sent by Tsar Boris Godunov on an important mission to Emperor Rudolph. Vlas'ev was also on the lookout for talented foreigners who might serve the tsar. Somewhere en route to Prague, probably in one of the German or Czech towns through which he traveled, Vlas'ev met Margeret and persuaded him to enter Russian service. Margeret accompanied Vlas'ev to Moscow in 1600, and there he was well received by Boris.[29] Margeret's military experience, linguistic ability, and lively intelligence were quickly recognized by the Russians. He received command of a cavalry company, a *pomest'e* land grant of 700 *chetverti* (nearly a thousand acres), and an annual salary of eighty rubles.[30] Margeret served Boris with zeal for several years, rising to share overall command of the tsar's foreign troops, which numbered several thousand.[31] During this time Margeret learned to speak and to read Russian.[32]

While in Boris's service Margeret had the opportunity to observe many activities at court, in Moscow, and in the field. He was in the tsar's army which was sent to repel the pretender Dmitrii Ivanovich's invasion of Muscovy in 1604-05. Margeret's actions at the battle of Dobrynichi were decisive in the defeat of Dmitrii's forces, for which he received special thanks from Boris.[33] Soon after the death of Boris, however, the tsar's army submitted to the pretender Dmitrii. To their credit, the foreign mercenaries resisted this temptation and remained loyal to Boris's son Fedor. But when the Godunov government was overthrown and the citizens of Moscow also submitted to the pretender, the foreign mercenaries had little choice but to join the Russians in recognizing Dmitrii as tsar. Along with most of his companions, Margeret entered Dmitrii's service, retaining his position of leadership.[34] Perhaps in part because Dmitrii's career reminded him of King Henri's, Margeret was quite willing to serve the new tsar well. Dmitrii was very impressed with the French captain, and in January 1606 Margeret became the commander of the tsar's new elite palace guard. He enjoyed many privileges and the complete confidence of Dmitrii. Contemporaries of Margeret who were in Russia at this time had great respect for him as an intelligent, sober, and valiant soldier.[35] He may even have made some contribution to military reform in Muscovy.[36]

When Dmitrii was assassinated in May 1606, Margeret was sick and not on duty. This probably saved his life and may even have been a factor in the conspirators' decision to strike when they did.[37] The new tsar, Vasilii Shuiskii, asked the Frenchman to stay on in Russian service, which he did. Shuiskii's request was, of course, virtually a command; but the miserable plight of those foreign troops Shuiskii did dismiss at this time may also have influenced Margeret's decision to remain in Muscovy somewhat longer.[38] He actually detested Shuiskii, however, and took the first available opportunity to leave Russian service in good standing. By mid-summer he managed to secure the tsar's reluctant permission to return to France. Shuiskii gave him rich presents in recognition of his long and faithful service to Muscovy. Margeret left for France from Arkhangel'sk in September 1606. It has been claimed that he "abandoned" Russian service in 1606 because he saw the whole country rising in mutiny against the boiar-tsar Shuiskii.[39] This is simply not true. Margeret received permission to leave Muscovy at a time when Shuiskii was still confident that his forces could easily overcome any rebellion, and he actually departed from Arkhangel'sk before news of the scope of Bolotnikov's rebellion reached him.[40]

Once Margeret returned to France he immediately presented himself to his former master Henri IV. The king listened with pleasure to his stories about Russia and ordered him to write an account of that mysterious land for publication. Margeret completed work on his book during the winter of 1606–07 and then returned home.[41]

In the years following Tsar Dmitrii's death, rumors persisted throughout Europe that he had somehow miraculously escaped assassination in 1606. Margeret was undoubtedly interested in these rumors, which he had first heard in Moscow in the days immediately following Dmitrii's assassination.[42] Never completely convinced of Dmitrii's death (because he had not been an eyewitness), Margeret decided to return to Russia to find out for himself if the rumors were true. By 1609 he appeared at Tushino, the camp of a man who claimed to be Dmitrii. Margeret quickly discovered, however, that the second pretender was a complete fraud—merely a convenient tool of the forces which had gathered in opposition to Vasilii Shuiskii. Real power at Tushino rested in the hands of several Polish-Lithuanian lords and a few Muscovite dignitaries Margeret knew personally, including the boiar Mikhail Saltykov and Filaret Romanov. With no illusions about the identity of the second pretender, Margeret remained in Tushinite service. No doubt he was a welcome addition, as much for the propaganda value of having the captain of Dmitrii's palace guard in camp as for his military skills. Margeret probably received generous land grants from the second Dmitrii Ivanovich.[43]

When the second pretender's camp broke up at the end of 1609, Margeret and the Tushinite dignitaries were faced with the unenviable choice of either submitting to the hated Tsar Shuiskii or entering into negotiations with King Sigismund III of Poland, whose forces were then invading Muscovy. Not surprisingly, the Tushinites chose to negotiate with the Poles and offered to support Sigismund's son Władysław as tsar once Shuiskii was overthrown.[44] This pleased Sigismund very much. He treated the Tushinite dignitaries as honored allies and promised them that, as tsar, Władysław would protect the Russian Orthodox church. Sigismund even planned to use the Tushinites as a directing staff for Muscovite affairs. Although Margeret has been criticized by some writers for joining Polish service at this point, in truth there were very few options open to him. He soon distinguished himself at the decisive battle of Klushino (June 1610) and on the subsequent march on Moscow.[45] Vasilii Shuiskii was at this point hastily overthrown by the Romanovs and other Russian lords, who joined the Tushinites in pledging support for Władysław if that prince was willing to convert to Orthodoxy. Once the Polish commander agreed to this, the gates of Moscow were opened to the Polish army. Margeret remained in Moscow for about a year, serving as one of the commanders (as well as paymaster) of an elite group of mercenaries in the occupation force. During this period he worked closely with Saltykov and the pro-Władysław government.[46]

By the winter of 1610–11, many disparate groups gathered to oppose the pro-Władysław government; and by March 1611 the Poles in Moscow found themselves besieged by a native Russian army headed by Prince D. M. Pozharskii. Accounts of that confrontation vary widely, but there is no doubt that it was Captain Margeret's own personal bravery, cunning, and daring assaults on the Russian positions which saved the day for the disheartened and greatly outnumbered Poles. Prince Pozharskii was seriously wounded in the battle, and the Russian army was forced to retreat.[47] The Poles then burned the outskirts of Moscow, retired to the inner city, and held what was left of the capital for another year. Charges that Margeret was personally responsible for the burning of Moscow appear to be groundless.[48]

By summer 1611 Margeret became aware that Sigismund had no intention of allowing his son Władysław to become the Orthodox tsar of Russia, that instead the Catholic king planned to rule Muscovy himself. While Margeret could support Władysław as an Orthodox tsar, there can be little doubt that as a Huguenot he opposed the plan of the "Jesuit King" to subjugate Muscovy for the Counter-Reformation. Joining the next embassy headed for Poland, Margeret left Moscow in the fall of 1611, never to return. Charges that he once again "abandoned" Moscow, perceiving the hopelessness of the Polish position there, are completely false. Margeret's correspondence in this period makes it quite clear that he actually feared the Catholic Poles would prevail in Russia.[49] Another serious charge leveled against Margeret at this time was that he plundered the Kremlin treasury before his departure. This is a gross exaggeration. Although Margeret received a very high salary while in the service of the pro-Władysław government, he did not plunder the Kremlin treasury.[50]

Back in Poland, Margeret was warmly received by Sigismund, who offered him a place on the Polish royal council. There, plans for the complete conquest of Muscovy were being discussed.[51] Margeret had very different plans, however, and departed from Poland for Germany as soon as he was able to do so. In January 1612 he wrote from Hamburg to John Merrick, chief agent of the English Muscovy Company, expressing concern that the Russians would probably be overwhelmed by Sigismund's planned offensive that year unless they could obtain foreign troops to help them.[52] By this time Margeret was already deeply involved in efforts to raise troops in Germany for Russian service. Along with several others, he wrote to the insurgent Russian government of Prince Pozharskii requesting permission to serve against the Poles.[53] Pozharskii's negative reply, however, made it clear that Margeret was not trusted. According to Pozharskii, Margeret was undoubtedly still in Sigismund's service and planned some further treachery against Russia. Pozharskii immediately ordered the reinforcement of Arkhangel'sk in order to stop Margeret from reentering Russia or from seizing that vital port.[54] Pozharskii was wrong about Margeret's intentions, but who could blame him? While some historians have criticized Pozharskii for not employing the talented Frenchman, Margeret really did appear too compromised by this time. Pozharskii, and the Romanov government after him, continued to fear Margeret for many months. Arkhangel'sk was again put on the alert in 1613, and a search was made for phantom spies Margeret had supposedly sent to North Russia. Scathing denunciations of this "enemy of Russia" were also sent to the French and English governments.[55]

Despite the fears of the Muscovite government, Margeret never did plan to seize Arkhangel'sk. He was not acting as a double agent for the Polish government, as some writers have claimed, but was probably sincerely interested in aiding Muscovy.[56] Denied reentry into Russian service, Margeret eventually settled in Germany. By 1619 he was a close confidant and financial consultant of the Calvinist Lithuanian Prince Janusz VI Radziwiłł and the margraves of Brandenburg. He was also by then acting as an agent of the French government, keeping it informed about military affairs in Eastern Europe.[57] Details of Captain Margeret's death have been lost, but it is known that his family continued its rise in French service.[58] Jacques' great-nephew, Pierre Margeret, eventually became *grand audiencier* of France, sat on the royal council of Louis XIV, and (as the seigneur de Pontault) obtained permanent noble status for the family. Pierre's eldest son served his country for nearly forty years as a cavalry officer and rose to the rank of brigadier-general by 1719.[59] Another member of the family who was ennobled in the mid-seventeenth century, Sébastien de Pontault, became a famous military engineer in the service of Louis XIV and is generally regarded as the first French military topographer.[60]

When Margeret's *Estat de l'Empire de Russie* appeared in 1607, Muscovy was still, to most French people, just as much an exotic *terra incognita* as the New World. But interest in that strange country was growing.[61] During the sixteenth century, accounts of voyages of discovery and histories of faraway lands enjoyed great popularity in France, especially when those works were written in French. In fact, the European discovery of new lands had stimulated an impressive quantity of French literature. Before 1610 more than five hundred fifty works in French were published on Asia, Africa, and America. The reading public delighted in detailed descriptions of faraway countries, their monarchies, courts, administrations, societies, customs, religions, military strength, and treasures. While at first these accounts merely attempted to convey a more or less accurate picture of newly discovered kingdoms and empires, gradually French writers began comparing some "barbarous" and exotic countries with those of "civilized" Europe. They did not hesitate to praise the "barbarians" for their effective government, valor, virtue, and fortitude when it seemed appropriate.[62] These later works are noteworthy for their increasing realism and their accurate, detailed study of such key issues as religious tolerance and political organization. By the late sixteenth century the accumulation of a relatively large body of knowledge about far-off countries led many thoughtful French writers to reexamine some of the values and directions of European civilization. In fact, twentieth-century scholarship on the French Enlightenment has rather convincingly traced the origins of *l'esprit philosophique* or rationalism back to the sixteenth century and the influence of travel literature on French Renaissance writers. Exposure to the unity as well as the diversity of human societies encouraged the growth of a sense of cultural relativism, religious tolerance and a critical spirit.[63] Montaigne (1533–92) and Jean Bodin (1530–96) were deeply influenced by travel literature, and they in turn influenced the writing of many later French accounts of foreign lands, including that of Captain Margeret.

Rabelais (1494–1553) had urged the French to travel to new lands, but it was Montaigne who really popularized travel and the study of other societies as an effective means to broaden one's knowledge. By studying travel and geographical literature, he discovered to his satisfaction the essential unity of mankind, long hidden by superficial and exaggerated differences as well as by the ignorance of self-centered cultures unwilling to look beyond themselves.[64] Montaigne's works and ideas were very influential during the reign of Henri IV, and it is not surprising to find echoes of Montaigne in Captain Margeret's book. Margeret undoubtedly had Montaigne in mind when he proposed using the example of Muscovy to help broaden the knowledge of Frenchmen.[65]

One of the greatest political theorists of the French Renaissance was Jean Bodin, whose writings helped to lay the intellectual foundation of French absolutism. It is often forgotten that "absolutism" as a political theory came rather late to France. The idea of a "limited monarchy" was probably the dominant theory until the second half of the sixteenth century; and during the French Wars of Religion questions about absolute monarchy and the legitimate power of royal government were fiercely debated in France and elsewhere—some seeing absolute monarchy as the only solution, others calling it "tyranny." In his writings Bodin did much to enhance the reputation of royal absolutism. Before formulating his political theories, he informed himself about all ancient and modern governments and thus was familiar with the abundant travel literature of the day.[66] His popular and influential works were certainly known to Margeret, whose portrayal of Muscovite absolutism echoes Bodin's ideas.[67]

In analyzing the surge of geographical and historical literature which appeared during Henri IV's reign, one quickly discovers that the French were then primarily looking east. It is often forgotten, in light of later French colonial efforts in Canada, that at the beginning of the seventeenth century they were most interested in Turkey and East Asia—during the period 1598–1609 twice as many French works on Turkey were published as on the New World (works on East Asia and Tartary also outnumbered those on America).[68] Despite religious differences, the Turks were much admired in sixteenth-century France for their honesty, sobriety, discipline, religious tolerance, and effective government.[69] The desire to read about and learn from the Turks, which had long been strong in France, increased dramatically during the Hungarian War (1593–1606). Many Frenchmen served in that war, and many more wished to understand the strengths and weaknesses of the Ottoman Empire. Some books on Turkey were phenomenally popular.[70] Much of this *turcica* contained implied criticism of Christian Europe and, by providing a standard for the critical examination of European politics, society, and culture, contributed to the development of a sense of cultural relativism among French intellectuals.[71] Montaigne was especially interested in Turkish religious tolerance, and Bodin greatly admired Turkish absolutism; Henri IV was interested in both.[72] At the time, the little-known state of Muscovy appeared similar in many respects to "barbarous" Turkey. Although armed with very limited information, a few French writers before Margeret did not hesitate to use Russia, like Turkey, to provide examples to compare with European politics and society. In fact, there are a great many parallels between the *turcica* and *rossica* of late sixteenth-century European writers; and similar images of the Ottoman and Muscovite states, rulers, and societies pervade the works of Frenchmen like Bodin. As with the Turkish example, Muscovite absolutism and religious tolerance were positively portrayed by some French writers. Margeret's work provides a good example of this.[73]

Outside France, a completely negative impression of Muscovy—of its government and people—held sway.[74] To most educated Europeans of the late sixteenth century, "barbarous" and "tyrannical" Muscovy appeared to have little by way of example to offer to "civilized" westerners. It was not just the exotic and oriental appearance of Muscovy which inspired such judgments. Equally important was the rapid emergence of Muscovy into the affairs of Eastern Europe and the Baltic. The Livonian War, for example, was very widely regarded, even in Western Europe, as one of the most significant developments of the sixteenth century. Fears of the growth of Muscovy's power were often reflected in portrayals of the tsar as a bloodthirsty Asiatic tyrant, poised to trample "Christian" Europe. Descriptions of the Russian people were equally distorted by hostile European writers.[75]

Perhaps because France was not in any immediate danger from Russian expansion, French writers maintained a more detached and objective view. In spite of increasing French interest, however, before Margeret's book was published very little accurate information about Russia was available in France—where the image of "barbarous" Muscovy still prevailed in the popular mind.[76] This is evident even in the works of writers who admired the Russians. Rabelais, for example, had written about Muscovy, relying upon ancient sources and foreign accounts. For him the question of where Europe stopped and Asia began was of particular interest. He had a very healthy respect for the power of Muscovy and hesitated to place it in Asia; yet he considered the Muscovites to be more Asiatic than European, associating them with the "Tartars." Montaigne also referred to the Russians, occasionally associating them with the "Tartars" or even with the ancient Scythians.[77] Bodin, who displayed one of the liveliest interests in "barbarous" Muscovy among sixteenth-century French writers, consistently blurred the distinctions among Russians, "Tartars" and Scythians. He believed them all to be given to drunkenness, cruelty, and beastly table manners. Yet the "barbarous" Muscovites, like the Turks, were worthy of study. Bodin's theory that climate determined character (a precursor to Montesquieu's) complicated his view of the Russians. The Russians occupied the north, as had the "Tartars" and Scythians; therefore, the Russians were brave and warlike, capable of defeating the wiser but weaker Europeans of more moderate climes. Bodin was very impressed by the power of the Muscovite state and regarded the "Muscovite Duke" as one of the few absolute rulers of Europe.[78]

Russia was also of considerable interest to the greatest French historian of the age, Jacques-Auguste de Thou (1553–1617). De Thou, a president of the Parlement of Paris and one-time chief custodian of Henri IV's royal library, probably knew more about

Russia than anyone in France until Margeret returned in 1606. He was a meticulous scholar who consulted a large number of foreign sources before writing about the Russians in his popular *Universal History*. That work was published in Latin and went through four editions by the time Margeret's book appeared. Although his Muscovites had some of the same legendary characteristics found in the works of Bodin and other French writers, he did not equate Muscovy with "barbarous" Turkey. In general, his understanding of Russian history was sophisticated and accurate.[79] However, his work on the Russians had so far only covered the period up to 1584, and it was not based upon personal experience and observation. Constantly seeking new information, he personally interviewed the knowledgeable Captain Margeret when the latter returned from Muscovy.[80] De Thou was also in a good position to urge Henri to commission a book that would correct the many inaccurate popular and scholarly views of the Russians. Although interest in Russia was growing at court, many French officials were still badly misinformed or uninformed about that land. Even the king's chief minister, Sully, considered Muscovy at least as much a part of Asia as Europe and placed it in the same category of "barbarous" countries as Turkey.[81]

Henri IV was considerably better informed about Muscovy than was his chief minister. He had corresponded with the tsars about French merchants in Russia[82] and had received second and third-hand reports about Muscovy from merchants, diplomats, and other travelers. He took a particular interest in the career of Tsar Dmitrii Ivanovich. One of his most trusted ambassadors in Venice kept him up to date on Dmitrii's campaign to win the Muscovite throne and the great hopes the Jesuits had of using young Dmitrii to help unite huge Orthodox Muscovy to the Roman Catholic church.[83] Although Henri already knew about Dmitrii's death by the time Margeret arrived at court in 1606, he was very impressed by

Margeret's extensive first-hand knowledge of Muscovy. The king's great interest in Dmitrii (and the debate over Dmitrii's true identity) may well have been an important reason for commissioning Margeret's book, which focused upon Dmitrii and was far more accurate than any of the other available sources.[84] He may also have seen the benefits of publicizing another example of royal absolutism and a powerful European ruler who practised religious tolerance. And no doubt the king, as well as de Thou, wished to eliminate some of the common misconceptions about Russia.

One of the least understood of Henri's motives for having Margeret's book published concerns his *grand dessein* of organizing an anti-Turkish coalition of Christian powers. Henri first spoke of the project in 1607, at about the same time that Margeret's book appeared. Although nothing ever came of the project, the king did not give it up completely until 1609.[85] Historians, invariably relying upon Sully's rather unreliable account of the project which was written many years later, have assumed that Muscovy was never included in the king's plans.[86] Yet it is clear from Margeret's account that Henri regarded the huge Christian state of Muscovy as one of the "main bulwarks of Christianity" protecting Europe from Islam.[87] He also knew that the Russians themselves were considering an anti-Turkish coalition that would include the French.[88] Dmitrii had been especially attracted by the idea of a crusade against Turkey, and this was undoubtedly one of the reasons why his cause was championed by Jesuit leaders. Antonio Possevino had long dreamed of including Muscovy in such a crusade, and during Henri IV's reign he kept the French government informed about the prospects of pulling Muscovy into a powerful Christian alliance.[89] Henri's *grand dessein* may well have been influenced by such diplomatic maneuvering. In this context, Henri may have wished to make available to the French people an accurate, eyewitness account of Christian Muscovy, a potential ally against the Turks.[90]

Whatever his motives for ordering publication of Margeret's book, Henri deserves much credit for its appearance. Without the king's great curiosity about Muscovy, the restless Captain Margeret very likely would never have taken the time to write his account.[91] With the king's commission, however, he set out to prepare a description of Muscovy which would respond to nearly all the views about Russia then current in France. He probably read Jean Bodin's *Method for the Easy Comprehension of History* (or at least the popular fourth chapter, "The Choice of Historians"), for he attempted to write an objective account that followed the guidelines for good history laid down by Bodin and the Ancients (primarily Polybius).[92] Margeret fit exactly Bodin's description of a most reliable historian: one who spent a great part of his life holding important offices and in warfare, a man of experience who did not praise himself in his writings but who attempted instead to present an accurate account devoid of all emotion and partisanship. Margeret sought to present only the truth about Muscovy, unadorned by "heroics" or literary flourishes, so that the French reading public might discern the truth in his words and learn from it.[93] In this he was very successful. Although Margeret was not a professional writer, his considerable knowledge of Russia, as well as his intelligence, honesty, keenness of observation, and careful differentiation between fact and opinion, made his account a work of lasting value.[94] Not only has the book been used by many French scholars since the seventeenth century, but, as noted before, it became one of the very first foreign accounts to be translated into Russian and to be used extensively by Russian historians. Margeret's book has long been regarded as an extremely valuable source for the early history of the Time of Troubles, and today Soviet scholars still regard his work as a particularly important account of Muscovy on the eve of the First Peasant War (1606–07).

At this point it may be useful to survey briefly the most significant evidence contained in Margeret's book. First of all, Margeret's geographic description of Russia is fairly accurate and is quite advanced when compared to most European accounts written in the sixteenth and seventeenth centuries. He was one of the first European writers to have a clear concept of the precise location of Christian Muscovy and its unique role in protecting Europe from Asia and Islam. Margeret's understanding of Siberian geography was also fairly advanced, and he provided Western Europeans with one of the first descriptions of the geography, colonization, and cultivation of the steppe along the southern and eastern frontiers of Muscovy. The book also contained one of the very earliest and most accurate printed discussions of the differences between "White Russia" and "Black Russia." Margeret's description of Russian agriculture and agricultural prices has been helpful to historians, and his view of Muscovy as a prosperous country at the end of the sixteenth century is particularly interesting. His awareness of the various ethnic groups within the Russian empire is worthy of note, as is his discussion of religious tolerance in Muscovy. Margeret's account contains valuable information about the Muscovite state bureaucracy, the tsar's revenue, finances, and justice. He provides much unique information on daily life at the tsar's court and is an especially important source concerning military affairs.

Margeret was struck by the power and prestige of the tsar, and his account provides historians with a very clear view of Russian absolutism devoid of the usual tirades against "tyranny" found in most European accounts of Muscovy. To Margeret, the Russian "emperor" was easily one of the most absolute princes in existence. He noted the role of councils and "estates" in the Muscovite political system, but he found the power of the tsar over his subjects, the economy, and the machinery of state to be virtually unlimited. For instance, Margeret viewed the entire Muscovite nobility as a class lacking any real independence. He accurately equated "nobility" with service in the tsar's cavalry force and duly noted the various groups and ranks within this service nobility. Margeret also provided a few details about "serfs" and "slaves" who labored to keep the tsar's cavalry force functioning. In one way or another, everyone in Muscovy had to serve. Margeret indicated that even the highest nobles were only paid employees of the tsar and regarded him as an autocrat. In his description of the tsar's actual exercise of power, Margeret distinguished between legitimate absolutism and occasional lapses into tyranny. Altogether, his view of the Muscovite political and social system was very sophisticated and accurate.

Margeret's description of Tsar Boris Godunov has also provided many details useful to historians. Margeret had a certain admiration for Boris, citing evidence of his humanity and goodness as well as his generally praiseworthy rule of Muscovy. In this respect, Margeret's account is similar to several other foreign and native accounts which present an ambivalent picture of Boris, mixing admiration with condemnation. The tsar's fatal flaw, according to Margeret and so many others, was that he was a usurper who was responsible for the murder of the last direct heir to the Muscovite throne. Although many scholars now dispute Boris Godunov's complicity, rumors that he had arranged Dmitrii Ivanovich's death in order to clear a path for his own rise to power circulated widely in Muscovy and caused him much trouble. Margeret's unique testimony concerning early circulation of contrary rumors—that Tsarevich Dmitrii had escaped Boris's assassins with the aid of the Romanov clan—has been of enormous value to historians in reconstructing the problems facing Boris. Margeret's evidence concerning clan politics and intrigue in this period is very interesting, as is his portrayal of Boris's drift into tyranny—troubled as he was by opposition and the "ghost" of Tsarevich Dmitrii.

It is in Margeret's portrayal of the pretender Dmitrii Ivanovich that his work differs substantially from several other contemporary foreign accounts as well as current scholarly views. His description of Dmitrii's invasion of Muscovy and of his accession to power in 1605 agrees substantially with other sources and provides valuable information on these events. However, there is much dispute over Margeret's characterization of the tsar himself. Margeret believed Dmitrii to have been the true son of Ivan IV. Most historians, on the other hand, believe Dmitrii to have been an impostor. For this reason, some historians have been reluctant to regard Dmitrii as an absolute ruler, focusing instead upon the many forces supposedly opposing him before he was actually murdered by a group of aristocratic conspirators in the spring of 1606. Margeret too focused upon the tragedy of Dmitrii's reign, claiming that he should have taken precautions against boiar intrigue, but he clearly indicated that until his death Dmitrii was a powerful and confident ruler who had no reason to fear mass revolt. In this, Margeret was arguing for continuity from Boris Godunov's reign to Dmitrii's. In contrast to Margeret's view, some historians believe that before his death Dmitrii was facing a growing popular revolt and that his reign should be seen as an extraordinary exception during which all basic assumptions of the Muscovite political order were somehow temporarily suspended. So far, however, the evidence used to dispute Margeret's account of Dmitrii's reign is not very impressive, and his image of Dmitrii cannot be easily dismissed.[95]

Margeret's consistent view of Muscovite absolutism is demonstrated in his brief remarks concerning the problems Tsar Vasilii Shuiskii faced in trying to establish his authority after the assassination of Dmitrii. He believed that Shuiskii would prevail over his opponents, that even an unelected tsar had so much power just by virtue of being tsar that he could in all likelihood

TSAR DMITRII, 1606

From D. A. Rovinskii, *Materialy dlia Russkoi Ikonografii,* vol. 2 (St. Petersburg, 1884). By permission of the British Library.

put down any potential rebellion. In this, Margeret made a good
point about the authority of the Russian tsar, but he greatly underestimated the threat to Shuiskii posed by the Bolotnikov rebellion.
The last section of Margeret's book concerns Dmitrii's true identity. It provides very clear evidence of the heated debates which
were prevalent all over Europe in the months and years following
Dmitrii's assassination, debates which may still be found in scholarly literature. Margeret's work does try to "prove" that Dmitrii was
authentic, but it is not just a propaganda tract. Rather, it is an
open, honest, and intelligent inquiry into the facts as they were
known to Margeret. Indeed, the evidence Margeret provided about
Dmitrii was so persuasive that his arguments dominated the debate
over Dmitrii's identity for many years.[96] Whether one accepts
Margeret's conclusion or not is less important than the fact that he
has contributed extremely significant evidence on that question.

Although Margeret's account has been used by scholars for over
two centuries, the work has long been available only in rare and
flawed editions. And, except for a few brief notes to the 1830 Russian translation, the work has never before been annotated.

All French editions of Margeret's text were published in Paris.
The original 1607 edition, which is now very rare, is the only
reliable French version. Later French editions were produced in
1669, 1821, 1855, 1860, and 1946; but all of them should be
approached with caution.[97]

There exist several editions of the old Russian translation
which was prepared by the historian Nikolai G. Ustrialov. This
translation first appeared in 1830 in St. Petersburg as
*Sostoianie Rossiiskoi Derzhavy i Velikago Kniazhestva Moskov-
skago* and in Moscow as *Istoricheskiia zapiski*. *Sostoianie* went
through four editions on its own (the last in 1913), and it was
included in Ustrialov's collection of translated foreign accounts,

Skazaniia sovremennikov o Dmitrii Samozvantse, which went through three editions by 1859. Ustrialov's translation is a useful version of Margeret's text, but it contains numerous errors.[98] The present English translation is based upon the original 1607 Paris edition. It is accompanied by notes which—beyond the usual definitions, identifications, corrections, and clarifications—are designed to place Margeret's specific evidence within the context of modern Soviet and western scholarship. In preparing the translation two works have been of considerable value—Randle Cotgrave's *A Dictionarie of the French and English Tongues* (London, 1611) and Edmond Huguet's seven-volume *Dictionnaire de la langue française du seizième siècle* (Paris, 1925). While the problems inherent in translating from Renaissance French into English have forced some compromises, every effort has been made to remain faithful to the original work. Except for the occasional repetition of a word, made necessary by problems of reference in English, all intrusions into the text are marked by brackets. The introduction of paragraph breaks into the English translation does not alter the original meaning in any way and should aid the modern reader. Finally, because this is a translation it was deemed proper to use modern spelling for Russian and Polish names and places. Margeret's spelling of Russian words was quite good by seventeenth-century European standards, but there is little reason to perpetuate his mistakes here.

STATE OF
THE RUSSIAN EMPIRE AND
GRAND DUCHY OF MUSCOVY

*WITH that which has happened there most memorable
and tragic during the reign of four emperors: that is to say,
from the year 1590 up to September 1606.*

BY CAPTAIN MARGERET

TO THE KING

SIRE,

If the subjects of your majesty who travel in faraway countries were to give a true account of what they saw and noted there of greatest interest, their own gain would be turned to the public advantage of your state: not only to have that which is good and industrious in other countries shown, examined, and imitated (it being very true that God has ordered all things in such a way that in order to improve relationships among men, some of them find elsewhere that which they do not have at home); but also this would give heart to a number of idle and stay-at-home young men to seek out and learn the virtue in the laborious but useful and honorable exercise of travel and foreign military service. It would also remove the false opinion held by many who believe that Christianity extends no further than Hungary; for I can truthfully say that Russia, of which I undertake the description here by the command of your majesty, is one of the main bulwarks of Christianity. That empire and country is larger, more powerful, more populous, and more abundant than is imagined, and it is better fortified and defended against the Scythians and other Mohammedan peoples than many judge. The absolute power of the prince in his state makes him feared and dreaded by his subjects, and the good order and civil administration within [the country] protect it from the usual incursions of the barbarians.

3

Sire, after your spoils of victory and your good fortune had acquired for your majesty the peace which France enjoys at present, and seeing from that time forward the service which I had rendered to your majesty and to my native land during the troubles (under the command of Sieur de Vaugrenant at Saint-Jean-de-Losne and other frontiers of your Duchy of Burgundy) as no longer useful, I went to serve the prince of Transylvania, and in Hungary the [Holy Roman] emperor, then the king of Poland as captain of an infantry company. And finally, fortune having carried me into the service of Emperor Boris of Russia, he honored me with the command of a cavalry company. After Boris's death, Dmitrii, in receiving the said empire, continued me in his service, giving me the first company of his guards. During this time I had the opportunity to learn, besides the language, innumerable things concerning his state, the laws, customs, and religion of the country which I have represented in this little discourse with so little fancy, indeed with such simplicity that not only your majesty, who has an admirably judicious and penetrating mind, but also everyone will recognize the truth in it, which the ancients have said to be the soul and life of history. That this discourse please your majesty, be it ever so little, would be my singular pleasure; seeing that after having deigned to listen to me, your majesty is so agreeable as to read me as well, assuring me that therein will be seen some very remarkable events from which the great princes may derive some benefit—even by the misfortune of my master Dmitrii, coming with great difficulty to his empire, elevated and overthrown all in less than two years, and his own death even followed by this woe that some judge him to have been an impostor or pretender. Therein will be seen in like manner many of the particularities of this state worth knowing and yet unknown, as much for the far-off setting of that land as for the dexterity of the Russians in hiding and keeping secret the affairs of their state.

I pray unto God, sire, to maintain your majesty in prosperity, your kingdom in peace, Monseigneur le Dauphin in the desire to imitate your virtues, and me in the zeal which I have always had to be able by my very humble services to merit the name,

SIRE, of

> most obedient subject, most loyal and most dedicated servant of Y[our] M[ajesty],

MARGERET

NOTE TO THE READER

THE Empire of Russia is a part of the country which in ancient times was called Scythia, from which comes the word Scythians—a name still used today for the Tatars, who were formerly lords of Russia.[1] The grand dukes of old paid homage to the Crimean Tatars.[2] These Russians for some time (and after having shaken off the Tatar yoke and having some knowledge of Christianity) have been called Muscovites, which comes from the capital city Moscow, which carries the title of Duchy. But that duchy is not the first of the country, for the prince formerly called himself grand duke of Vladimir, and continues to do so at present, styling himself duke of Vladimir and Moscow. Therefore, it may be said to be an error not only on our part, who are faraway, but also among their nearest neighbors to call them Muscovites and not Russians.[3] They themselves, when asked what people they are, respond *rusak,* which means Russians.[4] If one asks them from what place they are, they respond *iz Moskvy,* from Moscow, Vologda, Riazan, or other towns. It is also necessary to understand that there are two Russias—that is to say, this one which has the title of Empire (which the Poles call White Russia)[5] and another called Black Russia, which is a dependency of the kingdom of Poland and is adjacent to Podolia.[6] It is this Black Russia of which the king of Poland styles himself lord in his titles when he says "Grand Duke of Lithuania, Russia, Prussia," etc. I wished to inform the reader of this so that he may know that the Russians in question are those formerly called Scythians and since then Muscovites by error, inasmuch as Moscow is only a single town whose inhabitants are called Muscovites. It is as if one wished to call all Frenchmen Parisians because Paris is the capital of the kingdom of France (and with more reason, since Paris is the capital from earliest times, and Moscow has been for only one or two hundred years). Also, the short title of their prince is *Tsar', Gospodar' i Velikii Kniaz' N[ame] vseia Rusi,* which means, properly translated, King, Lord and Grand Duke N[ame] of all the Russians, or of all Russia (for it may also be understood in this sense, and not of the Muscovites or of Muscovy). And, so that one may distinguish Black Russia from this one, all of which lies beyond the Dnieper, the Poles called it White Russia. Otherwise, and without this distinction, one might often err in this treatise in which is discussed only White Russia, formerly Scythia and now Muscovy.

STATE OF
THE RUSSIAN EMPIRE AND
GRAND DUCHY OF MUSCOVY
1606

RUSSIA is a land of great expanse, filled with vast forests in the more settled parts. Along the borders of Lithuania and Livonia there are great marshes which serve as ramparts to Russia. The land is fairly well populated from Narva, which is a Swedish castle and seaport on the Livonian border, to Archangel, or Saint Nicholas, which is another seaport some twenty-eight hundred versts (four versts make a league) from Narva; and from Smolensk (a city on the Lithuanian border which Boris Fedorovich Godunov, then protector of the Russian Empire, had walled with stone during the reign of Fedor Ivanovich) to Kazan, a distance of about thirteen hundred versts.[7]

The land of Kazan was at one time an independent Tatar kingdom which was conquered by the [Muscovite] grand dukes Vasilii Ivanovich and his son Ivan Vasil'evich. The ruler of this country was taken prisoner in the city of Kazan by Grand Duke Ivan Vasil'evich and still lives in Muscovy. His name is Tsar Simeon.[8] The city of Kazan is washed by the famous Volga River, into which flows the Oka River. The Cheremissians live near that city.[9] Beyond Kazan

9

lies a vast uninhabited region of plains along the Volga (which flows into the Caspian Sea at Astrakhan). There are, however, some castles built along the river.

Some two thousand versts from Kazan is Astrakhan, a fortified city with more commerce than any other city in Russia. It furnishes nearly all of Russia with salt and salted fish. The land there is considered to be very fertile, for on the plains between Kazan and Astrakhan are found many small cherry trees which bear fruit in season, and some wild grapevines. In Astrakhan there are found many good fruits. Around there is also found the animal-plant about which some authors have written in times past. It is a sheep which grows out of the ground, rooted by a gut of two or three *brasses* in length which is attached to its navel.[10] The sheep eats the grass around itself and then dies. They are the size of a lamb, with curly wool. Some of the hides are completely white, others a little spotted. I have seen several of these hides.

This land of Astrakhan was conquered by [Grand Duke] Ivan Vasil'evich. During his lifetime the English traded there, and from there into Persia. Beyond the Volga live the Tatars who call themselves Nogai.

There is yet another large province sugjugated by Ivan Vasil'evich which they call the Empire or Realm of Siberia.[11] This country is full of woods, forests, and marshes. It is not yet fully explored. It is said that Siberia borders the great Ob River on one side.[12] From this land come nearly all furs such as black foxes (which are of great value even there), sables, and martens. These furs bring huge revenues to the emperors. They are beginning to till this land, which is fertile enough for grains. Four towns have been built there in which there are garrisons to hold the people in subjection.[13] The Siberians are very simple people of small stature. They look somewhat like the Nogai Tatars, with flat and large faces, deep-set noses, small eyes, and dark complexion. They have long hair. Few among them have beards. They dress in sable, the fur side out. Thirty years ago they did not know what bread was. Siberia is the principal place of exile for most of those who fall into disgrace with the ruler.

On the Tatar side [to the south] are those who are called Crimean Tatars. They are allied with the Turkish sultan, and they have aided him in Hungary several times, principally in 1595, in the great battle of Agria.[14] From 1593 to the present time many towns and castles have been built on the plains of Tartary to repulse incursions of the Tatars. However, this region is inhabited only as far as Livny, which is about seven hundred versts from Moscow. Beyond Livny there are various towns, such as Tsarev-Borisov, Belgorod, and others. Tsarev-Borisov is nearly one thousand versts from Livny.[15] These towns are still increasing steadily in population. The soil there is very fertile, but they only dare to till near the towns.[16] They say that Tsarev-Borisov is only a week's journey from the great [Crimean] khan. It was in times past the point of rendezvous for the Tatars when they assembled to ravage Europe.

To conclude, Russia is a land of great expanse, for it borders Lithuania, Podolia, Turkey, the Crimean Tatars, the Ob River, and the Caspian Sea, as well as Livonia, Sweden, Norway, Novaia Zemlia, and the Arctic Ocean.[17]

This country is very cold—I mean in the more settled parts, the north and west mentioned above. Although in the plains of Tartary, along the Volga, in Kazan and Astrakhan, and on the eastern side of the Ob River are very temperate regions; in the said cold provinces there are six months of winter. During winter there is always snow up to one's waist, and one can cross entire rivers on ice. Nonetheless, the land there is very fertile, yielding an abundance of all kinds of grains which we have in France. Rye is sown at the beginning or middle of August, wheat and oats, according to the length of winter, in April or May, and barley at the end of May. There are fruits such as huge melons (better than I have eaten elsewhere), plenty of cucumbers, good apples, cherries, but few pears and plums. There is also a great quantity of nuts, strawberries, and such fruit. There is little rain in the summer and none in the winter.

In Kholmogory, Archangel, and Saint Nicholas, likewise in some other places in the north, in summer one can always see the sun, day and night, for the space of a month or six weeks; at midnight one can see it two or three *brasses* above the horizon. In winter, for the space of a month, there is hardly any daylight, because the sun is not visible at all.

Moreover, there are in Russia all sorts of wild game and animals which are found in France, except wild boars. Stags, hinds, and wild goats are found in large numbers to the east and south, in the plains of Tartary and between Kazan and Astrakhan. Everywhere in Russia are to be found a great many elk, called the "great beast." Rabbits are very scarce there. Pheasants, partridges, thrushes, blackbirds, quail, and larks are found there in great abundance, besides infinite other fowl. However, very few woodcocks are seen. In August and September there are great numbers of cranes. Swans, geese, and wild ducks are found there in winter. I saw only one stork, which was entirely black. The carnivorous beasts of Russia include black and white bears in great quantity, five kinds of foxes, and plenty of wolves, which live in the large forests and do great damage to livestock. Besides this, reindeer are found in some places in the north. They are smaller than stags and have large, beautiful antlers. Their coat is gray, almost white. Their hooves are more cloven than stags' hooves. These reindeer serve as food, clothing, and horses for the people of that region. They harness one of them to a sleigh built especially for the purpose and go more quickly than any horses can. Most of the time the reindeer feed on what they find under the snow. In the winter all the hares in Russia turn white, and in the summer they are the same color as in France. In summer and winter white partridges are found there, as well as falcons, hawks, and other birds of prey. In all of Europe there are no better nor more diverse kinds of freshwater fish than the Russians have in great abundance. These include sturgeon, beluga, *belaia ryba* (which means "white fish" and is larger than a salmon), sterlet, and all the varieties of fish which we have in France, except trout.

Fish and every other type of foodstuff is cheap, for, notwithstanding the great famine (of which I will speak below) which depopulated nearly all the country of livestock, I bought on my departure from Russia a lamb as big as one of our sheep in France, or almost as big, for ten *dengi*, which is worth about thirteen sols, four deniers.[18] (I also bought a chicken for seven deniers tournois; there are no capons in Russia, except among the foreigners.) The reason why lambs are so cheap is that each ewe ordinarily has two or three of them, and these lambs the following year become themselves mothers of just as many lambs. As for beef and cows, they also increase in numbers extraordinarily, for they do not eat any veal at all in Russia, since it is against their religion. Moreover, they observe fifteen weeks of fasting each year, besides Wednesday and Friday of each week. That makes nearly a half year of fasting, which causes meat to be cheap. Given that grains (of which there are a great many varieties) are not exported, they too are cheap. The land itself is so rich and fertile that, except for a few places, it is never manured. And thus, a child of twelve to fifteen years and a small horse will plow an arpent or two of land each day.[19]

Although there is a great abundance of food, and at low cost, the common people content themselves with very little. They cannot afford the cost, having no industry, and being very lazy. They do not apply themselves to work; rather, they are given to drunkenness more than to anything else. Their principal drink when they make merry is aqua vitae and mead, which they make from honey (which comes to them without labor and in great abundance, as one can judge by the great quantity of wax which is taken out of the country annually). They also have beer and other beverages of little value. All, without distinction (men as well as women, girls and boys, and the ecclesiastics as much or more than the others), are addicted to this vice of excessive drinking. Whenever there is liquor (which they are permitted to make for the principal festival days of the year) they can be expected to keep drinking day and night until it is gone. Here I am speaking of the common people, for the gentlemen have liberty to make such liquor as they wish and to drink whenever they want.

It is maintained that the grand dukes are descended from three brothers who came from Denmark. According to the Russian Chronicles, they invaded Russia, Lithuania, and Podolia about eight hundred years ago.[20] Riurik, the eldest brother, had himself called grand duke of Vladimir. From him are descended all the grand dukes in the male line up to Ivan Vasil'evich, who was the first to receive the title of emperor from the [Holy] Roman Emperor Maximilian, after the conquests of Kazan, Astrakhan, and Siberia.[21]

Now, concerning the title which the grand dukes hold, they think that there could be no title greater than their own, having themselves called *tsar'*. They call the [Holy] Roman emperor *tsesar'*, which they derive from Caesar, and they call kings *korol'* in imitation of the Poles.[22] They call the king of Persia *kizilbasha*[23] and the Turkish sultan *velikii gospodar' turskoi,* which means "great lord of Turkey," in imitation of *grand seigneur*. But this word *tsar'*, they say, is found in the Holy Scripture. Everywhere mention is made of David or of Solomon or of other kings, they are called *Tsar'* David, *Tsar'* Solomon, which is, as we interpret, King David, King Solomon, etc. Thus they keep for themselves the more authentic name of *tsar'* with which God was pleased to honor David, Solomon, and others ruling over the house of Judah and Israel in olden times.[24] They say that the words *tsesar'* and *korol'* are only human inventions, which names someone acquired by great feats of arms. For that purpose, after Fedor Ivanovich, tsar of Russia, raised the siege of Narva (which he had besieged), and when the deputies and ambassadors of both sides were assembled to conclude peace between Russia and Sweden, they debated for more than two days on the title of emperor which Fedor wanted to have, the Swedes not wanting to recognize him as such.[25] The Russians say that the word *tsar'* is even greater than emperor, so the accord was made that the Swedes would always call Fedor "Tsar and Grand Duke of Muscovy," each of the parties thinking the other had been outwitted in the use of the word *tsar'*. The king of Poland writes to [the grand duke] in the same way. The [Holy] Roman emperor gives him the title of emperor, as did the late Queen Elizabeth and as do the king of Great Britain, the king of Denmark, the grand duke of Tuscany, and the king of Persia.[26] All [the sovereigns] of Asia give him the titles that he claims. As for the Turkish sultan, given that there has been neither correspondence nor ambassadors between them in my time, I do not know what title he gives him.

This Ivan Vasil'evich had seven wives (which is against their religion, which does not permit the taking of more than three), from whom he had three sons.[27] There is a rumor that he killed his eldest son by his own hands, which is not true. Although he did hit him with the end of a staff tipped with a steel point (which staff is in the form of a crook, none daring to carry it but the emperors—a staff given in homage to the grand dukes of old by the Crimean Tatars), his son was only somewhat wounded by the blow and did not die of it. He died, rather, some time later on a pilgrimage.[28] The second son was Fedor Ivanovich, who succeeded his father. The third son, namely Dmitrii Ivanovich, was from Ivan's last wife, who was of the house of Nagoi.

Ivan Vasil'evich, surnamed the Tyrant,[29] not being certain of the loyalty of his subjects, tested them in various ways, but principally by elevating the above-mentioned Tsar Simeon to the imperial throne in his place. Ivan had him crowned and resigned to him all the titles of the empire. Ivan then had built for himself a palace opposite the castle and called himself *Velikii Kniaz' Moskovskii.*[30] Tsar Simeon reigned for two whole years conducting the internal as well as the foreign affairs of the country, that is, after requesting [Ivan's] counsel, which was worth as much as an absolute commandment. At the end of two years Ivan deposed him as ruler and gave him much property.[31]

Then, after the death of his eldest son, Ivan had his second son, namely Fedor, marry the daughter of Boris Fedorovich Godunov, who was a gentleman from a reputable family, called *moskovskie dvoriane.*[32] Little by little Boris Fedorovich gained the favor of the Emperor Ivan, who died in March 1584. After Ivan Vasil'evich's death, Fedor succeeded him to the throne. Fedor was a simple-minded prince who amused himself most of the time by ringing bells or by going to church. Boris Fedorovich, who was at that time liked well enough by the people and greatly favored by Fedor, intervened in the affairs of state.[33] Being subtle and very clever, he satisfied everyone. After some rumblings about deposing Fedor for his simple-mindedness, Boris finally was chosen to be protector of the country.[34] From that time, they say, he began to aspire to the throne, seeing that Fedor had no child save a daughter who died at age three.[35]

In order to secure the throne for himself Boris began to attract the people by good deeds. He had the above-mentioned city of Smolensk walled. He had the city of Moscow enclosed with a stone wall to replace the wooden one which was there previously.

He had some castles built between Kazan and Astrakhan, as well as on the frontiers of Tartary. Thus, being assured of the good will of the people, and even of the nobility (except the more clear-sighted and the high officials), Boris sent into exile under some pretext those he thought to be most opposed to him.[36] Boris then sent the empress, wife of the deceased Ivan Vasil'evich, with her son Dmitrii Ivanovich, to Uglich, a town 180 versts from Moscow.[37] It seems that the mother and some other lords saw the end toward which Boris headed and knew the danger the child Dmitrii could fall into, because several lords sent into exile by Boris already had been poisoned on the journey.[38] They devised a means to hide the child and to put another in his place after Boris had several more innocent lords put to death, so that he no longer feared anyone except Dmitrii.[39] To destroy this one last barrier, he sent to Uglich to have the changeling prince murdered. This was accomplished by the son of one whom Boris had sent as a secretary to Dmitrii's mother.[40] The assassin was killed on the spot, and the changeling prince, being aged seven or eight, was buried very simply.[41] When news of Dmitrii's death reached Moscow, it gave rise to differing opinions, the people murmuring and talking about it in various ways. Boris, being informed of all, had the principal shops, merchants' houses, and other places set afire during the night, to keep the people busy until the rumors had died down a little and minds were settled.[42] Boris himself attended the fire, giving orders for putting it out. In this he took such pains that one might have thought the damage to be of great importance to him. Then, having gathered together all those whose property had been damaged, he made a long speech to console them and to show them his regret for their loss, promising them to entreat the emperor for some recompense for each of them, so that they would be able to rebuild their homes. He even promised to have stone shops built to replace those which before were made only of wood. This he carried out so well that it made each one content, considering himself happy to have such a good protector.

Finally Fedor died in January 1598. (Some say that Boris was the author of his death.)[43] Then Boris began more than before to intrigue for the empire, but so secretly that none but the most clear-sighted perceived it. Even they did not dare to oppose him in this, for he feigned to work on behalf of his sister, widow of the late Fedor, although this was against the laws of the country, which do not permit any woman [to rule]. As I understand it, the widows of grand dukes or emperors, living free, take the veil in an abbey within six weeks of the funerals of their husbands.[44] [Boris] even appeared to refuse to see those from the empress's council who came before his door. [He also refused to enter] the council chamber (which all are at liberty to enter during the interregnum).[45] Boris then required much persuading to accept the title of emperor. Reproving the Muscovites, he warned them that they were wrong to be so hasty and that the affair merited a more mature deliberation. Boris stated that nothing pressed them, considering that they were at peace with everyone and that the empire would continue in the same state as in the time of the late Fedor (when he himself was the protector) until with mature counsel they might choose another tsar.[46]

And yet the truth was that the country had not received injury in Boris's time. He had augmented the treasury, had constructed several towns, castles, and fortresses, and had even made peace with all their neighbors. And in this matter of choosing a new emperor, he wished to convoke in due course the estates of the country—namely, eight or ten persons from each town, to the end that all the land would have a voice in who should be chosen. This convocation would take time, for Boris's desire (so he said) was to satisfy everyone.[47] During this time Boris had a rumor circulated that, according to the information which he had from prisoners that the Cossacks brought in, the Tatar khan was coming in person with great forces to plunder Russia.[48] On hearing this news the people begged Boris more urgently to receive the crown. He made several protestations that it was against his wishes to accept it, considering that there were several born of more noble lineage than he, to whom the crown belonged with greater right than to him. Even without the crown he would prove his affection for the people like a father, with as much diligence in public affairs as he had shown before. But seeing how much the people wanted him to be tsar and seeing also that no one else wanted to interfere, he was content to take upon himself so weighty a burden. [But he would not do this] before having repulsed the infidels, who came with an army of one hundred thousand men to ravage the empire, and [before] having dictated the law [to the Tatars] as well as to the rest of their neighbors. From this time on Boris was given the titles of his predecessors.[49]

To meet the Tatar threat Boris had the troops assemble at Serpukhov, a town situated on the Oka River and a common passage of the Tatars. It is ninety versts from Moscow. Boris went there in person after his sister the empress entered *Devichii Monastyr'*, which means "Cloister of the Virgins," located three versts from Moscow.[50] At Serpukhov Boris reviewed the army in July, and according to accounts by foreigners or by Russians who were present, there were five hundred thousand men there, whether of infantry or cavalry.[51] I say there were at least this many, for Russia has never had greater power than at that time. And since this number seems improbable, I will note below the method which they use to levy so many men, according to what I have seen and learned. But to finish this war, there appeared no other enemy but an ambassador, with about one hundred very well mounted men dressed in sheepskins (according to their custom). They came to negotiate a treaty between Russia

and the Tatar khan, about which Boris was well informed be-
forehand. This treaty acquired for him very great renown. After
having shown all the forces of Russia to the ambassador, all the
cannon (which were lined up on both sides of a road about two
versts apart, with the pieces of ordnance at some distance one
from another) were fired several times. Boris had the ambassador pass several times between the said ordnance. Finally he
sent him away with many presents. After having dismissed the
army, Boris Fedorovich returned to Moscow in great triumph.
Reports then spread that the Tatar khan heard of Boris's ap-
proach and had not dared to enter Russia. Boris was crowned
on the first day of September 1598 [O.S.] which is their first
day of the year.[52]

This country first received Christianity about seven hundred
years ago, from a bishop of Constantinople. The Russians follow the Greek religion. They baptize their children, plunging
them three times into the water: in the name of the Father, of
the Son, and of the Holy Spirit. Then the priest hangs a cross
around the child's neck, which he receives from the child's god-
father, in witness of the baptism. This cross is worn until
death. They believe in the Trinity; nevertheless, they differ
from us in that they do not confess that the Holy Spirit pro-
ceeds from the Father and the Son alike, but rather from the
Father alone, through the Son. They have many sacred images,
but none carved except the cross, for all the others are paint-
ings.[53] The Russians claim to have the Virgin Mary painted by
the very hands of the Evangelist St. Luke.[54] Their greatest pa-
tron is St. Nicholas. In addition to the saints which they have
from Greece, they have canonized several; however, there is no
female saint among them except the Virgin Mary.[55]

The Russians have a patriarch, who was created in the time
of Ivan Vasil'evich by the patriarch of Constantinople. There

are, if I am not mistaken, five archbishoprics, several bishoprics and abbeys.[56] The priests alone administer the sacraments. These priests are married. If their wives die, they can no longer administer the sacraments. If they do not remarry, they can become monks. The monks are not married, nor are the patriarch, bishops, and abbots. Because of this they cannot administer the sacraments nor eat meat. Instead, each one of them must receive the sacrament from these priests. They administer the sacrament under both kinds to everyone alike, clerics and lay, after the auricular confession. This is customarily done once a year. If the priests remarry, they become laymen. The Russians do not consider anyone to be duly baptized except those who are baptized in the Greek manner, although they dispense Catholics from rebaptism.[57]

They observe holy days precisely, and even Friday just as much as Sunday. However, there is no holy day so great that it is not permitted to open the shops and to work at whatever is necessary after noon. They fast on Wednesdays and Fridays. Moreover, they have four fasts a year: Great Lent, of which we will speak below, two others each of fifteen days, and the fourth which begins a week before [the winter feast of] St. Nicholas and ends at Christmas. They observe these fasts as strictly as they can, not eating eggs or any flesh products.

They have the Holy Scripture in their language, which is Slavonic. They esteem highly the Psalms of David. In the Russian churches they never preach; instead, at some holy days they have certain lessons which they read from some chapter of the Bible or New Testament. But ignorance is so great among the people that there is not one out of three who knows what the Lord's Prayer or the Apostles' Creed is. Indeed, one may say that ignorance is the mother of their devotion. They abhor any kind of studying, and especially the study of Latin. They have no school or university. The priests alone teach the children to read and write, to which few apply themselves. The greater part of their alphabet is Greek. Nearly all of their books are written by hand, except for some printed Bibles and New Testaments which they get from Poland. It is only ten or twelve years since the Russians learned to print, and still today handwritten books are more sought after than the printed ones.[58]

Twice a year the rivers and running waters in Russia are blessed, and after the benediction the emperor and the nobles are accustomed to jump into the water. I have even seen them cut the ice for this purpose and the emperor jump in.[59] On Palm Sunday the patriarch is mounted on an ass, on which he sits sidesaddle. (For want of an ass a horse is covered with white linen so that one can see nothing but the horse's eyes. Large ears are also made for the animal.) The emperor leads the patriarch's mount by the bridle to a church called Jerusalem outside the castle, and from there he leads him to the Church of Our Lady.[60] There are people appointed on that day who throw off their cloaks and spread them out on the path. In the procession they follow the priests and other clergy from the city. [The clergy] have among them an order of those who, having received the last rites and then recovered, are obligated to wear a [monastic] habit different from the others for the rest of their lives. They consider this to be a very holy thing. The wives of these men can remarry. No one may enter their churches except those of their religion.[61] The patriarch, bishops, and abbots are appointed at the emperor's will. All cases involving the church are judged by the patriarch, unless they are of some importance, in which case it is necessary to submit the matter to the emperor. (A Russian may repudiate his wife under any pretext whatever, sending her against her will to a cloister, of which there are many. He may remarry up to the third time.)

The emperor grants freedom of conscience to everyone, allowing all to exercise their religious devotion publicly except

Roman Catholics.[62] The Russians have not permitted any Jews among them since the time of Ivan Vasil'evich, surnamed the Tyrant. He had all of them who were in the country assembled and led onto a bridge. After having their hands and feet bound, he made them renounce their belief and forced them to say that they wanted to be baptized and to believe in God the Father, the Son, and the Holy Spirit. He then immediately had them all thrown into the water.[63]

In Russia there are Livonians who were taken prisoner in Livonia thirty-eight or forty years ago when Ivan Vasil'evich conquered the greater part of them and brought all the inhabitants of Dorpat and Narva into Muscovy. These Livonians, who were Lutherans, obtained two churches in the city of Moscow, there making public exercise of their faith.[64] However, because of the arrogance and vanity of these people, their churches ultimately were demolished by order of Ivan Vasil'evich, and, without regard for age or sex, their houses were sacked.[65] Although they were thus in wintertime left naked like new-born babes, they could blame no one but themselves for this reminder of past misdeeds. They had been brought out of their homeland, despoiled of their possessions and reduced to servitude under the power of a thoroughly rude and barbarous people governed, moreover, by a tyrant prince. But instead of being humbled by their adversities, their bearing was so haughty and their dress so sumptuous that one might have thought them all to be princes or princesses. Livonian women going to church were clothed in nothing less than velvets, satin, damask, or at least taffeta, even though they might not have anything else of value. The principal source of income for these Livonians was in the franchise which they had to sell aqua vitae, mead, and other sorts of beverages on which they gained not ten percent, but rather one hundred percent. This may seem unbelievable, but nevertheless it is true.[66]

Although the Livonians have always been like that, one might believe that they had been taken into Russia to make them see their vanity and insolence, which in their own country they would not have dared to practice because of the laws and the judicial administration. Finally they were given a place outside the city to build their houses and one church. None of them has since been permitted to dwell in the city of Moscow.

Even Tatars, Turks, and Persians, besides the Mordvinians and other Mohammedan peoples, are found under the domination of the Russians, each retaining their own religion.[67] There are also Siberians, Lapps, and others who are neither Christian nor Mohammedan, but rather worship certain animals according to their fancy without being forced into [the Russian] religion.

They never keep their dead as long as twenty-four hours, be he prince or slave. Instead, if he dies in the morning, he is interred in the evening. They ordinarily have a number of women to lament their dead, who ask him why he has died — if he was not favored by the emperor, if he did not have enough wealth, enough children, an honest wife. If it is a woman, they ask if she did not have a good husband, and similar foolishness. They put a new shirt on the deceased, leggings, shoes which are like slippers, and a cap. Then they place him in the coffin and into the ground. The kinsfolk and friends take part in this. After the interment they begin to cry over the grave, asking the same questions as before. Then they leave. At the end of six weeks the widow and some close friends gather together at the grave, bringing things to drink and to eat. After they have cried a lot, asking the same questions again, they eat the food which they brought. Then they distribute the remainder which they were unable to eat to the poor. That is the way it is among the common people. However, if it is someone of quality who has died, a feast is held in the home after the closest relatives have returned from the sepulcher, where they themselves asked the questions or hired women to do it and distributed to the poor all the food brought to the sepulcher. These feasts in commemoration of the dead are continued thus once each year. At the end of six weeks a widow can remarry, the period of mourning then being past.

The observation of Lent is as follows. During the week before Lent, which they call *Maslenitsa* (which means *semaine grasse*), although they dare not eat any flesh, they do eat everything derived from flesh, namely butter, cheese, eggs, and milk.[68] During this week they visit one another, kissing each other, taking leave, and requesting pardon if they were offended by past words or deeds. Even meeting one another on the streets, although they might never have seen each other before, they kiss one another, saying *Prosti menia, pozhalui,* which means "Pardon me, I beg you." The other responds, *Bog tebia prostit,* "God pardons you; forgive me also."[69]

Now before going further, it is necessary to know that it is not in this season alone that they kiss one another, but rather at all times. Kissing each other is a kind of salutation used as much by the men as the women in taking leave from one another or in meeting each other after a long interval.

At the end of [*Maslenitsa*] they all go to the baths. They leave their houses seldom or not at all during the following week. Most of them eat only three times that week, but no flesh or fish, rather honey and all sorts of roots. The following week they go out of their houses, but very simply dressed as if in mourning. For the rest of Lent (except the last week) they eat all sorts of fish, fresh as well as salted, without butter or anything else coming from flesh; on Wednesday and Friday they eat little fresh fish, only salted fish and roots. The last week of Lent is observed as strictly as the first or even more so, for then they all customarily receive the sacrament.

Now on the day of Easter and for the week following, they visit one another (as during [*Maslenitsa*]) carrying red eggs which they present to each other, saying *Khristos voskrese*, which means "Christ is risen." The other responds, *Vo istinnu voskrese*, "In truth He is risen." They give an egg or exchange them and kiss each other, which they happily do in celebration of the Resurrection. The emperor observes the following custom: as on the last day of [*Maslenitsa*] when everyone comes to kiss his hand, so, on the day after Easter as well as the next day, each of the high nobles and dignitaries comes to kiss his hand while the emperor is going to church. He gives them one egg, two, or three according to whom he favors more or less. There is nothing but feasting for the space of two weeks after Easter.

They have many bells in Russia. In this they seem to differ from the Greeks, who have none on their churches, as one may see by observing those who follow the Greek religion—the Wallachians, Moldavians, Retzes, and others.[70] It is not that church bells are against the Greek religion; rather, these people, being under the domination of the Turks whose Koran permits no bells on their temples (as with the Jews), do not dare to have them. The Catholics, Protestants, and Arians did have bells in Transylvania when Stephen, later king of Poland, and after him Sigismund Bathory held that country in fief to the Turkish sultan.[71] But the Greeks did not have any bells.

All the routes out of Russia are so closed that it is impossible to leave without the permission of the emperor. They have not allowed any of those who carry arms to leave the country in our times; for I was the first.[72] Even if there is a war against the Poles, they do not cast out any Poles although they have a goodly number of them. Instead, they send them to the frontiers of Tartary.[73] They do likewise with the other non-Russian peoples among them, out of fear that these foreigners will run away or surrender to the enemy, for this is the most distrustful and suspicious nation in the world.

All their castles or fortresses are of wood, except Smolensk, the castle of Ivangorod or Narva, the castle of Tula, Kazan, Astrakhan, the castle of Kolomna, and the castle of Putivl on the frontiers of Podolia, and the city of Moscow.[74]

Moscow is a large city, through which flows a river larger than the Seine. The city is enclosed by a wall of wood which has a circumference, as I estimate, greater than Paris. Inside there is a big wall which has a circumference half that of the wooden wall, but which does not extend across the river.[75] Inside this there is a third made of brick which encloses all the stone shops of the merchants.[76] Then there is the castle, which is large and was built by an Italian in the time of Vasilii Ivanovich, father of Ivan Vasil'evich.[77] In the castle there are several stone churches, among which are four covered with gilded copper. The city is full of wooden buildings, each building having only two stories. There is a large yard around each dwelling because of fires, to which they have been very subject lately. They have built many stone churches; there is also an infinite number of wooden ones there. Even the streets are paved or planked with wood.

The high nobility always reside in Moscow. There are the *kniaz'ia* (that is, the dukes), then those of the council who are called *dumnye boiare,* then the *okol'nichie* (who are marshals), then the *dumnye dvoriane*, and other *moskovskie dvoriane*.[78] From these are chosen the principal officers and governors of the towns. There is in the council no fixed number, for it is up to the emperor to appoint as many as he deems proper.[79] I have known there to be as many as thirty-two [in the council]. The privy council is customarily made up of those closely related by blood to the emperor and meets in matters of great consequence. One takes (as a matter of form) the advice of the clergy, summoning the patriarch with some bishops to the council.

Strictly speaking, however, there is no law or council save the will of the emperor, be it good or bad. He has the power to put all to fire and sword, be they innocent or guilty. I consider him to be one of the most absolute princes in existence, for everyone in the land, whether noble or commoner, even the brothers of the emperor, call themselves *kholopy gosudaria*, which means "slaves of the emperor."[80] Moreover, they admit to the council two *dumnye d'iaki,* whom I take more for secretaries than chancellors, however they may interpret their function.[81] One of them holds the office from which all ambassadors are dispatched and foreign relations are conducted.[82] The other holds the office from which all troops receive their orders, including lieutenants general, governors of towns, and others, except for the *strel'tsy,* the best Russian infantry (who are harquebusiers) who have an office of their own.[83]

Beyond this, each province of the land has an office in Moscow where a member of the council or an *okol'nichii,* together with a *d'iak,* judge all differences among those who serve the emperor. It must be noted that no judges or officers dare to take any gifts from those who have business with them. If they are accused by their own servants or by those who gave them gifts (which happens often when things do not come out as the giftgiver wished) or by anyone else, and if they are convicted, all their possessions are confiscated. After restitution of the gifts, the guilty ones are placed on the *pravezh* (of which we will speak below) to make them pay a fine of five hundred, a thousand, or two thousand rubles, more or less, as ordered by the emperor according to the rank of the individual concerned.[84] If the guilty one is a *d'iak* who is not well favored by the emperor, he is whipped through the streets. If it is money which he has taken, a purse full of money is hung around his neck. And it is the same with all other things, for if they have taken furs, pearls, or anything whatsoever, including salted fish, this is

usually hung around the guilty one's neck when he is beaten.
This is done not with canes, but rather with a whip. Then the
guilty are sent into exile. In this they are looking not only to
the present, but to the future as well.⁸⁵ Notwithstanding this
punishment, these officials do not stop taking [gifts]. They
have found a new trick, which is that one offers [the gift] to the
[ikon] of whomever he has business with. (Everyone has a large
number of these [ikons] in his house, which the more simple
people call *Bog,* which means "God", and the others call *obraz,*
which means "image" or "representation.") The gift is hung on
the [ikon]. This does not always excuse the official if the gift
surpasses seven or eight rubles in value and if the emperor is informed of it. It is also somewhat permissible for them during
the week after Easter to accept some little thing when they
meet, kiss each other, and exchange eggs. However, they may
not take any gift if it be presented to them in hope thereby of
gaining favor, for they are not exempted should they be accused by parties from whom they have received [a gift] at Easter-
time, inasmuch as [accusers] can testify to having given them [a
gift] for such and such a reason; otherwise they are exempt during this time from all other accusations. Thus all judges and officials must be content with their annual salaries and the lands
which they possess from the emperor.⁸⁶

There is no appeal from a given sentence. Except for inhabitants of towns, everyone, including those from faraway provinces, must come to be judged in Moscow. As for the inhabitants
of towns, they have in each town a *gubnoi starosta* who judges
all cases. His decisions may be appealed to Moscow. These sub-
altern judges also have the power to search out and imprison all
murderers, robbers, and thieves; to interrogate and torture
them; and, after their confession, to forward this information
to a special office in Moscow which they call *Razboinyi
Prikaz.*⁸⁷ Nowhere in Russia can a man be executed without

express order from the sovereign court of Moscow.[88] Their laws provide that everyone plead his own case or have some kinsman or servant of his assigned to do this, for they have no lawyers at all. All differences, except those which one may judge on sight, end with an oath which one of the parties swears against the other. To do this he must kiss a cross with some ceremony in a church designated for this purpose. It must be noted that those who serve the emperor on horse are exempt from making this oath in person. They can have a servant kiss the cross for them, except when they swear an oath of homage to princes.

Those who are indebted to the emperor or to someone else, and who cannot or do not wish to pay, are put on the *pravezh*. This is a place where they must go at sunrise on weekdays to be beaten and lashed on the calves of the legs with a rod or switch by men appointed for this, who are called *nedel'shchiki*.[89] [The punishment] lasts until ten or eleven A.M. I have seen several brought back on wagons to their homes after they have been beaten. This continues until the debt is fully repaid.[90] Those who serve the emperor on horse are exempt from this, putting one of their men in their place.

The nobility, by which I mean all those receiving an annual salary and possessing lands from the emperor,[91] maintain this regimen: During the summer they ordinarily get up at sunrise and go to the castle (if they are in Moscow), where the council meets [from five A.M. until ten A.M.].[92] Then the emperor, attended by the council, goes to hear the church service. This lasts from eleven until noon. After the emperor leaves the church, the nobles go home to eat dinner, and after dinner they lie down and sleep for two or three hours. At about [six o'clock P.M.] a bell rings, and all the lords return to the castle, where they remain until two or three hours after sunset. Then they retire, eat supper, and go to bed.

Now one should mention that all the nobles go on horseback in the summer and in winter on sleighs, so that they get no exercise. This makes them stout and obese. They even hold in honor those who have the biggest bellies, using the name *dorodnyi chelovek,* which signifies "a brave man."[93] The nobles dress very simply except on festival days or when the emperor goes out in public or some ambassador is due to have an audience.

Noble women ride in a carriage in summer and in a sleigh in winter. However, when the empress goes into the country there are a number of women who follow her carriage riding on horseback like men. These ladies all wear white felt hoods, similar to those that the bishops and abbots wear in the countryside, except that the hoods of the latter are dark gray or black. These women are dressed in [long gowns], as wide at the shoulders as at the bottom. These gowns are ordinarily of scarlet or some other beautiful red cloth. Under this gown they have another dress of silk, with great sleeves more than an ell of Paris wide.[94] The cuffs of these sleeves are of some cloth of gold a third of an ell long. If she is a woman she wears a cap embroidered with pearls; but if she is a girl she wears a tall hat of black fox fur, as do the nobles when audience is given to an ambassador. A woman who has not had any children may wear the same hat as a girl. They all wear a collar of pearls a good four fingers in width and earrings which are very long. They wear boots made of red and yellow moroccan leather, with heels three fingers high. These boots are hobnailed like the boots of the Poles or Hungarians. They all paint themselves, but very crudely. They consider it to be a disgrace not to paint oneself, whether old or young, rich or poor.

Russian women are held under close supervision and have their living quarters separate from that of their husbands. One never sees them, for to present their wives is the greatest favor that Russian men extend to one another (except to close kin). Even if someone wants to marry, he must talk to the kinsmen of the girl, who, if they are content to enter into alliance with the prospective bridegroom, allow one of the suitor's most loyal kinsmen or friends to go see the girl and to make his report. On the basis of this report the marriage is contracted. If either party backs out, a sum of money mutually agreed upon must be paid. After the contract has been signed, the prospective bridegroom may go to see his intended wife.

On the day of the marriage the bride is led to the church with a veil on her face (like Rebecca, when she was informed that it was Isaac that she saw coming from far away) so that she can see no one and no one can see her face.[95] After the ceremony she is brought back in the same fashion and seated at the table. She continues so veiled until the marriage is consummated. Then the husband and wife go to the baths; or, if they do not go, they have a bucket of water poured over their heads, for they consider themselves to be unclean until that moment, following in this the Jews and the Turks. They must receive a blessing from a priest or monk before entering their church or even before presenting themselves before any [ikons], of which each house has a good number. They do the same every time that they have sexual intercourse. The entire dowry and everything else given for the marriage are evaluated at double or triple [their real worth], and, should she die without children, the husband pays the full amount to her closest kin according to the evaluation.

The wealth of one and all is measured by the number of men and women servants that one has and not by the money that one possesses.[96] They have retained this practice from the Ancients. The servants, of whom they have a great number, are slaves; and they, along with their children, remain serfs belonging to the heirs of their first master.[97] They follow several other practices from antiquity, as in their writing. Their registers, reports, and requests or petitions are rolled in parchment and not registered in books or folded as among us. So it is with all their other writings.

In this they imitate the Ancients, and even the Holy Scripture, as we read from the Prophet Ezekiel, ch. 3.[98] They also imitate the Ancients in the way in which they invite a man to a banquet or to dinner. Even the emperor, inviting ambassadors, does not say anything but *Khleba esh' so mnoi,* which means "Eat some bread with me." Their greatest reproach to someone who appears ungrateful is to say, "Thou hast forgotten my bread and my salt." Even if the emperor makes some journey, or when he is crowned or marries or [when there is an imperial] baptism, the common people individually come to offer him, among other presents, a loaf of bread and some salt.

The Russian way of showing reverence is to remove one's hat and to bow low. This is not done in the fashion of the Turks or the Persians and other Mohammedans, who put their hand on their head or on their chest, rather it is done by lowering the right hand to the ground, or not so low, according to the respect which they wish to show. However, if an inferior wishes to entreat something from his superior, he will prostrate himself before his master, with his face against the ground as they do in their prayers before some [ikons]. They know no other signs of respect. They do not regard kneeling as such, because the Mohammedans (they say) customarily kneel merely to sit down on the ground. The Russian women show respect in the same way [as the men].

There are among the Russians many people aged from 80, 100, to 120 years. They are not so subject to illness as in these parts. Except for the emperor and some principal lords, they do not know about physicians. They even consider to be unclean several things which one uses in medicine. Among other things they do not take pills voluntarily. As for enemas, they abhor them, along with musk, civet, and other such things. If the common people are sick, they usually take a good draught of aqua vitae, place in it a charge of harquebus powder or a peeled clove of garlic, stir this and drink it. Then they go immediately to a hot-house which is so hot as to be almost unendurable, and remain there until they have sweated an hour or two. They do the same for all sorts of maladies.

Now let us consider the revenue of the empire. First, the demesne of the emperor comes under an office which is called the *Dvorets*.[99] The master of the house has superintendence over this office and, along with two *d'iaki*, judges matters related to it. Beyond this, the country is divided into five offices, which they call *chetverti*, to which offices are brought the ordinary revenues.[100] In addition, there is another office which they call the *Bol'shoi Prikhod*, which supervises these *chetverti*. If there are any extraordinary taxes, they are all brought to the *Bol'shoi Prikhod*.[101]

The revenue of the emperor, beyond his demesne, consists in direct property taxes, which not only the towns must pay, but also all the peasants, including even those on the hereditary lands of the emperor's kinsmen. Then there are imposts and excise taxes on all sorts of merchandise and on the drinking houses where aqua vitae, mead, hydromel, and beer are sold. None dare sell those beverages anywhere in Russia except those who have leased the drinking houses in each town or village. There is also revenue from furs, wax, and other merchandise.

The revenue from the emperor's demesne consists for the most part in food, such as grains, aqua vitae, honey, wild game, meat, poultry, fruits, and other things necessary for the kitchen and larder. This notwithstanding, everything is taxed at a particularly high rate, and those who are a little distant from the city pay in money instead of in kind.[102] There are even many who are taxed in money for each *vyt'*, which contains seven or eight *desiatiny* of tilled land, depending on where it is located.[103] A *desiatina* is a piece of land on which one may sow two *chetverti* of grain.[104] (A *chetvert'* is also what one would call an arpent of land [in France].)[105] They pay an annual tax on each *vyt'* of ten, twelve, fifteen, even up to twenty rubles, according to the fertility of the land, each ruble making about six livres and twelve sols.[106] This tax adds up every year to a great amount, so that there is found in the [*Dvorets*] the clear sum of up to one hundred twenty thousand, indeed up to one hundred fifty thousand rubles each year.[107] The actual total depends on the costs and expenses of the foreign ambassadors and other extraordinary expenditures which are incurred by this office.

Some of the five *chetverti,* such as that of Kazan and the *Novaia Chetvert',* yield each year a clear sum of eighty or one hundred thousand rubles, after all costs are met (for these are the offices from which all pensions and salaries of most of the soldiers are paid).[108] Beyond this, the *Bol'shoi Prikhod* receives, in addition to the extraordinary levies made on all the land by the command of the emperor, the income from casual forfeitures, such as the confiscated possessions of those who fall into disgrace.

Furs and wax come to an office called the *Kazna* which is where the treasury is located.[109] The returns from the government seal are also contained in this office. For each sealed document the goverment receives a quarter of a ruble. All sorts of merchandise taken for the emperor are paid for out of the *Kazna.*

Moreover, each office of the provinces yields a good sum of money at the end of the year, for the emperor has the tenth part of all penalties and judgements in legal disputes. Besides that, there are two more offices. One handles the land grants and is called the *Pomestnyi Prikaz.*[110] For each grant the recipient must give two, three, or four rubles, according to the extent of the land of which he takes possession. Then if one of these landholders falls into disgrace, the revenue from said

land returns to the *Pomestnyi Prikaz* until the emperor grants
the land to someone else. The other office is called the *Koniushennyi Prikaz,* which is the office of the equerry.[111] This office also
has several sources of revenue and casual income. All horses
which are sold in the country, except by the peasants, must be
registered (at a cost of twenty sols each) by the purchasers to
avoid any danger of someone claiming that the horse had been
stolen. Then there are great revenues from horses that the
Nogai Tatars bring to sell in Russia. First, the emperor takes
the choice tenth part of these horses. Then, for each horse
which they sell he takes from either the seller or buyer, as
agreed upon by them, 5 percent of the price. Now after being
raised for two or three years, the emperor's tenth part of the
Tatar horses, which are young horses or colts when received, are
sold. This amounts to a great sum of money, for I have seen the
Nogai Tatars lead at one time nearly forty thousand horses into
the country. They come two or three times a year and bring more
or less each time, so that one cannot be exactly certain of the
revenue of the emperor.

Nevertheless, Russia is a very rich land, for no money leaves
it, while there is a good amount coming in every year.[112] All
payments are made with merchandise, of which they have a great
quantity, including all sorts of pelts, wax, tallow, hides of cows
and elk, other hides dyed red, flax, hemp, all sorts of cordage,
caviar (which are salted eggs of fish, of which a great quantity is
sent to Italy), salted salmon, plenty of fish oil, and other merchandise. Although there is a great abundance of grain in Russia,
they do not dare to transport it out of the country through
Livonia. Beyond this, they have much potash, linseed, thread,
and other merchandise which they barter or sell. The Russians,
including the emperor, buy nothing from foreigners with ready
money. If the emperor owes a sum such as four of five thousand rubles, he will make the payment in furs or wax.

By his thrift the emperor has a treasury which he never touches and which he adds to, more or less, every year. Besides this, there is the *Raskhodnaia Kazna,* which is the treasury where money is taken for extraordinary expenditures.[113] It is full of all sorts of jewels in great number, but principally pearls—for they wear more of them in Russia than in all the rest of Europe. I saw in the treasury at least fifty of the imperial robes, around which were jewels instead of lacing; also, robes entirely [embroidered] with pearls, and others bordered all around with about a foot, a half foot, or four fingers of pearls.[114] I saw bedspreads by the half dozen, all bordered with pearls, and diverse other things. There are also costly jewels, for they buy them every year. These remain in the treasury, along with those that the emperor receives from ambassadors. There are four crowns: three of the emperor and a fourth with which the grand dukes were crowned in former times. This does not include the crown that Dmitrii had made for his wife, the empress, which was left unfinished, for it is not the custom of the country to crown the wives of emperors or grand dukes. Dmitrii was the first. There are at least two scepters and two golden orbs. All this I saw, having the honor several times of accompanying Dmitrii Ivanovich to the vaults in which the treasury is located. The Russians maintain that everything belongs to the treasury, be it clothes, jewels, cloth, or money.

Also in the treasury there are two intact unicorn horns and a crosier which the emperors carry, the entire length of which is made of one piece of unicorn [horn]. The transverse part of the crosier, on which one leans, is made of another piece of unicorn [horn].[115] There is also another half unicorn [horn] which is for everyday use in medicines. I have seen there yet another crosier, this one of gold, but a little hollowed inside because of the weight. There are a great number of gold dishes large and small, and cups to drink from. Beyond this, there are innumerable vessels of silver, gilded and plain, as one can judge by this account: After the election of Boris Fedorovich, when he had assembled the army at Serpukhov as we have mentioned above, he held a feast six weeks long, entertaining ten thousand men at a time nearly every day. They dined under tents, and all ate from silver dishes, according to the word of those who were there. I have seen in the treasury a half dozen casks made of silver which Ivan Vasil'evich had made from silver vessels which he found in Livonia when he conquered that country. One of these casks is nearly the size of a half *muid;*[116] the others are not so large. There are also a great number of silver basins, very large and very deep, with handles on the side to carry them. Four men customarily bring to each table these basins full of mead, three or four, more or less, according to the length of the table. There are large silver cups to draw the mead from these basins because two or three hundred men would not suffice to pour drinks for those invited to the emperor's banquet. All these vessels are works of Russia. Moreover, there are a great number of silver vessels from Germany, England, and Poland, which are either presents of princes sent by ambassadors, or which have been purchased for the rarity of the workmanship.

There is in this treasury an abundance of all sorts of fabric — cloth of gold and of silver from Persia and from Turkey, all sorts of velvets, satin, damask, taffeta, and other silk cloth. In truth they need a great quantity of fabrics, for all those who come to serve the emperor have their "welcome" as they call it, which consists of money and, according to the quality of the man, a robe of cloth of gold or enough velvet, satin, damask, or taffeta to make him a garment. Moreover, when the emperor recompenses someone, be it for service done in war or in some other matter, he gives him fine cloth. Also, all ambassadors coming from the Nogai Tatars, the Crimean Tatars, or of some other nation of Asia receive, along with their attendants, robes of silk cloth, each according to his quality. To keep the treasury perpetually supplied, all merchants, foreigners as well as Russians, are obliged to bring all fine cloth and other things of value to the treasury where some are chosen for the emperor. If it is found that a merchant sold or concealed, for example, ten or twelve écus worth of merchandise before bringing it to the treasury, all the rest of his merchandise would be confiscated, even though the merchant had paid the excise tax and all imposts.[117]

They have no minerals except iron, which is very soft. However, I do not doubt that in such a large country there are other metals, but they have no person knowledgeable in such matters.[118]

There is no other coin among them but *dengi* or kopeks, which are worth about sixteen deniers tournois, and some *moskovskie dengi,* which are worth eight deniers tournois. There are a few *polushki,* which are worth four deniers. This money is of silver, a little finer than the *reals de ocho.* They pay all sums with these coins, for there are no others in all of Russia. They convert all their sums into rubles, which are equal to one hundred *dengi.* (A ruble is worth, as we have already mentioned, six livres and twelve sols.) They also convert sums into half rubles or quarter rubles, then into *grivny,* which are ten *dengi,* and into *altyny,* which are three *dengi* (which is worth four sols).[119]

Foreign merchants bring to Russia plenty of reals and reichstalers on which they make a profit.[120] Russians buy them for twelve *altyny* apiece (thirty-six *dengi* or about forty-eight sols). Then they resell them to the mint at which, after just a little refining takes place, what we call a real of forty sols [thirty *dengi*] is restruck as forty-two *dengi.*[121] Beyond this, these merchants bring to Russia a great number of ducats, which are bought and sold like other merchandise, and on which they often make a considerable profit.[122] I have seen ducats bought for up to twenty-four *altyny* apiece, which makes about four livres and sixteen sols. I have also seen them sold for sixteen *altyny* or half a ruble apiece; but the most common price is from eighteen to twenty-one *altyny*. Ducats become very valuable when an emperor is crowned or marries and [when there is an imperial] baptism, for everyone comes to offer him presents. The common people join together in groups which vie with one another in offering rich presents. Among these presents there are customarily a number of ducats, be they in goblets or silver cups, or in plates covered with taffeta. Ducats also increase in value some days before Easter, because for a week after Easter the custom is to visit one another, to kiss, and to present red eggs (as was mentioned above). However, when one goes to visit the great nobles and those with whom one has some business, one offers them, along with the egg, some jewels, pearls, or some ducats. This is the only season of the year in which they dare to take gifts. Yet it is necessary that this be done secretly, for this season does not excuse anyone from taking something of greater value than ten or twelve rubles.

The greatest office of Russia is that of grand master of the stable, called by them *boiarin koniushii*.[123] After him comes the one who supervises the doctors and apothecaries, and who is called *aptechnyi boiarin*. Then there is the master of the household; and after him, the emperor's taster.[124] These four offices are the principal ones of the council. After them there are various offices, such as *stol'niki, chashniki, striapchie,* pages, and others, in great number.[125]

The guard of the emperor is composed of ten thousand *strel'tsy,* who reside in the city of Moscow. These are harquebusiers. They have only one general. The *strel'tsy* are divided into *prikazy,* which are companies of five hundred. Each *prikaz* is commanded by a *golova,* whom we shall call a captain.[126] Each hundred men is commanded by a centurion, and each ten men a *desiatnik,* whom we shall call a corporal. They do not have lieutenants or ensigns. Each captain, according to the services which he has done, receives a salary of thirty, forty, up to sixty rubles annually, and he receives up to three, four, or five hundred *chetverti* of land. (Each *chetvert'* is comparable to an arpent of land and is to be understood as such throughout this work.) Most of the centurions have lands, and they receive from twelve to twenty rubles annually. The corporals receive up to ten rubles and the *strel'tsy* four or five rubles each year. Beyond this, each one receives twelve *chetverti* of rye and as much of oats every year.[127] When the emperor goes into the countryside, even if it is only six or seven versts from the city, most of the *strel'tsy* go with him, receiving horses from the stables of the emperor.[128] If the *strel'tsy* are sent somewhere with the army or are garrisoned somewhere, they are given horses. There are men designated to feed them, and every ten *strel'tsy* have a wagon to carry their provisions.

Besides these soldiers who reside in Moscow, those called *dvoriane vybornye* are selected from the principal gentlemen of each town within the jurisdiction of which they hold their lands.[129] According to the size of the town, sixteen, eighteen, up to twenty or, indeed, thirty *vybornye dvoriane* are chosen, who reside in the city of Moscow for three full years. Then others are chosen, and those in Moscow are dismissed.[130] This means that there is always a multitude of cavalry, so that the emperors seldom go out without eighteen or twenty thousand riders with them.[131] All those attached to the court ride horses. Most of them sleep in turns at the castle, without any weapons.

In receiving some ambassador whom the prince wishes to honor, he sends some of his *strel'tsy* with their harquebuses to place themselves in rows on each side of the road up to the ambassador's lodging, starting from the entry gate of the wooden or stone wall of the city, depending on the emperor's orders. Then a number of his *moskovskie dvoriane* and *vybornye dvoriane* go to meet the ambassador, accompanied by the principal merchants, who are very richly dressed if necessary. This depends on the degree of respect one wishes to show the ambassador. Everyone has three or four changes of clothes for this purpose. Sometimes the emperor has them dress in his cloth of gold and silver from Persia, with the tall hat of black fox. Sometimes he has them dress with the *tsvetnoe plat'e* (which are robes of *tabis* or camlet of silk, or of scarlet, or some other beautiful fine cloth of light color, laced with gold) and with the black tall hat. Otherwise, they wear what they call *chistoe plat'e,* which is simpler, but comely attire.[132] The number of men of quality meeting the ambassador is increased or diminished according to the honor that one wishes to show. They go to receive the ambassador at an arrow's flight from the city, or sometimes a quarter of a league away. To this meeting place one brings horses from the stable of the emperor for the ambassador and his attendants to ride into the city. Thus the ambassador is conducted all the way to his lodging, before which are placed guards. These guards do not permit anyone to enter the ambassador's residence except those who are assigned to do so. Nor, for that matter, do they allow anyone to leave who does not have a guard with him to see where he goes, what he will do, and what he will say. There are men appointed for this task and others who supply the ambassador's party with all kinds of necessary victuals at the emperor's expense. This service is provided from the time the ambassador crosses the border. Not only ambassadors, but all foreigners who come to serve the emperor are provided with all food necessary for themselves as well as for their horses, both in the city of Moscow and on the journey—each according to his quality. This is called *korm,* [the amount of which] given to the ambassadors is augmented or diminished according to the emperor's orders.[133] All this is furnished from the office called *Dvorets,* as has been mentioned above.

Concerning the military, we must first speak of the *voevody,* who are the generals of the army. They are chosen customarily from the *dumnye boiare* and *okol'nichie* — that is to say, if some enemies appear. Otherwise, they are chosen annually from the *dumnye dvoriane* and *moskovskie dvoriane,* who are sent to the frontiers of Tartary to stop the incursions of any assembled forces of Tatars, who come sometimes to steal the grazing horses of some garrisons. If they were to meet no resistance, they would ravage all the more. The *voevody* separate their army into five units: the advance guard, which is near some town close to the confines of Tartary; the right wing, which is near some other town; the left wing; then the main force of the army; and the rear guard — all separated one from another. However, the generals must be ready at a moment's notice to join the main force. There are no other officers in the army but these generals. However, all the men-at-arms, both cavalry and infantry, are led by captains, without lieutenants, ensigns, trumpets, or drums. Each general has his own banner, which is identifiable by some saint who is painted on it. These banners are blessed by the patriarch, just as other images of saints. There are two or three men designated to hold the banner upright. Moreover, each general has his own *nabat,* as it is called. These are the brass drums which are carried on horseback. They each have ten or twelve of them, as many trumpets and some shawms. These are never sounded except when they are about to give battle or during a skirmish. One of the drums is used to signal the cavalry to dismount or to mount up.[134]

The method they use to discover the enemy in these great plains of Tartary is as follows: There are routes which they call the road of the emperor, the Crimean road, and the road of the great khan.[135] In addition, there are some oaks scattered here and there on the plains, eight, ten, up to forty versts from one another. Under most of these trees there are certain sentinels — that is to say, two men, each with a fresh horse.[136] One of them keeps watch while perched in the tree, and the other one feeds the horses, which are kept saddled. They exchange places every four days. In case the sentinel in the tree spots some thick dust rising in the air, he has orders to descend, without saying a word until he is in the saddle, and to ride as fast as he can until he comes to the next tree, shouting from afar and making signs that he has seen men. The sentinel who guards the horses of this second tree mounts a horse on the command of the sentinel in the tree, who sees the first rider while he is still far off. As soon as they are able to hear or discern in what direction the approaching rider indicates that he has seen the cloud of dust, this second rider gives his horse free reign and rides as fast as he can to a third tree. Here they do the same thing, and so on, from one to the next, up to the first fortress. From there a message is sent to Moscow, without any other news except that men have been sighted. It turns out often to be only a herd of wild horses or of some other wild animals. But if the sentinel who remained in the first tree comes and continues the news, and in this manner further word is relayed, then they take to arms and the above-mentioned generals join together.[137]

They send men to try to reconnoiter the forces of the enemy. Also, those sentinels scattered from the route which they are taking spread out on both sides, waiting for the enemy to pass. Then they come to their trail and reconnoiter the approximate size of their forces by the width of the path which they make across the grass. The prairie grass is taller than a horse, but in this region the Russians put fire to it every spring, so that the land is desolate. This is done so that the Tatars cannot find pasture so soon and in order to make the grass grow even taller.[138] If the Tatars come by any of the above-named roads, the Russians survey their approximate strength by exact measurement of the depth of the path which they make. They also know the approximate size of the Tatar force by the dust which they see rising into the air, for the Tatars do not go voluntarily across the grass for fear of putting their horses out of breath.

These sentinels come by some secret paths which they know to bring news of the enemy's forces. To resist these forces, the generals withdraw toward some rivers and woods to block their passage. However, the Tatar is an enemy so nimble and so skillful that, knowing this, he will divert the Russian army with twenty or thirty thousand horses, while he sends some force to ransack the country by some other route. This they will effect with such swiftness that they will strike their blow before the Russian army receives any warning of it. Now the Tatars do not burden themselves with any booty except prisoners. They carry no baggage with them, although each one of them has a change or two of horse, which are so well trained that they are no trouble at all. Tatars are so skillful that they can descend from a trotting horse and leap onto another. They carry no arms except a bow, arrows, and a scimitar. They shoot much more steadily and more surely in retreat than otherwise. The provision which they carry is a little sun-dried meat, which is sliced very small. Moreover, they have plenty of rope attached to their pommel. In short, a hundred Tatars will always put to flight two hundred Russians, unless the latter are elite troops.

The Russian infantry or harquebusiers, being on the bank of a river or in some woods, make the Tatars retreat exceedingly fast, although in truth they are more adept at frightening them than they are at inflicting any damage to their forces. If any [Tatar] battalion of fifteen or twenty thousand horses should move against them a little, no more than three or four thousand come within cannon range, the rest seeming more like phantoms on asses than horsemen. So the Tatars retreat without ever sustaining great loss—unless one holds the passage in some woods or on a river, waiting for their return, which does not often happen.

The Russian forces consist mostly of cavalry. Besides the *dvoriane* mentioned above, one must add here the rest of the *dvoriane—vybornye dvoriane, gorodovye dvoriane*, and the *deti boiarskie,* who together constitute a great number.[139] The companies call themselves by the name of the towns under which they have their lands.[140] Some cities have three, four, up to eight or twelve hundred men, such as Smolensk, Novgorod, and others. There are a great number of towns furnishing a great multitude of men. Now each of these men must provide, beyond himself, a man on horse and a foot soldier for each one hundred *cheverti* of land which he possesses; but this is only in times of necessity. Normally, there is need for only the *dvoriane* themselves. This makes an incredible number of shadows rather than men.[141]

The stipend of the lords of the council ranges from 500 rubles up to 1200 rubles.[142] The latter amount is the salary of Prince Fedor Ivanovich Mstislavskii, who has always had the first place during the lives of four emperors.[143] The *okol'nichie* receive from 200 up to 400 rubles and from 1000 to 2000 *chetverti* of land; I have known there to be fifteen *okol'nichie* at the same time. The *dumnye dvoriane,* who customarily do not exceed six in number, receive from 100 rubles to 200 rubles and from 800 up to 1200 *chetverti* of land. The *moskovskie dvoriane* receive from 20 up to 100 rubles and from 500 up to 1000 *chetverti* of land. The *vybornye dvoriane* receive from 8 up to 15 rubles; the *gorodovye dvoriane,* from 5 up to 12 rubles. Each receives up to 500 *chetverti* of land.[144] All of these are paid annually out of the *chetverti* [or fiscal departments] and must furnish two men for each one hundred *chetverti* [of land], as mentioned above.[145] As for the *deti boiarskie,* their pay is from 4 to 6 rubles, paid for six or seven years at a time.[146] They all hold from 100 to 300 *chetverti* of land from the emperor. Their service, which is more to fill out the number [of troops] than anything else, customarily corresponds to their salary.

The important nobles mentioned above must have a shirt of mail, a helmet, a lance, bow and arrows. So must each of their servitors, along with a good mount. The *dvoriane* must have fairly good horses, a bow, arrows, and a scimitar. So must their servitors. This makes a multitude of men badly mounted, without order, courage, or discipline. Many often do more damage to the army than good. Beyond this, there are the forces of Kazan, which, joined together with the Cheremissians, are said to make nearly twenty thousand horses. Then there are the Tatars who serve the emperor. These, along with the Mordvinians, will make seven or eight thousand horses.[147] Their annual pay is from 8 up to 30 rubles. Then there are the Cherkasy, who are from three to four thousand.[148] The foreigners, as many Germans and Poles as Greeks, number two thousand five hundred.[149] They draw a salary of from 12 to 60 rubles. Some captains have up to 120 rubles and from 600 up to 1000 *chetverti* of land.

Finally, there are the *datochnye liudi* that the patriarch, bishops, abbots, and all other ecclesiastics who possess lands must furnish. As mentioned above, they must provide a man on horse and one on foot for each one hundred *chetverti* of land they hold.[150] Depending on the army's needs, one sometimes takes from these ecclesiastics a great number of horses in place of men. These horses transport the artillery and other munitions of war, and they serve as mounts for the *strel'tsy* and others to whom horses must be furnished. That is all that need be said about the cavalry.

Most of their horses come from the Nogai Tatars, which horses they call *koni*.[151] They are of a middling size, very good for work, and they can run for seven or eight hours without being winded. However, if they become tired and winded, they need four or five months to recover completely. They are very wild and are greatly terrified by the noise of a harquebus. They are never shod; nor, for that matter, are the horses which come from Russia. They eat little or no oats, and they must be made accustomed little by little to that feed if one wants to give it to them.[152] They also have jennets from the Georgians; but these are not common. They are very beautiful and good horses, but they do not compare to the *koni* for long wind or speed, unless it is just for a short run. Then they have some Turkish horses and some from Poland, which they call *argamaks*.[153] There are some good ones among them. These horses are all geldings. Beyond this, there are found a few very good ponies among the Nogai Tatars. These are all white and spotted with black, like a tiger or leopard, so that one might think them to be painted. The horses native to the land are called *merina*.[154] They are usually small and good, especially those which come from Vologda and that region. They are quicker to train than the horses of Tartary. A very beautiful and good horse of Tartary or of Russia can be bought for twenty rubles. This horse will do more service than a Turkish *argamak* horse, which costs fifty, sixty, up to a hundred rubles.

All their horses are subject to greater illnesses than in France. They are very subject to a malady which they call *maritsa*. This disease first appears in the chest; and if one does not cure it quickly, it goes into the legs and nothing more can be done about it. However, as soon as they perceive this malady, they pierce the skin of the horse's chest, almost between the legs, and push through this hole a cord made of hemp and of bark (which one rubs with tar). The horse is made to run two or three times a day, until it is all in a lather, and the cord is moved around often. At the end of three or four days the pus comes to maturity and leaves through the hole. This process continues up to two or three weeks. Then they withdraw the cord, the hole closes itself, and the horse is very sound after that. To avoid this malady they send all the horses into a river after the ice is melted. There they are kept in the water up to their necks for one or two hours, until they are almost unable to stand upright because of their shivering. This makes the horses very thin, for they continue this remedy for two weeks. Afterward, the horses are very agile. These horses are also very subject to short-windedness.

They do not think a horse of Tartary or of Russia to be fit for work until it is seven or eight years old, and these horses continue to work until they are twenty years old. I saw horses twenty-five to thirty years of age still render good service. They consider horses to be young at ten or twelve years, and they find very good pacers among these.

The best infantry consists of the above-mentioned *strel'tsy* and of Cossacks, of whom we have not yet spoken. Besides the ten thousand harquebusiers of Moscow, there are *strel'tsy* in each town within a hundred versts of the frontiers of Tartary. According to the size of the castles located there, sixty, eighty, up to a hundred fifty *strel'tsy* may be in each town. The towns on the actual frontier are well garrisoned.

There are Cossacks who are sent in winter to the towns in the vicinity of the Oka River. They receive pay equal to that of the *strel'tsy,* with grain; moreover, they are furnished with powder and lead by the emperor. There are other Cossacks in arms, numbering perhaps from five to six thousand, who possess lands and do not leave their garrisons.[155] Then there are the true Cossacks who maintain themselves along the rivers in the plains of Tartary, like the Volga, the Don, the Dnieper, and others. They often do much more damage to the Tatars than the whole Russian army. They do not have large stipends from the emperor, but they do have liberty, it is said, to do the worst they can against the Tatars. They are permitted to withdraw sometimes to the frontier towns, there to sell their booty and to buy what they need. When the emperor wishes to make use of them, he sends them powder, lead, and some seven, eight, or ten thousand rubles. It is the Cossacks who usually bring in the first Tatar prisoners, from whom one learns the designs of the enemies. The custom is to give to whoever captures and brings in some prisoner enough good cloth and damask to make a garment from each, forty martens, a silver cup, and twenty or thirty rubles. On these rivers there are found up to eight to ten thousand Cossacks who will join the army on the command of the emperor, which happens in time of need.[156] However, those Cossacks from above the Dnieper support themselves most often in Podolia.[157]

In time of need a man from each hundred *chetverti* of land is added to the army. These recruits are all peasants, more fit to handle a plow than a harquebus, although one cannot tell them by their dress for they must be dressed like Cossacks.[158] This means that each one wears a robe which comes to below the knees, is close to the body like a doublet, and which has a large turned-back collar descending to the waist. Half of these peasants must have harquebuses, two pounds of powder, four pounds of lead, and a scimitar. The others, at the discretion of those who send them, carry a bow, arrows, and a scimitar or a kind of spear more proper to pierce a bear coming from its den than for any military service they might perform with it. Moreover, in times of necessity the merchants must furnish men according to their means, be it three or four, more or less.[159]

Now, as noted above, at about the beginning of Lent the Cossacks bring in prisoners from whom one learns if the Tatars are assembling. According to this information, orders are issued throughout the country, while the snow is still on the ground, that each member of the military send his provisions into the towns near which it had been resolved to await the enemy.[160] These provisions are brought on sleighs to these towns. They consist of *sukhari*, which is bread cut in little pieces and dried in an oven like a biscuit. Then there is *krupa*, which is made of millet and hulled barley, but principally of oats. Then they have *tolokno*, which is made of oats scalded, dried, and ground to flour. This they use in various ways, in both food and drink, putting two or three spoonfuls of that flour in a good draught of water, along with two or three grains of salt, stirring it, and drinking it; they consider this to be a good and wholesome beverage. Then they have pork, beef, and mutton, salted and dried in smoke. There is also butter and dried cheese, pounded fine like sand. With a spoonful or two of this they make good soup. Then there is plenty of aqua vitae and some dried and salted fish which they eat without cooking. This is the provision of the most important persons; as for the others, they content themselves with biscuit, some *krupa* of oats, and *tolokno,* with a little salt.

The Russians seldom place themselves in the field against the Tatars until they begin to see grass underfoot. As for other enemies, if they do not come unexpectedly, the same plan of defense is used against them. In this way the emperor spends little more for the army in wartime than during times of peace, apart from recompense for those who have performed some service, such as taking a prisoner or killing one of the enemies, receiving a wound, or other such things. They are given money; and, depending upon the quality of the person, each one receives a piece of cloth of gold or other silk cloth to make a garment for himself.

The emperors of Russia have correspondence with the [Holy] Roman emperor, the kings of England and of Denmark, and with the king of Persia. They also have had from olden times correspondence with the kings of Poland and Sweden; but at present this is only a formality, for they continually mistrust one another, never knowing when war between them will break out. As for the Turks, since they lifted the siege of Astrakhan, which they had besieged with the Nogai Tatars and some Piatigorskie Cherkasy (Georgians) around forty years ago, there have been only two Turkish ambassadors in Russia and two Russians at

Constantinople—so that the emperors and the sultans have no war with one another.[161] But they have not had the advantage of correspondence and felicitous exchanges between them for thirty years, as if they lived very far apart. In that time the Russians have fought only with the Crimean Tatars and the Piatigorskie Cherkasy (Georgians).[162] This is because the Russians have built on the lands and frontiers of these peoples four or five towns and castles, the principal ones being Terek and Samara.[163] In the year 1605, the Georgians, assisted by some Turks, took one of the neighboring Russian castles; but this was of no great consequence.[164] The Georgians are warlike men and are very well mounted. Most of their horses are jennets. The Georgians are outfitted in a kind of light armor; but since the armor is well tempered, they are very agile in it. They all carry lances or javelins. They would do great harm to Russia if they were as numerous as some of their other neighbors, even though the Volga separates them [from the Russians], for they live between the Caspian Sea and the Pont Euxine.[165]

Let us return to Boris Fedorovich, who was crowned emperor on the first day of September 1598. Beginning his reign in peace and in greater prosperity than any of his predecessors,[166] he changed from his former practice, which was to hear personally the needs and requests of everyone. Instead, he held himself aloof, seldom appearing before the people; and when he did, it was with much more ceremony and reluctance than any of his predecessors. Boris had a son named Fedor Borisovich and a daughter.[167] He began then to work to ally himself with some foreign princes, to assure his own position and to establish his dynasty on the imperial throne.[168] Besides this, he began to exile those of whom he was suspicious.[169] Boris also arranged advantageous marriages, allying to his house the greatest of those whom he was of a mind to use. This left in the city of Moscow only five or six houses with which

Boris was not allied. One of these was that of Mstislavskii, who was not married and had two sisters. One sister had married Tsar Simeon. The other, not being married, was forced by Boris to enter a convent against her will. Prince Mstislavskii himself was not permitted to marry.[170] Then there was the house of Shuiskii, consisting of three brothers. To ally himself with that house, Boris had his wife's sister marry the second brother, named Dmitrii.[171] He did not permit the eldest brother to marry. This was *Kniaz'* Vasilii Ivanovich Shuiskii, who is at present reigning in Muscovy and of whom much more will be said below. [Boris was prompted to take such action] out of fear that some houses, joining together, might resist his authority. Finally, he sent into exile Tsar Simeon, who has been amply discussed above and who had married the sister of *Kniaz'* Mstislavskii. While Simeon was in exile, the said Emperor Boris sent him on his birthday (a day which they celebrate greatly in all of Russia) a letter by which he was given hope that he would soon be returned [from exile]. He who carried the letter also brought some Spanish wine sent by Boris. He had Simeon and his servant drink to the health of the emperor. They both soon after became blind, and Tsar Simeon is still blind. I have heard Simeon himself recount this.[172]

The second year of his reign, Boris managed to lure into the country Gustavus, son of King Erik of Sweden (who was deposed by his brother Johan, [who then became] king of Sweden).[173] This was done in hope of giving his daughter in marriage to Gustavus if that prince were found to be such as Boris hoped. He was in truth very magnificently received and honored with great gifts from the emperor—namely, silver dishes for his entire house, much cloth of gold and silver from Persia, velvet, satin, and other silk cloth for his entire retinue, jewels, chains of gold and [strands of] pearls, many beautiful horses with all the trappings, pelts or furs of all kinds, and a sum of money which truly did not correspond to such presents, some ten thousand rubles.[174] Gustavus made his entry into Moscow as a prince; but he did not behave well and was finally sent in disgrace to Uglich (the town where Dmitrii Ivanovich was supposed to have been murdered). There his annual revenue, had it been well managed, would have amounted to four thousand rubles.[175]

In the year 1600 a large embassy came from Poland. The ambassador from Poland was Lew Sapieha, at present chancellor of Lithuania, with whom peace was concluded for twenty years. Sapieha was detained for a long time against his will, for he remained in Moscow from the month of August until the end of Lent 1601.[176] Boris was sick during that time.[177] On the day that [Sapieha] was to take his leave, he kissed the hand of the emperor, who was in the audience chamber. Boris was seated on the imperial throne, the crown on his head, the scepter in his hand, and the golden orb before him. His son was seated next to him on his left. Seated on benches all around the chamber were the lords of the council and the *okol'nichie* wearing robes of very rich cloth of gold bordered with pearls, with tall hats of black fox on their heads. On each side of the emperor two young lords stood dressed in white velvet garments, bordered all around with ermine to the height of half a foot. Each wore a white tall hat on the head, with two large chains of enameled gold crisscrossed around the neck [and over the chest]. Each of them held a costly battle-ax of Damascus steel on his shoulder, as if in readiness to let fly a blow, this giving an impression of great majesty.[178] The great hall through which the ambassadors pass is full of benches on which other *dvoriane,* similarly dressed, are seated. They do not dare to appear unless dressed in robes of cloth of gold, and they do not stir when the ambassador goes by on a pathway reserved for this purpose. There is such silence that one would think the hall and audience chamber to be empty. That is the customary manner of receiving ambassadors.

Lew Sapieha and up to three hundred of his people dined in the presence of the emperor. They all ate from the emperor's great quantity of golden vessels, by which I mean shallow dishes, for plates and napkins are not used at all even by the emperor. They ate very good fish, but poorly prepared, considering that this was during Lent, when the Russians do not eat eggs, butter, or any milk products. They drank several toasts from one side to the other. Then Sapieha was sent back with good and worthy presents.

Now it should be noted that the emperor has his meals served very sumptuously, according to the ancient custom of the country, by two or three hundred gentlemen dressed in cloth of gold or of silver from Persia, with large turned-back collars a good half-foot wide at the shoulders, and trimmed with pearls. Each wears a round cap on his head, also trimmed with pearls. This cap has no brim, but rather is made like a porringer without handles. Above this cap is a tall hat of black fox. Then there is a heavy chain of gold around the neck. These two or three hundred gentlemen, who are increased in number according to the number of invited guests, are ordered to bring the meat dishes before the emperor, and to hold them until he asks for such and such. The custom is that, after the emperor is seated and the ambassadors or other guests are too, these gentlemen come in two by two, dressed as described above. They pass before the table of the emperor, bow low to show their respect, and leave two by two in a long line to fetch the meat dishes from the kitchens, and to bring them before the emperor.

But before the meat comes, aqua vitae in large silver flasks is brought in and placed upon all the tables, with little cups for pouring and drinking. On these tables there is only bread, salt, vinegar, and pepper; no plates or napkins. After everyone has drunk, or while everyone is drinking aqua vitae, the emperor sends to each one individually a morsel of bread from his table, calling aloud the name of each recipient. Each one thus favored stands up and is given the bread, with the words: *Tsar', Gospodar' i Velikii Kniaz' N[ame] vseia Rusi zhaluet tebe* ("the Lord Emperor and Grand Duke N[ame] of all the Russians favors you").[179] He takes it, bows, and then sits down. This process is repeated for everyone individually.

Then the meat comes. The emperor sends to each one of the principal guests a plate full of meat. After that, all the tables are furnished with meat in great abundance. Then the emperor sends to each one individually a goblet or cup full of some Spanish wine, with the same words and ceremonies as above. Then when everyone is a little more than half finished dining, the emperor sends again to each one a large cup full of some red mead, of which they have various kinds. After that, large silver basins full of white mead are brought in and placed on the tables. Everyone draws from them with large cups. As soon as one is empty, another is brought in, full of some other kind, stronger or less strong, according to what is requested. Then the emperor sends for the third time to each one a cup full of some strong mead or claret.[180] Then, finally, when the emperor has dined, he sends for the fourth and last time to each one another cup full of *patochnyi med* (which means mead of virgin honey), which is not strong but is clear like spring water and very delicate. After that the emperor sends to everyone individually a plate of meat, which each sends to his home. This presentation is made repeating the abovementioned words and ceremonies. The emperor tastes a little of these meats before sending them to those whom he favors most. Besides the invited guests, the emperor sends to the house of each noble and to all those that he favors a plate of meat called a *podacha*.[181] This is not done just during banquets, but rather once each day, a ceremony observed as strictly as possible.

If the emperor is not disposed to feast an ambassador after he has had his audience, then, according to the custom of the country, the emperor sends a dinner to the ambassador's own lodging. This is done with the following ceremony: First, one of the principal gentlemen, dressed in cloth of gold, his collar and cap trimmed with pearls, is sent before the dinner on horseback to announce it, to proclaim the favor of the emperor to the ambassador and also to keep the ambassador company during the dinner. He has fifteen or twenty servitors around his horse. After him walk two men, each one carrying a tablecloth which is rolled like a parchment. After them follow two others who carry saltcellars and two others with two bottles full of vinegar. Then come two others, one of whom carries two knives and the other two spoons, which are very costly. After them follows the bread, which six men carry, going two by two. Then, after that, comes aqua vitae. And after them follow a dozen men, each carrying a silver pot holding about three pints,[182] full of various kinds of wine, though most are strong wines from Spain, the Canary Islands, and other places. A dozen large goblets of German craftsmanship are brought after this. Then the meat dishes follow. First come those that one eats cold, then the boiled and roasted ones, and finally the pastry. All these meat dishes are carried in large silver plates; however, if the emperor favors the ambassador, all the dishes placed on his table are of gold. After the food come eighteen or twenty large flagons, each carried by two men, full of mead of various kinds. After these follow a dozen men, each carrying five or six large drinking cups. And after everything else come two or three wagons full of mead and beer for the ambassador's servants. All these things are carried by *strel'tsy* appointed for this task, who are very handsomely dressed. I have seen up to three and four hundred carry food and drink for a single dinner, and I have seen during one day three dinners sent to various ambassadors, more to one, less to another—nevertheless, all with such ceremony as described above.

In the year 1601 began that great famine which lasted three years. A *mesure* of wheat, which sold for fifteen sols before, sold for three rubles, which is nearly twenty livres.[183] During these years things so atrocious were committed that they are unbelievable. To see a husband quit his wife and children, to see a wife kill her husband or a mother her children in order to eat them—these were ordinary enough occurrences. I have even seen four women, neighbors, abandoned by their husbands, who conspired together so that one woman would go to the market to buy a cart full of wood. This done, she would promise payment to the peasant upon delivery to her lodging. But after having unloaded the wood, when he entered the [dwelling] to receive his payment, he was strangled by these women.[184] His body was placed where the cold would preserve it until his horse had been eaten first. When the body was discovered the women confessed the deed. That peasant was their third victim. In short, this famine was so great that, not counting the number of dead in other towns of Russia, more than one hundred twenty thousand people died from it in the city of Moscow and are buried in three public places outside the city designated for this purpose.[185] This was done by order of and at the expense of the emperor, who even provided shrouds for their burial. The reason for such a great number of dead in Moscow is that the Emperor Boris had alms given every day to as many poor as were found in the city. Each received a *moskovskaia denga* worth seven deniers tournois, so that everyone, hearing of the liberality of the emperor, rushed to Moscow; this, even though some of them still had enough to live on. When they arrived in Moscow, they could not live on those seven deniers, even though on the principal holidays and Sundays they received a *denga* worth twice as much as a *moskovskaia denga.* [186] So, falling into even greater weakness, they died in that city or on the roads leading out of it. Finally, informed that all too many hastened to Moscow and that the country was becoming depopulated little by little by those coming to die in the capital, Boris stopped giving alms to them. They could be found in the streets dead or half dead, suffering from cold and hunger. This was a strange spectacle. The sum that the Emperor Boris spent on the poor is incredible. Besides the disbursement which was made in Moscow, there was not a town in all of Russia to which Boris did not contribute something for the care of these poor. I know that he sent to Smolensk by a man known to me twenty thousand rubles. He had the good quality of ordinarily giving great alms and much property to the clergy, who were all devoted to him. [187] This famine has greatly diminished the strength of Russia and the revenue of the emperor.

At the beginning of the month of August, in the year 1602, Duke Johan, brother of Kristian, king of Denmark, arrived to marry the daughter of the emperor. [188] He received great honors, according to the custom of the country. There were some two hundred men in his retinue. His guards were twenty-four harquebusiers and twenty-four halberdiers. Three days after his arrival, Duke Johan had an audience with his majesty. The emperor received him very amiably, calling him his son. There was a seat prepared in the audience chamber next to that of the emperor's son, on which Duke Johan was seated. After the audience he dined with the emperor at his table, which had not been seen before — for it is against the custom of the country for anyone except the emperor's sons to sit at his table. The tables having been cleared, Duke Johan received rich presents and was conducted to his lodging. About two weeks later Duke Johan fell ill, allegedly from overindulgence, of which he died some time later. The emperor, along with his son, went to see him three times during his illness. Boris regretted his death greatly. All the physicians were disgraced.[189] The emperor did not wish to permit his body to be embalmed, which practice is against their religion. The duke was interred in the church of the Germans, two versts outside the city.[190] All the nobles conducted his body into the church, where they remained until the end of the entire ceremony. The emperor and all his nobles were in mourning for three weeks. A short time later the empress, Boris's sister, widow of the Emperor Fedor Ivanovich, died. She was interred in a monastery for women.[191]

During all this time Boris's jealousy and suspicion were always growing.[192] He exiled several times the Shuiskii brothers, suspecting them more than the others even though the second brother was married to the sister of Boris's wife.[193] Several innocent people were tormented for having visited the Shuiskii brothers even when they were in Boris's favor. None of the physicians dared, on pain of being exiled, to visit any lords or to administer anything to them without the express order of the emperor. (There have never been in all of Russia any physicians except those who serve the emperor, nor even any apothecary shops.)

Well, rumors had been circulating since the year 1600 that some people considered Dmitrii Ivanovich still to be alive.[194] From then on there was nothing but torturing and racking every day because of this. From that time forward if a servant came to accuse his master, however falsely, with the hope of freeing himself, he was rewarded by Boris. Then the master or one of his principal servants would be tortured to make him confess to that which he had never done, or seen, or heard.[195] The mother of this Dmitrii was taken out of the monastery where she lived and was sent about six hundred versts from Moscow.[196] In the end there were very few good families who had not felt the suspicion of a tyrant, even though Boris had been considered a very clement prince—for not ten persons were publicly executed during his reign before Dmitrii's arrival in Russia, except for some thieves who had assembled in a band of up to five hundred, of whom several were secretly hanged upon being taken prisoner.[197] A large number of persons were tortured, sent into exile, and poisoned on the journey; and an infinite number of persons were drowned. However, this did not relieve the emperor in the least.

Finally, in the year 1604 there occurred that which [Boris] had feared so much. Dmitrii Ivanovich, son of the Emperor Ivan Vasil'evich, who was supposed to have been killed at Uglich, as has been mentioned above, appeared in Russia. Along with about four thousand men he entered the country by way of the frontiers of Podolia, besieged first a castle called Chernigov which surrendered, then another castle which also surrendered.[198] Then they came to Putivl, a very large and rich city which surrendered, along with several other castles including Ryl'sk, Kromy, and Karachev.[199] On the Tatar side [to the south] Tsarev-Borisov, Belgorod, Livny, and other places surrendered. And so, with his forces growing in number, he came to besiege Novgorod Severskii, which is a castle situated on a mountain.[200] Its governor was named Petr Fedorovich Basmanov, of whom we will speak below, who offered such good resistance that Dmitrii could not take the castle.[201] Finally, the army of the Emperor Boris encamped on December 15 some ten versts from Dmitrii's forces. Prince Fedor Ivanovich Mstislavskii, general of the main body of the army, was still awaiting reinforcements. Nevertheless, on December 20 [O.S.] the two armies met. After skirmishing for two or three hours both sides retired without heavy losses, except that here Dmitrii missed a good opportunity, his captains showing how little experienced they were in military art.[202] In skirmishing,

Dmitrii sent three Polish companies to charge one of the Russian battalions so furiously that this battalion dissolved into the right wing and into the main force of the army with such disorder and confusion that the entire army, except for the left wing, was shaken and started to retreat. If another hundred horses had come to make a flanking move or to attack the other battalion, which was half wavering, there is no doubt that four companies would have defeated the emperor's entire army. This Mstislavskii, general of the Russian army, was thrown from his horse and received three or four blows on the head. He would have been taken prisoner by Dmitrii, except for a dozen Russian harquebusiers who made Dmitrii's men forgo their captive. In fact, one might have said that the Russians had no arms to strike with, although there were forty or fifty thousand of them.[203]

The armies withdrew from one another and refrained from doing anything until after Christmas.[204] The prisoners were sent to Moscow, among whom there was a captain of the Polish cavalry named Domoracki.[205] On December 28 [O.S.] Dmitrii Ivanovich lifted the siege of Novgorod Severskii, seeing that he could do nothing [to take the castle], and withdrew into the province of Severia, which is very fertile, where most of the Poles left him. Notwithstanding this, he assembled all the forces that he could, Russians and Cossacks as well as Poles, with a good number of peasants who were practised at arms.[206] Boris's army was also reinforced every day, and although there was another [Muscovite force] near Kromy, they followed Dmitrii so slowly that it might be said that they did not wish to strike.[207] In the end, after having kept to the woods and the forests, through which the army was conducted for an entire month, the Russians again approached Dmitrii's forces.[208] When warned that the Russians were quartered in a village so crowded together that they could not move, Dmitrii ordered a surprise attack during the night.[209] First, some peasants who knew the ways into the village were sent to put fire to it, but they were discovered on all sides by the Russian scouts. Thus, the [emperor's army] remained alert until morning, which was the twenty-first of January 1605 [O.S.]. Then the armies approached each other. After some skirmishing, with cannon play from both sides, Dmitrii sent his main cavalry along a small valley to attempt to cut between the village and the Russian army.[210] Mstislavskii, warned of this, sent forward the right wing of his army, with two companies of foreigners. The Poles, seeing that they had been forestalled, played for double or nothing.[211] Led by ten cornets, they charged the [Russian] right wing with such fury that, after some resistance made by the foreigners, all turned their backs and scattered except the main body of the army, which stood there as if in a trance, as motionless as if dead — giving [the Poles] access to the village, at the entrance to which were located most of the [Russian] infantry and some cannon. The infantry, seeing the Poles so near, fired a volley from ten or twelve thousand harquebuses which so frightened the Poles that they turned back in great confusion. Meanwhile, the rest of Dmitrii's cavalry and infantry approached as quickly as possible, thinking to have gained a total victory. But on seeing their own cavalry turn back in such disorder, they took to their heels and were pursued by five or six thousand horses for more than seven or eight versts. Dmitrii lost nearly all his infantry, fifteen ensigns and cornets, and thirteen pieces of artillery. Five or six thousand men had been killed, not counting the prisoners taken by the Russians. Of these, all who were found to be Russian were hanged by the army; the others were taken, along with the cornets and ensigns, buglers, and drummers, in triumph to Moscow. Dmitrii with the remainder of his forces withdrew to Putivl, where he remained until the month of May.[212]

Boris's army went to besiege Ryl'sk, which had surrendered to Dmitrii.[213] However, after staying there for two weeks without doing anything, the Russians lifted the siege with the intention of dismissing the exhausted army for a few months.[214] When Boris was informed of this, he wrote to his leaders expressly prohibiting them from dismissing it.[215] Thus, after the army had rested and refreshed itself for awhile in the province of Severia, Mstislavskii and Prince Vasilii Ivanovich Shuiskii (who was sent from Moscow to be Mstislavskii's associate commander) set out toward the other [Russian] army, which after having heard of Dmitrii's defeat had besieged Kromy.[216] The two armies, joined, remained before Kromy without accomplishing much of anything. They only made fools of themselves until the death of Boris Fedorovich, who died of apoplexy on Saturday, April 23 [N.S.] of that year.[217]

Now before going further, it must be noted that there are no duels among the Russians. First, they carry no arms except to war or on a journey. And if one is offended by words or actions of another, there is no other satisfaction except by means of the law. Whoever has offended the honor of another is condemned to pay a penalty which they call *beschestie,* which means "reparation of honor."[218] This penalty, however, depends on who has been offended. The guilty party may be beaten with *batoga,* which is executed in the following way: One uncovers his back down to the shirt. Then he is made to lie down on his belly. Two men hold him, one by the head and the other by the legs. Then, with rods the thickness of a finger, they beat him on the back. This is done in the presence of the judge, the offended party, and all those who happen to be there. It continues until the judge says, "Enough!" Or, the guilty person may have to pay to the satisfaction of the person he offended the sum of [the offended party's] annual salary from the emperor. However, if [the offended party] is married, [the guilty person] must pay twice as much for the reparation of the honor of [the former's] wife. Thus, if [the offended party] has an annual salary of fifteen rubles, [the guilty person] pays fifteen rubles for the reparation of honor, and thirty rubles for that of the wife; which amounts to forty-five rubles.[219] This same penalty is exacted whatever the [the offended party's] salary. But the injury may be such that the guilty person will be whipped publicly, forced to pay the above-mentioned sum, and then exiled. If by chance, as I have seen one time in six years, there occurs a duel between foreigners and one of the parties be wounded, whether the challenger or the challenged (for both are considered the same), the other is punished like a murderer. He can offer no excuse. Moreover, even if a man is greatly injured by words, he is not permitted to strike his foe, even with his hand, on pain of being punished as above. For if he does, and the other returns the blow, and a complaint is lodged, they are both condemned to be beaten as above or to pay a fine to the emperor. This is because, they say, whoever has been offended, in wreaking vengeance for the injury or in answering a blow, took upon himself the authority of the law, which reserves to itself alone the recognition of wrongs committed and the punishment of them. In consideration of this, justice is quicker and much more rigorous in these disputes, injuries, and calumnies than in any other thing. This is observed very exactly, not only in the towns in time of peace, but also in the armies in time of war. It is to be understood that this is the procedure followed for the nobility; the reparation of honor for the common people and the bourgeoisie is only two rubles. It is true that they do not take offense at every word, for they are very blunt in their speech (seeing that they use only the familiar form of address) and used to be even simpler. For if one were to say that something dubious were not so, instead of saying "That's your opinion," or "Pardon me," or something similar, they say, "You have lied!"—even the servant to his master. Although Ivan Vasil'evich was surnamed and taken for a tyrant, even he did not take offense at being called a liar. However, now, since there have been foreigners among them, the Russians do not "give the lie" so liberally as they did twenty or thirty years ago.

Immediately after the death of Boris, the princes Mstislavskii and Shuiskii were summoned [to Moscow] by the empress and Fedor Borisovich, wife and son of the deceased. This was done before the army was informed of the emperor's death.[220] On the twenty-seventh [of April] Petr Fedorovich Basmanov, who had been governor of Novgorod Severskii when Dmitrii had besieged it, and another general reached the emperor's army, as much to get the soldiers to swear an oath of loyalty to Boris's son as to supplant Mstislavskii and Shuiskii.[221] The army swore an oath of loyalty and obedience to Fedor Borisovich, son of the deceased, recognizing him as emperor.[222] Fedor sent very favorable letters to the army, admonishing them to continue the same loyalty toward him that they had shown to his father, the late emperor, and assuring them of his generosity toward each of them after the expiration of the six weeks of mourning.

Prince Vasilii Vasil'evich Golitsyn and Petr Fedorovich Basmanov, with several others, surrendered to Dmitrii Ivanovich on the seventeenth of May [N.S.].[223] Two *voevody,* Ivan Ivanovich Godunov and Mikhail Saltykov, were taken prisoner.[224] The rest of the *voevody* and the remainder of the army fled toward Moscow, leaving all the cannon and other munitions in the trenches.[225] Day after day towns and castles surrendered to Dmitrii, who set forth from Putivl to reach [the Russian forces which had surrendered].[226] He had only six companies of Polish cavalry numbering six hundred men, some Cossacks from above the Don and Dnieper rivers, and a few

Russians. He immediately sent orders to dismiss from the army for some three or four weeks of refreshment those who held lands on this side of Moscow. And he sent the rest of the army to cut off supplies from the city of Moscow.[227]

Dmitrii, with some two thousand men, set off on a slow journey toward Moscow, daily dispatching letters to that city, both to the nobles and to the common people, assuring them of his clemency if they would surrender, and admonishing them that God first and then he would punish them for their obstinacy and rebellion if they should continue to resist. In the end, the people, having received one of these letters, assembled themselves on the public square before the castle.[228] Although Mstislavskii, Shuiskii, Bel'skii, and others were sent to calm the tumult, the letters were read publicly nonetheless; and after one and all were agitated, the people ran to the castle and took prisoner the empress, widow of the late emperor, her son and daughter, along with all the Godunovs, Saburovs, and Veliaminovs—who are all of the same house.[229] Everything that the people found was plundered.

Dmitrii Ivanovich was at Tula, a town some one hundred sixty versts from Moscow, when he received news of this. He sent Prince Vasilii Golitsyn to receive the oath of loyalty from the city. All the important officials came from Moscow to Tula to meet Dmitrii.[230] Finally, on June 20 [N.S.] the dowager empress and her son Fedor Borisovich were, it is maintained, strangled.[231] However, a report was circulated that they had poisoned themselves. Boris's daughter was kept under guard, and all the other kin of the late emperor were exiled here and there.[232] At the request of the lords, the late Boris Fedorovich was disinterred from the church named Archangel, the place of the sepulcher of the grand dukes and emperors, and was interred in another church.[233]

Finally Dmitrii made his entry into Moscow on the thirtieth of June [N.S.]. Having arrived, he dispatched Mstislavskii,

Shuiskii, Vorotynskii, Mosal'skii, and others to fetch the empress his mother, who was in a monastery some six hundred versts from Moscow.²³⁴ Dmitrii went to receive her one verst from the city, and, after a conference lasting a quarter of an hour in the presence of all the nobles and people from the city, the empress got into a carriage.²³⁵ The emperor and all the nobility on foot around the coach led her to the emperor's residence, where she remained until quarters for her were completed in the cloister where the empress, widow of the emperor Fedor and sister of Boris, was interred.²³⁶

At last Dmitrii had himself crowned on the last day of July [N.S.], which was done with little ceremony, except that all the paths from the chamber to the Church of Our Lady, and from there to Archangel [Cathedral], were covered with a scarlet cloth, and on top of this a cloth of gold from Persia, on which Dmitrii walked. When he arrived in the Church of Our Lady, the patriarch and all the clergy were waiting for him.²³⁷ After prayers and other ceremonies, the crown, the scepter, and the golden orb were brought from the treasury and were delivered to him. Then, while Dmitrii was leaving from that church to go to Archangel [Cathedral], little gold pieces were thrown along his path. (These were worth half an écu, an écu, and some two écus; they were minted for this occasion, since no gold coins are struck in Russia.) And from Archangel [Cathedral] Dmitrii returned to his palace, where there was a banquet open to all those who could find a place to sit.²³⁸ This is the usual custom practised by the Russians at coronations.

A short time later Prince Vasilii Shuiskii was accused and convicted, in the presence of persons chosen from all estates, of the crime of lese majesty.²³⁹ He was condemned by the Emperor Dmitrii Ivanovich to be beheaded, and his two brothers were sent into exile. Vasilii Shuiskii was led four days later to the public square. When his head was already on the chopping block his pardon came, procured by the dowager empress and by a Pole named Buczyński and others.[240] Nevertheless, Shuiskii was sent into exile with his brothers, where he remained for only a short time. This was the greatest mistake that the Emperor Dmitrii was ever known to make for, in the end, this Vasilii Shuiskii procured Dmitrii's death.[241]

Meanwhile, Dmitrii dispatched Afanasii Ivanovich Vlas'ev on an embassy to Poland.[242] This was, it is believed, to fulfill a secret promise made to the palatine of Sandomierz by the emperor, to marry his daughter when it pleased God to restore Dmitrii to the throne of his deceased father, Ivan Vasil'evich. This promise was made in return for the palatine's assistance in Dmitrii's conquest of the Russian empire.[243] Afanasii arrived at the Polish court and negotiated so well that the wedding was solemnized at Krakow. The king of Poland personally attended the ceremony.[244]

During this time the Emperor Dmitrii set up a foreign guard, which had not been seen before in Russia. It included a company of one hundred archers for his bodyguard, which I had the honor to command, and two hundred halberdiers.[245] Dmitrii gave freedom to marry to all those who in the time of Boris had not dared to marry, such as Mstislavskii, who then married a cousin of Dmitrii's mother. [The emperor] attended this marriage celebration for two days in a row.[246] Vasilii Shuiskii, recalled from exile and in as much favor as before, was already betrothed to one of that same house.[247] His marriage was to be solemnized a month after that of the emperor. In short, nothing was seen but weddings and joy at the contentment of everyone, for Dmitrii made them feel little by little that this was a free country, governed by a clement prince. He went every day once or twice to see his mother the empress. He sometimes showed a bit too much familiarity toward the lords, who are brought up in such subjection and fear that they would almost not dare to speak in the presence of their prince without command.[248] However, this emperor knew otherwise how to maintain a majesty and grandeur worthy of the prince that he was. Moreover, he was wise, having enough understanding to serve as schoolteacher to all his council.[249]

Notwithstanding this, some secret plots were discovered.[250] A secretary or *d'iak* was apprehended who was tortured in the presence of Petr Fedorovich Basmanov, the emperor's favorite. The *d'iak* did not confess, nor did he accuse the leader of this conspiracy, who was, it later became known, Vasilii Shuiskii. So, this secretary was sent into exile.[251]

At last the empress, wife of Dmitrii, arrived at the frontiers of Russia with her father, one of her brothers, a brother-in-law named Wiśniowiecki, and several other lords.[252] On April 20 Mikhail Ignat'evich Tatishchev, a lord held in great favor by the emperor, was dismissed in disgrace for a scornful word spoken to Dmitrii in favor of Prince Vasilii Shuiskii, who was then disputing with the emperor over a roast veal which was on the table (for this is against their religion).[253] Tatishchev was finally returned to favor on Easter day at the solicitation of Petr Fedorovich Basmanov; although everyone suspected, even the emperor (although he was not a suspicious prince), that Tatishchev was involved in some conspiracy, for he did not show himself as much as before his exile. His recall was a mistake approaching that of recalling Shuiskii, for Tatishchev was known to have a malicious temperament and to be incapable of forgetting any injury.[254]

At the end of April the Emperor Dmitrii received news that between Kazan and Astrakhan about four thousand Cossacks had assembled. (These Cossacks are infantry, like all those mentioned above and hereafter, and not cavalry, as are the Cossacks who live in Podolia and Black Russia under the domination of the king of Poland.[255] These latter Cossacks have been seen here and there in the armies of Transylvania, Wallachia, Moldavia, and other places. They were from olden times mounted and armed like the Tatars and still continue to be, although in recent years most of them use harquebuses. They carry no defensive arms, except a number of them who have scimitars.) They caused harm along the Volga.[256] They were said to have with them a young prince named Tsar Petr who was the true son (as they had it bruited about) of the Emperor Fedor Ivanovich and of the sister of Boris Fedorovich, who reigned after the said Fedor. He was supposedly born around the year 1588 and a girl was supposedly put in his place secretly, who died at the age of three, as was mentioned above.[257] This Tsar Petr could have been aged from sixteen to seventeen years if their story had been true, but it was well known that this was only a pretext to pillage the land. These Cossacks were discontented with Dmitrii, reckoning that they had not been recompensed by him as they had hoped to be.[258] Notwithstanding this, the emperor wrote Tsar Petr a letter by which he sent for him, saying that if he were the true son of his brother Fedor he would be welcome. All provisions (which they call *korm*) for his journey would be provided by the emperor. However, Dmitrii also wrote, if he were not the true son of Fedor, he should withdraw from the emperor's lands.[259] During the time that the messengers went and returned, Dmitrii was miserably assassinated, as I will touch upon below. But before my departure from Russia, these Cossacks sacked three castles situated along the Volga, captured some small cannon and other munitions of war, and separated. Most of them went into the plains of Tartary. The others withdrew to a castle which is halfway between Kazan and Astrakhan, hoping to rob the merchants taking goods to Astrakhan or at least to force them to come to terms.[260] But while I was at Archangel I received news that all was calm along the Volga, and that the Cossacks had all left.[261]

On Friday, May 12 [N.S.], the empress, wife of Dmitrii, made an entry into Moscow more magnificent than any other that had been seen before in Russia. Harnessed to her carriage were ten Nogai horses which were white, spotted with black (like tigers or leopards), and which were matched so well that one could not distinguish one from another. She was accompanied by four companies of Polish cavalry, very well mounted and richly dressed, and a company of Haiduks for her guard.[262] She had several lords in her retinue. She was led to the cloister of the dowager empress, where she remained until May 17 [N.S.], at which time she was led to her upstairs quarters in the palace. She was crowned the next day, with a ceremony similar to the emperor's, escorted on the right by the ambassador of the king of Poland, the castellan of Małogoszcz, and on the left by the wife of Prince Mstislavskii.[263] Upon leaving the church the Emperor Dmitrii led her by the hand, and Vasilii Shuiskii escorted her by the left arm.[264] On this day only Russians were at the banquet.[265] On the nineteenth began the wedding celebration attended by all the Poles except the ambassador. This was because the emperor refused to allow him to sit at his table. Although is was against the custom of the Russians to allow any ambassadors to sit at the table of the emperor, this did not stop the castellan of Małogoszcz from protesting to the emperor that the Russian ambassador had been granted the same honor by the king, his master, for he was always seated at the same table as the king of Poland during the wedding ceremony [in Krakow].[266] On Saturday and Sunday the castellan dined at a separate table near that of their majesties.

During this time Dmitrii was warned by his father-in-law the palatine of Sandomierz, his secretary, and by Petr Basmanov and others that there was a conspiracy against him. Some prisoners were taken, but the emperor did not seem to give much credence to this matter.[267]

As it turned out the fatal day on which the Emperor Dmitrii Ivanovich was cruelly assassinated was Saturday, May 27 [N.S.], at six o'clock in the morning, an hour when nothing of the kind was expected.[268] It is believed that 1,705 Poles were also massacred; this, because their lodgings were very far apart from one another.[269] Vasilii Ivanovich Shuiskii was chief of the conspirators. Petr Fedorovich Basmanov was killed in a gallery right next to the emperor's quarters. He received the first blow from Mikhail Tatishchev, whose freedom Basmanov had secured not too long before. Some archers of the emperor's bodyguard were killed.[270] The empress, wife of Dmitrii, was taken prisoner along with her father, brother, brother-in-law, and all others who escaped the fury of the people. Each was held in a separate house.

The dead and naked Dmitrii was dragged before the monastery of the empress, his mother, and onto the public square, where Vasilii Shuiskii ought to have been beheaded.[271] There Dmitrii was placed on a table of about one ell in length, his head hanging over one side and his legs over the other. The body of Petr Basmanov was laid under that table. Both bodies remained as a public spectacle for three days, until the chief of the conspiracy, Vasilii Ivanovich Shuiskii, about whom so much has already been said, was chosen emperor.[272] (Although this is not an elective but a hereditary monarchy, Dmitrii was the last of the ruling house. Inasmuch as none remained who were of the imperial blood, Shuiskii was chosen through his intrigues and scheming, as had been Boris Fedorovich after the death of the Emperor Fedor.) Shuiskii had Dmitrii's body buried outside the city near a major road. The night after Dmitrii was assassinated there occurred a great frost which lasted for a week and ruined all the grain, the trees, and even the grass in the fields—something which had never happened at this time of year before. Because of this, Dmitrii was dug up some days later at the request of those who followed Shuiskii's faction. His body was burned and reduced to ashes.[273]

During this time there were nothing but murmurings of discontent.[274] Some were crying, others lamenting, and still others rejoicing. In short there was a true metamorphosis. The council, the people, and the country divided against one another, beginning new treacheries. Provinces revolted, and for a long time it could not be known how things would turn out.[275] The ambassador of Poland was kept closely guarded. All those who had been in any way favored by Dmitrii were exiled. Finally, the empress, widow of the late Emperor Dmitrii Ivanovich, was led under very close guard to the lodging of her father, the palatine, along with all the maids of honor and other Polish women.

Now to attempt to calm the tumult and discontent of the people, Vasilii Shuiskii sent his brother Dmitrii, Mikhail Tatishchev, and others of his faction to dig up the body or bones of the true Dmitrii, whom they claimed to be the son of Ivan Vasil'evich, murdered some seventeen years before in Uglich, as was mentioned above.[276] They found the corpse (as they had it bruited about) intact. Dmitrii's garments were also as unspoiled and whole as they were when he was interred (for it is their custom to bury a person in the same clothes he was wearing when murdered). They even found some whole nuts in his hand.[277] The body being disinterred caused, so they say, several miracles, both in the town and along the roads back to Moscow.[278] Dmitrii was brought into the capital in a procession which included the patriarch and all the clergy, with all the holy relics (of which they have a great number), the Emperor-elect Vasilii Shuiskii, the mother of the dead Dmitrii, and all the nobles.[279] In Moscow he was canonized as a saint by the command of Vasilii Shuiskii.[280] This hardly appeased the people. Vasilii was twice very near to being deposed, although he had himself crowned on the twentieth of June.[281]

Shuiskii sent a great number of Poles back to Poland, servitors and people of little quality, retaining the important ones as prisoners to force the Poles to make peace. He sent the palatine of Sandomierz with his daughter the empress to Uglich, there to be guarded. The palatine was at this time very ill.[282]

To conclude, the late Emperor Dmitrii Ivanovich, son of the Emperor Ivan Vasil'evich, surnamed the Tyrant, was about twenty-five years old [at his death]. He was beardless, had a moderate stature and strong, sinewy limbs. He had a dark complexion and a wart very near his nose, under his right eye. He was agile, generous, had a magnanimous disposition, and a forgiving nature. Quick to take offense, Dmitrii was also quickly appeased. In short, he was a prince who loved honor and made great account of it. He was ambitious and determined. His aim was to make himself known to posterity, and he had already ordered his secretary to prepare to leave with the English ships in August 1606 to come to France to congratulate the Most Christian King and to exchange letters with him.[283] He spoke to me of the king of France several times with a great reverence. In short, Christianity has lost much in his death, if dead he be. It seems very likely that he is dead, but I speak in this manner because I did not see him dead with my own eyes, for I was sick at the time of his assassination.

Some days after Dmitrii's murder, there began to circulate a rumor that the emperor had not been killed, but rather it was one who resembled him, whom Dmitrii had put in his place. This was done after Dmitrii had been informed some hours in advance of what was about to happen and had left Moscow to see just what would occur. I believe this was done (if it is true) not out of any fear that Dmitrii might have felt, considering that he could have taken other action to protect himself. Rather, it was done to identify those who were loyal to him, which could not very well be done except by choosing this most dangerous path. His decision could be attributed to the virtual lack of suspicion that he had of his subjects' loyalty.[284] This rumor persisted until my departure from Russia, which was the fourteenth day of September 1606. In truth, I thought that this was a plot of some new faction to render Vasilii Ivanovich Shuiskii, leader of the conspiracy and at present reigning, odious to the people. This would make it easier for them to accomplish their own designs. I can no longer believe it to be anything else in view of what will be touched upon below.[285]

Now to make this rumor plausible, the Russians allege first that after midnight someone came in the name of the Emperor Dmitrii to fetch three Turkish horses from the castle's small stable. These were not brought back and no one knew what had become of them. The one who delivered the horses was later tortured to death by the command of Shuiskii to make him confess what had happened. Besides this, they allege that the master of the first lodging where Dmitrii would have eaten after his departure from Moscow attested to speaking to Dmitrii. This man even brought a letter written by Dmitrii (so he said) in which the emperor complained about the Russians, reproaching them for their ingratitude and disregard for his kindness and clemency, and assuring them that he would soon revenge himself on the guilty. Moreover, there were found several notes and letters scattered on the roads saying much the same thing. Dmitrii was even recognized at most of the places where he had taken post horses. In August there were also found several other letters testifying that they had failed in their coup and that Dmitrii would come to see them shortly, on the first day of the year [1 September, O.S.].

I shall touch in passing what was reported to me by a French merchant from Kazan named Bertrand.[286] Returning from the square where the corpse of Dmitrii was lying, Bertrand told me that he had been under the impression that Dmitrii had no beard, seeing that he had not noticed it during the emperor's life. (Dmitrii did not, in fact, have a beard.) However, the corpse lying in the square had a thick beard, as one could see, although it had been shaved. Bertrand even told me that the corpse had much longer hair than he thought Dmitrii had, for he had seen the emperor the day before his death. Moreover, he was assured by Dmitrii's secretary, who is a Pole named Stanisław Buczyński, that there was a young Russian noble, much loved and favored by Dmitrii, who strongly resembled the emperor, except that he had a little beard. According to what Russians say, no trace of this young noble was ever found, and no one knew what had become of him.[287]

Then I was informed by a Frenchman who was a cook for the palatine of Sandomierz that the empress, wife of Dmitrii, having been informed of the rumor which was circulating, was entirely persuaded that Dmitrii was alive, declaring that she could not believe otherwise.[288] From then on she appeared much more cheerful than before.

Some time after the election of Shuiskii five or six principal towns on the frontier of Tartary revolted. They took their generals prisoner and killed or disbanded a part of their garrisons.[289] However, before my departure in July, they sent to Moscow to request a pardon, which they obtained, excusing themselves by saying that they had been informed that the Emperor Dmitrii was still alive.[290] During this time there was great division in Moscow among the nobles and the others over the election of Vasilii Shuiskii, who had been chosen without their general consent and agreement, and Shuiskii came close to being deposed.[291] Finally, everything calmed down, and he was crowned on the twentieth of June.[292]

After Shuiskii's coronation there began new secret plots against him, in favor (as I imagine) of Prince Fedor Ivanovich Mstislavskii.[293] Mstislavskii is of the foremost house in all Russia, and he had several votes in the election. The election would have gone to him if all the land had been assembled.

Notwithstanding this, he refused to be elected, according to the rumor which circulated, declaring that he would become a monk if the choice fell on him. The said Mstislavskii married a cousin of Dmitrii's mother, who is, as mentioned above, of the house of Nagoi. Thus, it appears that this plot in Mstislavskii's favor was made more by his wife's kin, as I suppose, than by his consent. Then a great lord named Petr Nikitich Sheremetev, of the said house of Nagoi, was accused and convicted by testimony given in his absence of being chief of this plot. He was sent into exile from the town where he was, and, I have heard, was later poisoned on the way.[294]

At about this same time, a writing appeared one night on the doors of most of the nobles and foreigners to the effect that Emperor Vasilii Shuiskii commanded the common people to ransack these houses, considering that traitors lived in them. To accomplish this, the common people assembled. (They are attracted to booty by the recent changes and, I believe, would be content under such conditions to have a new emperor every week.) These people were appeased with some difficulty.[295] On a Sunday, some time later, without Shuiskii's knowledge someone convoked the common people before the castle in his name, under the pretext that he wished to speak to them.[296] By chance I found myself near the Emperor Shuiskii when he went out to go to church. Upon being informed that the common people were assembled in his name on the square, he was quite astonished and ordered a diligent search for those who had convoked this assembly. He did not budge from the spot where he was informed of it. As everyone hastened to that spot, Shuiskii began to cry, reproaching them for their inconstancy, saying that they did not need to use such cunning to be rid of him, if that is what they desired. It was they who had chosen him to be emperor, and they had a similar power to depose him if he was not acceptable to them. He said that his intention was not to oppose them in this. And so, in handing over his hat and the crooklike staff that none carry but the emperors, he said to them, "If such is the case, choose another who seems good to you." Then immediately taking back the staff, he said: "I am tired of such plots. Sometimes you want to murder me, sometimes it is the nobles and even the foreigners [you want to massacre]. At least you want to plunder them. If you recognize me as your chosen emperor, I do not want this to go unpunished." At this, all those present cried out that they had pledged an oath of loyalty and obedience to him, that they all wanted to die for him, and that those who were found guilty should be punished. Before this, an order had been given to the common people to return to their homes. Five men were apprehended who were the instigators of this convocation of the people. It is believed that if Shuiskii had gone out or if all the common people had been assembled, he would have run the same risk as Dmitrii. Some days later these five men were condemned to be whipped through the streets, which is the ordinary punishment, and then exiled. When the sentence was pronounced mention was made that Msistlavskii, who had been accused as leader of this conspiracy, was innocent. The guilt fell upon the above-mentioned Petr Sheremetev.[297]

Vasilii Shuiskii ran another risk when the body of the true Dmitrii (as they had it bruited about), murdered seventeen years before, as I have touched upon above, was brought to Moscow. When Shuiskii, along with the patriarch and all the clergy, went to receive the body outside the city, it is said that the emperor just missed being stoned there, although the nobles had appeased the common people before they were assembled.[298]

During this time the duchy of Severia revolted, even though, according to the Russians, it had already sworn the oath of loyalty to Shuiskii.[299] Maintaining that Dmitrii was alive, the rebels put seven or eight thousand men in the field. However, they had no leaders and, as I was informed at Archangel, were defeated by the forces that Vasilii Shuiskii sent there, composed of fifty to sixty thousand Russians and all the foreigners.[300] Those rebels who escaped retired to Putivl, which is one of the principal cities of Severia. It was even said that this city had surrendered and that all these revolts were brought about by some Polish troops amassed within the confines of Russia and Podolia who had the rumor circulated that Dmitrii was alive in Poland.[301] This is all that has happened up to September 14, 1606, to verify the notion that Dmitrii was still alive.

As for the opinions of those who do not hold Dmitrii Ivanovich to be or to have been the son of Ivan Vasil'evich, surnamed the Tyrant, but rather an impostor, I shall respond to them with my own views on the matter.[302]

The first objection by the Russians is that of Boris Fedorovich (a very cunning and crafty prince while he ruled) and of Dmitrii's other enemies. It is that Dmitrii was an impostor, considering that the true Dmitrii Ivanovich was killed at the age of seven or eight years at Uglich, some seventeen years ago, as I have mentioned above. It is claimed rather that he was a *rasstriga,* which means a monk who has quit his monastery, named Grishka or Grigorii Otrep'ev.[303]

Those who consider themselves most perceptive, whether the foreigners who knew him or others, allege that he was not Russian but rather Polish, Transylvanian, or of some other nation, brought up for that purpose.[304]

To respond, I have above touched upon the reason why Boris Fedorovich, protector of the empire under Fedor Ivanovich (son of Ivan Vasil'evich and brother to this Dmitrii Ivanovich), sent Dmitrii with his mother the empress into exile at Uglich. It can be judged from this discourse that this was not the work of the Emperor Fedor, whether because of his simple-mindedness or because Dmitrii was then only a child aged four to five years who could not hurt Fedor in any way. Rather it was the result of scheming by Boris Fedorovich.[305] Now it is enough to conjecture that Dmitrii's mother and some of the high nobles who were left, like the Romanovs, the Nagois, and others, seeing the end to which Boris was headed, tried by every means to deliver the child from the danger he was in.[306] Now I know and believe that it will be admitted that there existed no other means to save Dmitrii except to put another in his place and to bring him up secretly, waiting for time to change or halt completely the designs of Boris Fedorovich. This they accomplished so well that no one, except those involved, knew anything of it. Dmitrii was brought up secretly.[307] After the death (I believe) of Emperor Fedor, when Boris Fedorovich was elected emperor, Dmitrii, in a monk's habit, was sent to Poland along with the above-mentioned *rasstriga* Grishka Otrep'ev (it is maintained) to get him out of the confines of Russia.[308] Once in Poland Dmitrii put himself into the service of a lord named Wiśniowiecki, son-in-law of the palatine of Sandomierz.[309] Finally, he came into the service of that palatine and revealed his identity to him.[310] The palatine brought him to the Polish court where Dmitrii received some small assistance.[311] The above will serve as a response to the first objection and to verify that it was not Dmitrii but rather a substitute who was murdered at Uglich.

Concerning this *rasstriga,* it is very certain that a short time after the election of Boris Fedorovich there was a monk named Grishka Otrep'ev who fled to Poland from his monastery, for which reason he is called *rasstriga.* (He had once been the secretary of the patriarch.)[312] It was from that time on that Boris began to have doubts about what was happening, as one can see by the subsequent course of his life. To respond to this, I say that it is a certainty that there were two who fled in the habit of monks, this *rasstriga* and another who up to now has been nameless.³¹³ The Emperor Boris, then reigning, sent couriers to all the borders, with express orders to have all passages watched and to detain everyone, not allowing even those who had passports to pass. This was done because (so his order read, as I have learned) there were two traitors to the empire who were fleeing to Poland. The roads were closed so that for the duration of three or four months no one could enter or leave to go from one town to another, which was assured by the *zastavy,* guards who controlled the roads and who are never posted except in time of contagion.³¹⁴

Beyond this, it is confirmed and certain that this *rasstriga* is aged thirty-five to thirty-eight years, whereas Dmitrii could only have been twenty-three to twenty-four years old when he returned to Russia.³¹⁵ Otrep'ev was brought back with Dmitrii, and everyone who wanted to could see him.³¹⁶ His brothers are still alive, having lands within the jurisdiction of the town of Galich.³¹⁷ Before his flight this *rasstriga* was known to be an insolent man, given to drunkenness. It was this insolence which led the Emperor Dmitrii to have Grishka confined to Iaroslavl, 230 versts from Moscow.³¹⁸ In Iaroslavl there is a house of the English Company, and one [of the Company] who was staying there when Dmitrii was assassinated knew this *rasstriga.*³¹⁹ He has affirmed to me that, when news came that Dmitrii had been murdered and that Vasilii Shuiskii had been chosen emperor, Grishka Otrep'ev assured him that Dmitrii was the true son of the Emperor Ivan Vasil'evich and that he, Otrep'ev, had accompanied Dmitrii out of Russia when Boris Fedorovich was emperor. This he attested to with great oaths, affirming that no one could deny that he himself was Grishka Otrep'ev, surnamed *Rasstriga.* This is his own confession, and there are few Russians who believe otherwise.³²⁰ Sometime later Emperor-elect Vasilii Shuiskii sent for him, but I do not know what came of this.³²¹ This will suffice for that objection [to Dmitrii's authenticity].

The objection that most of the foreigners make is that Dmitrii was a Pole or Transylvanian, an impostor on his own or one raised for this purpose. They wish to prove this by the fact that he did not speak Russian so smoothly as he should have; that he did not do things in the Russian manner, which he ridiculed; that he observed their religion only in form; and other similar allegations. In conclusion (they say), all his gestures and manners revealed him to be Polish.[322]

Now if he were Polish, raised for the purpose, by whom this was done would have to be known. Moreover, I think it unlikely that a child would have been taken from the streets, inasmuch as I would say in passing that not one out of fifty thousand will be found capable of accomplishing that which Dmitrii undertook at the age of twenty-three or twenty-four years. But beyond that, what reason might have persuaded the leaders of this plot to undertake such a thing, considering that in Russia no one doubted the murder [at Uglich]?[323] Furthermore, Boris Fedorovich was then reigning in greater prosperity than any of his predecessors, as feared and respected by the people as he could be. Add to this that the mother of Dmitrii, along with several of his living kin, could testify as to who he was. It is probable that if this were a Polish plot it would have been done with the consent of the king of Poland and the estates. There is not the slightest indication that a thing of such consequence would have been undertaken without the knowledge of the king, for, if unsuccessful, it would have brought all the damage upon Poland through a great war at a disadvantageous time.[324] Now if this had been done with the king's consent, the war would not have been started with four thousand men and Dmitrii would have had, I believe, some councilors and men of quality, some Polish lords assigned by the king to advise Dmitrii in this war. Moreover, I believe that Dmitrii would have been assisted with money. It is also unlikely that most of the Poles would have deserted him when he lifted the siege of Novgorod Sever-skii, as I have mentioned above, considering that he already held nearly fifteen towns and castles and his army was growing stronger every day.[325]

As for those who say that Dmitrii was an impostor who undertook these things on his own, it seems to me that it would be simpleminded to believe that Dmitrii, being only twenty or twenty-one years old when he revealed himself, could have learned for this purpose how to speak and even to read and write the Russian language so long a time before.[326] Considering that he must have had the necessary knowledge and discernment to respond to each question put to him, as I imagine, when he revealed himself in Poland, one may also ask where he would have learned this; for Russia is not a free country which may be entered to learn the language and to become informed of certain matters and then leave.[327] Besides the fact that it is a closed country, as I have already touched upon, all things there are so secret that it is very difficult to learn the truth of a thing unless it has been seen with one's own eyes. Also, I do not think it to be likely that an impostor could have managed this scheme without someone knowing about it. Now if any had known about it, they would have revealed themselves during his lifetime or after his death. Finally, had he been Polish, he would have behaved differently toward some of them.[328] And I do not think that the palatine of Sandomierz would be so impetuous as to make any promise to Dmitrii before having been better informed of who this person really was. To say that he knew [Dmitrii was an impostor] is not probable, as we will discuss below.[329]

As for those who hold that he was brought up by the Jesuits, from what nation do they believe he came?[330] He was not Polish, as appears above and will be touched upon below. Still less did he come from another nation than Russia. If they admit that he was Russian, it must be known whence they took him since there had been no Jesuits in all of Russia before the arrival of Dmitrii, except accompanying ambassadors, who are held and watched so closely that it would have been impossible for them to be able to lead a child out of Russia. Now it is impossible to take a child out of the country by any means other than during the wars that Stephen, king of Poland, waged in Russia some thirty years ago or during the wars between Sweden and Russia, when they would surely have had occasion to procure one.[331] Yet how is it possible that they procured a child who is without equal in Russia? Furthermore, I think that they would not have been able to raise him so secretly that some of the estates of Poland and, consequently, the palatine of Sandomierz, ultimately would not have been informed of it.[332] At the very least we must admit Dmitrii to have been ignorant of who he was [if he was an impostor] and that, had he been raised by the Jesuits, he undoubtedly would have been taught to speak and to read and to write in Latin. However, it is very certain that he spoke no Latin. I can testify to that. He knew even less how to read and write it, which I can show by the poor manner in which he signed his name.[333] Dmitrii would also have favored the Jesuits more than he did if he had been raised by them.[334] Yet there were only three of them in all Russia, who came after the Polish soldiers, who had no other clerics [with them].[335] One of these Jesuits, after Dmitrii's coronation, was sent to Rome at their solicitation.

Concerning the objection that he did not speak native Russian, I respond that I heard him speak shortly after his arrival in Russia. I found that he spoke Russian as well as could be expected except that he sometimes mixed in a Polish phrase to embellish the language. I have even seen letters that he dictated on various subjects before he was received in Moscow, which were so correct that no Russian could find fault with them.

And though he sometimes made errors in pronunciation of some words, that is not sufficient evidence to condemn him considering his long absence from the country and [that he left Russia] at a very young age.

As for the argument that he ridiculed the customs of the Russians and that he did not observe their religion except in form,[336] it is not necessary to marvel at this—especially if one considers their customs and life-styles, for they are rude and gross, without any civility. And Russia is a nation of liars, without loyalty, without law, without conscience—sodomites and corrupted by infinite other vices and brutalities. Boris Fedorovich, who was above suspicion, detested not so much the Russians as their vices, and he brought to the country what little reform there is. How then could Dmitrii (who knew something of the world, having been brought up for some time in Poland, which is a free country, and among the high nobles) have done less than to desire some reform and civility among his subjects?[337]

It should be added that his observation of the Russian religion was no different than that of many Russians that I know, among others a man named Postnik Dmitriev who, as a member of an embassy sent by Boris Fedorovich to Denmark, learned something of what religion is about. Upon his return from Denmark, when among friends he openly ridiculed the ignorance of the Muscovites.[338] Why should Dmitrii not have abhorred their ignorance? For his age he did not lack judgement and was devoted to reading the Holy Scripture. And he had, no doubt, heard religious differences discussed in Poland and had learned the meaning of the articles of faith which all Christians must believe. In this I speak only to the charges leveled, although I have been assured that no foreigners accuse him of this, nor are there any but a very few Russians who could have detected in him anything by which he could be accused of sacrilege, for he observed all their ceremonies generally.[339] However, I am not unaware that he was resolved to found a university.[340]

To conclude, if he were Polish, this did not seem to disturb anyone. The Russians, including Boris and his faction as well as the now reigning Emperor Vasilii Shuiskii, would not have passed up so sure a weapon if they could have seriously alleged that Dmitrii was a foreigner.

[Consider] those who are inclined to object, as do some Russians, that whoever Dmitrii was, the palatine of Sandomierz would have known. If this be so, and Dmitrii could have been other than the true son of Ivan Vasil'evich, why was the palatine so quick to ally himself with him, considering that he was informed of the treason of which Shuiskii was convicted shortly after Dmitrii arrived in Moscow?[341] Moreover, should he have wanted to ally himself with [an impostor], it seems reasonable to believe that the palatine would have counseled him not to dismiss the Poles and the Cossacks that Dmitrii kept with him, since he could retain them without any suspicion inasmuch as Dmitrii's predecessors had always tried to attract as many foreigners to their service as possible. This Dmitrii did not do, for he dismissed them all except for a company of one hundred horse. Similarly, I believe that the palatine would have brought a larger force with the empress, his daughter, than he did, and he would have found means to have the Poles quartered close to one another. Instead, they were lodged very far apart and at the discretion of the Russians, this even after the consummation of the marriage when there was so much talk of treason, as was mentioned above. The palatine would have procured these things by request from Dmitrii, and he would have warned and counseled him so that they might have easily prevented the massacre.[342]

There is greater proof that Dmitrii was Russian, that he was the true son of Ivan Vasil'evich. First, I believe that during his life or after his death his adversaries would have done their utmost to find his kin, whoever they might be, especially if we consider the Russian system and way of doing things.[343] Then, it is probable that, if Dmitrii felt himself to be culpable, he would have worked above all and everywhere to please the Russians. He knew very well that Boris could do no more to discredit him than to call him a heretic. Thus, he would not have allowed any Jesuits to enter Moscow.[344] He knew well enough that Boris had incurred the ill will of the Russian people by trying to ally himself with a foreign prince, so Dmitrii might have prevented this ill will by allying himself with a Russian house, as all his predecessors had done.[345] This would have fortified his position. However, when we come to consider Dmitrii's confidence we shall see that he could not be less than the son of a great prince. He had an eloquence which charmed all the Russians. There even shone in him a certain inexpressible majesty not seen before among the lords in Russia, much less in one of low quality as he would necessarily have been had he not been the son of Ivan Vasil'evich. Dmitrii's enterprise also seems enough to prove his rightful claim—to assail so great a country with so few men when that country was flourishing more than ever and was governed by a wily prince who was feared by his subjects, who was allied with most of the principal houses of Russia, and who had driven out, put to death, or exiled all those whom he suspected.[346] [Boris also] had the good wishes of the clergy, and, insofar as one might have judged, he had by favors and alms attracted and acquired the heart of everyone in Russia. He was at peace with all his neighbors, and he had reigned eight or nine years peacefully.[347] Let us also not forget the mother of Dmitrii, who, along with several of his living relatives, could have [called Dmitrii an impostor] had he been one.[348]

Next, let us consider his condition when he was abandoned by most of the Polish troops. What boldness this was to place himself in the hands of the Russians (upon whose loyalty he could not yet count, their forces numbering no more than eight or nine thousand men, of whom a large part were peasants) and to resist an army of more than a hundred thousand men. And when he lost the battle and lost the small number of cannon that he had, along with all his munitions, he returned with thirty or forty persons to a town named Ryl'sk (which had surrendered to him a short time before) without any assurance of the townspeople's loyalty.[349] From there he went to Putivl, which is a large and rich city, where he stayed from January until the following May, without ever showing in the midst of his adversities anything but his former [confidence]—even though Boris made every effort, both through secret plotting and by overt means, to have Dmitrii poisoned, killed, or imprisoned.[350] Boris also made numerous false allegations to persuade the people that Dmitrii was an impostor—but without ever being inclined to question Dmitrii's mother in public to find out who he really was.[351] And Boris was finally compelled to say that, although Dmitrii was the true son of Ivan Vasil'evich, he ought not to be accepted because he was not legitimate (as the son of the seventh wife, which is against the Russian religion) and because he was a heretic. Yet this proved to be of no avail against Dmitrii.[352]

Next, let us speak of Dmitrii's clemency toward everyone after he was received in Moscow, and especially toward the present emperor, Vasilii Shuiskii, who had been convicted of treason. That Shuiskii and his house had never been loyal servitors of their princes was confirmed by the Russian Chronicles and by his behavior toward Boris, and Dmitrii was even implored by everyone present to have Shuiskii put to death, considering that he had always been a disturber of the public peace.[353] (I heard and saw all this with my own eyes and ears.) Notwithstanding these things, Dmitrii pardoned him, although he knew well that only the house of Shuiskii would dare aspire to the crown. Dmitrii also pardoned many others, because he was without any suspicion.

Moreover, if he had been an impostor, as they say, and the truth of this was known only a short time before his assassination, why was he not taken prisoner? Or, why did they not take him alive to the public square to prove before the people assembled there that he was an impostor instead of killing him and throwing the country into such great division in which many have lost their lives? And must all the country believe, without any other proof, the word of four or five men who were the principal conspirators?[354] Further, why is it that Vasilii Shuiskii and his accomplices have taken so much trouble to devise lies to render Dmitrii odious to the people?[355] They have had letters read publicly which stated that Dmitrii wanted to give the greater part of Russia to the king of Poland and to his father-in-law the palatine—in short, that he wanted to split up Russia.[356] Likewise, [they claimed] that he had sent all the treasury to Poland[357] and that, had he lived, he would have had all the common people and the nobility assemble outside the city on the next day, which was a Sunday, on the pretext that he wished to amuse himself and the palatine, his father-in-law, and that he wished to show the palatine all the cannon, which would have to be brought out for this purpose. But Dmitrii's real purpose, [they claimed,] was to have all the Russians cut to pieces by the Poles, to have their houses plundered, and to put the city to fire.[358] [It is also alleged] that he had sent word to Smolensk for the same thing to be done there. To infinite other lies they added that the body of the true Dmitrii, murdered seventeen years ago, was found completely uncorrupted. As has already been mentioned, this Dmitrii was canonized as a saint by the command of Shuiskii. All this was done to make the people believe Shuiskii's words.

And so I conclude that if Dmitrii had been an impostor, the pure proven truth would have been sufficient to render him odious to everyone. And if Dmitrii had felt himself to be culpable in anything, he would have had just cause to believe the machinations and treasons plotted and contrived against his person. He was well aware of them and could easily have overcome them.[359] I believe that neither during his life nor after his death could anyone prove that he was an impostor. Moreover, Boris suspected [that he was the true Dmitrii] and for this reason resorted to tyranny.[360] [Dmitrii's authenticity is also supported] by the sheer diversity of opinions about him, not to mention his own bearing, his confidence, his boldness, his lack of suspicion, and the other princely qualities that he had—qualities which are not found in an impostor and usurper.

Bearing in mind everything which has been said above about this Dmitrii, I conclude that he was the true Dmitrii Ivanovich, son of the Emperor Ivan Vasil'evich, surnamed the Tyrant!

END

NOTES

BIBLIOGRAPHY

INDEX

NOTES

INTRODUCTION

1. Zhordaniia, *Ocherki*, I, pp. 295, 375–76; Adelung, *Kritisch-literärische Übersicht*, II, p. 20.

2. Mansuy, *Le Monde*, pp. 430–32; Albert Lortholary, *Le Mirage russe en France au XVIIIe siècle* (Paris, 1951), p. 14.

3. N. M. Karamzin (1766–1826) made extensive use of Margeret's book in composing volume eleven of his famous *Istoriia Gosudarstva Rossiiskago*. It was Karamzin's high opinion of Margeret as a source which led Nikolai Ustrialov to translate the work into Russian in 1830.

4. Paris, *Chronique*, I, p. 425; Ustrialov, *Skazaniia sovremennikov*, I, pp. 240–41; Mongault, "Mérimée," p. 195; Margeret, *Sostoianie* (1913), pp. 3–7; Kliuchevskii, *Skazaniia inostrantsev*, p. 20; Seredonin, *Sochinenie*, p. 342; Pirling, *Iz Smutnago Vremeni*, p. 193; Kostomarov, *Smutnoe Vremia*, p. 7; Platonov, *Boris Godunov*, p. 189; Platonov, *Moscow and the West*, pp. 29, 37, 48; Smirnov, *Vosstanie*, pp. 88, 368–69; Koretskii, *Formirovanie*, pp. 231, 253–54; Alpatov, *Russkaia mysl'*, pp. 29–35; Leitsch, "Herberstein's Impact," p. 165.

5. See G. Lozinski, "La Russie dans la littérature française du moyen age," *Revue des Études Slaves* 9 (1929), 71–88, 253–69; H. Pirenne, "Draps d'Ypres à Novgorod," *Revue Belge de Philologie et d'Histoire* 9 (1930), 563–66.

6. Prior to 1555 a few Russians had apparently traveled in France. See Kirchner, *Commercial Relations*, pp. 56–57, 94–95.

7. Kirchner, *Rise of the Baltic Question*, pp. 45, 237–40.

8. Kirchner, *Commercial Relations*, pp. 95–106; Zhordaniia, *Ocherki*, I, pp. 3, 140–79; Haumant, *La Culture française*, pp. 3–4.

9. Kirchner, *Rise of the Baltic Question*, pp. 241–42; Zhordaniia, "Les premiers marchands," p. 11.

10. Alexandra Kalmykow, "A Sixteenth-century Russian Envoy to France," *Slavic Review* 23 (1964), 701–05.

11. See Zhordaniia, *Ocherki*, I, pp. 59, 209–10, 372; Jehan Sauvage, *Memoire du voiage en Russie fait en 1586* (Paris, 1855).

12. Kirchner, *Commercial Relations*, p. 104; Zhordaniia, *Ocherki*, I, p. 372; Ikonnikov, *Snosheniia*, p. 6.

13. Zhordaniia, "Les premiers marchands," p. 11; Zhordaniia, *Ocherki*, I, pp. 95–116; Platonov, *Moscow and the West*, p. 33.

14. Paris, *Chronique*, I, pp. 404–22; Hellie, *Enserfment*, p.169; Howe, *False Dmitri*, p. 131; Zhordaniia, *Ocherki*, I, pp. 265–67; Pierre de La Ville, *Discours sommaire de ce qui est arrivé en Moscovie* . . . ,Vol. 5 of *Bibliothèque Russe et Polonaise* (Paris, 1859), p. 17.

15. Due to the general neglect of Margeret's biography, for a long time there was considerable debate over his nationality. More than one seventeenth-century source listed him as coming from Franche-Comté, then part of the Spanish Habsburg Empire. This mistake has been repeated by some of Margeret's later biographers. Haumant, *La Culture française*, p. 5; de Thou, *Histoire*, XIV, p. 492; Margeret, *Estat* (1860), pp. ii–iv; Claude Courtépée, *Description générale et particulière du duché de Bourgogne*, 4 vols. (Dijon, 1847–48), II, p. 426.

16. Although there is no way to know for certain, the Margerets seem to have made a fortune in the salt trade, perhaps even trading with the East Baltic and Russia in the 1560s. Claude Margeret was still active in the salt trade in 1580; and the family expertise in the salt market was eventually tapped by King Henri IV. Margeret, *Estat* (1860), pp. iii–iv; Kirchner, *Commercial Relations*, pp. 95–99; Zhordaniia, *Ocherki*, I, pp. 169–70; Drouot and Gros, *Recherches*, pp. 126–27.

17. Margeret, *Estat* (1860), pp. iii–iv; Drouot and Gros, *Recherches*, p. 157.

18. It is possible that Jacques' father was Guillaume Margeret, but there are no French records to confirm this. (See Zhordaniia, *Ocherki*, I, p. 247.) Nor are there records of Jacques' birth, which may have occurred as late as the 1570s. Koretskii's estimate of 1550 is too early. See *Great Soviet Encyclopedia* (New York, 1977–), XV, p. 463.

19. Zhordaniia, *Ocherki*, I, p. 249; Bussov, *Khronika*, p. 112; Mansuy, *Le Monde*, p.429; Margeret, *Estat* (1607), pp. Aii–Aiii, 9, 16–16(v), 51.

20. The traditional view of Margeret's religion may be found in Adelung, *Kritisch-literärische Übersicht*, II, p. 20; Platonov, *Moscow and the West*, p. 29; and Margeret, *Sostoianie* (1830), p. xx. Evidence indicating that he was a Protestant includes his family background, his early and continued support for Henri IV, the persecution of his family by the Catholic League, his position of leadership in Muscovite service when most of his German and Livonian troops were Protestant, his ties to Tsar Dmitrii's inner circle of Protestant advisors, comments about him by Western European Protestants, his close contact with members of the English Muscovy Company, his efforts to aid Muscovy against Catholic Poland, and his close ties with several zealously Calvinist princes in Germany. See Margeret, *Estat* (1860), pp. xix–xxvi; Bussov, *Khronika*, p. 112; Pirling, *Iz Smutnago Vremeni*, pp. 182–94; Purchas, *Hakluytus Posthumus*, XIV, pp. 225–26; Boldakov, *Sbornik*, pp. 91–98, 123.

21. Henri Drouot, *Mayenne et la Bourgogne*, 2 vols. (Dijon, 1937), I, pp. 340–41, 413.

22. Drouot and Gros, *Recherches*, pp. 3–4, 49–52, 112–14, 118.

23. Margeret, *Estat* (1860), pp. iv–v, xxx.

24. Drouot and Gros, *Recherches*, pp. 126–27.

25. Mansuy, *Le Monde*, p. 426.

26. Early reports of the progress of imperial troops against the Turks were enthusiastically reported in Europe in 1595, and many French soldiers joined the crusade. See Fernand Braudel, *The Mediterranean and the Mediterranean World in the Age of Philip II*, 2 vols. (New York: Harper and Row, 1975), II, p. 1201.

27. Adelung wrongly asserted that Margeret served Stephen Bathory, who was already dead by this time. Adelung, *Kritisch-literärische Übersicht*, II, p. 18.

28. Margeret, *Estat* (1860), pp. v, xxx.

29. There has been considerable confusion over just when Margeret reached Muscovy. Adelung incorrectly guessed 1601. Richard Hellie believed that Margeret was in Muscovy in the 1590s, probably basing

this erroneous assumption on the fact that Margeret's book covered the period 1590–1606. See Margeret, *Sostoianie* (1830), p. ix; Zhordaniia, *Ocherki,* I, pp. 248–49; Adelung, *Kritisch-literärische Übersicht,* II, p. 18; Hellie, *Enserfment,* pp. 169, 353 n.77.

30. Alpatov, *Russkaia mysl',* p. 28; Zhordaniia, *Ocherki,* I, pp. 248–49; SGGD, II, p. 605.

31. Hellie, *Enserfment,* p. 169; Margeret, *Sostoianie* (1830), p. ix; Massa, *Kratkoe izvestie,* p. 118. Margeret was not the captain of Boris's bodyguard as some historians have assumed. See Kliuchevskii, *Skazaniia inostrantsev,* p. 20; Ustrialov, *Skazaniia sovremennikov,* I, p. 237.

32. Alpatov, *Russkaia mysl',* p. 30; Mansuy, *Le Monde,* p. 426; Margeret, *Sostoianie* (1830), p. xviii; Zhordaniia, *Ocherki,* I, p. 245; Ikonnikov, *Snosheniia,* p. 9; Kliuchevskii, *Skazaniia inostrantsev,* p. 21.

33. Bussov, *Khronika,* p. 102; Massa, *Kratkoe izvestie,* pp. 86–89; Ustrialov, *Skazaniia sovremennikov,* I, p. 237. Margeret's daring action at Dobrynichi was immortalized in A. S. Pushkin's *Boris Godunov,* pp. 86–88.

34. Zhordaniia, *Ocherki,* I, pp. 250–51; Mansuy, *Le Monde,* p. 425; Barbour, *Dimitry,* pp. 137–38.

35. Zhordaniia, *Ocherki,* I, p. 257; Massa, *Kratkoe izvestie,* p. 118; Bussov, *Khronika,* p. 112; de Thou, *Histoire,* XIV, p. 492; Ustrialov, *Skazaniia sovremennikov,* I, p. 238.

36. The traditional view is that military reform did not take place until after 1607, when Karl IX of Sweden sent Vasilii Shuiskii a book on modern military tactics—the result being the eventual production of a Russian book on the subject, Mikhailov's *Regulations.* However, more than one Soviet military historian claims that the Muscovite army was actually more advanced than has traditionally been thought and that work on the book of military regulations must have begun under Tsar Dmitrii. Since several sources credit Margeret with the victory at Dobrynichi (where the Muscovite infantry used a linear battle formation for the first time) and since Dmitrii often used Margeret's troops to train the Muscovite forces in the art of war, it is quite possible that Captain Margeret provided some of the "advanced" training of the Muscovite army prior to 1607. On Margeret's military skills and the debate over the arrival of "modern" tactics in Muscovy, see Bussov,

Khronika, pp. 102, 186–87; Massa, *Kratkoe izvestie*, pp. 86–89; Alpatov, *Russkaia mysl'*, pp. 17, 33; Zhordaniia, *Ocherki*, I, pp. 250, 255, 273–76; Hellie, *Enserfment*, pp. 162–68; L. G. Beskrovnyi, *Ocherki po istochnikovedeniia voennoi Rossii* (Moscow, 1957), p. 61; Razin, *Istoriia*, III, pp. 68–76.

37. Had Margeret been on duty the night before the murder, chances are that he would not have allowed Vasilii Shuiskii (whom Margeret knew to be Dmitrii's enemy) to dismiss most of the guards in the Kremlin. As it was, the tsar had only a few guards and not even one officer with him when he was killed. See de Thou, *Histoire*, XIV, p. 494; Howe, *False Dmitri*, p. 44.

38. See de Thou, *Histoire*, XIV, p. 504.

39. Zhordaniia, *Ocherki*, I, pp. 258–60; Massa, *Kratkoe izvestie*, p. 154; Margeret, *Sostoianie* (1830), p. xii.

40. Margeret, *Estat* (1607), pp. 41(v)–42, 45(v)–46, 47–47(v).

41. Margeret, *Estat* (1860), pp. iv, viii; Pirling, *Iz Smutnago Vremeni*, pp. 193–94. Henri Chevreul incorrectly claimed that Margeret had been financially ruined by Dmitrii's assassination and implied that he was forced to return home to make a financial recovery. This appears to be a misreading of de Thou, *Histoire*, XIV, p. 504.

42. Margeret, *Estat* (1607), pp. 44(v)–47(v).

43. This may explain the remarkable similarity between some of the land grants issued by the second pretender and ones later received by Margeret from the king of Poland. See Zhordaniia, *Ocherki*, I, pp. 262–63; Koretskii, *Formirovanie*, pp. 326–27; SGGD, II, p. 605.

44. Margeret's Soviet biographer believed that he joined a group of Polish-Lithuanian mercenaries at this time and did not enter Sigismund's service for many months. There is no evidence to support this claim. Margeret was closely associated with Mikhail Saltykov, and it is very likely that the two men entered Polish service together. (The relationship between Saltykov and Margeret has never been appreciated by Russian or Soviet scholars, even though the two men served together as early as 1603 and worked closely together until the end of 1611.) See Zhordaniia, *Ocherki*, I, pp. 263, 267; Bussov, *Khronika*, p. 32; SGGD, II, pp. 605–06.

45. Zhordaniia, *Ocherki*, I, pp. 264–67.

46. Ibid., pp. 268–69, 283–89; Margeret, *Estat* (1860), pp. viii–ix.

47. Margeret received very generous land grants from Sigismund for his decisive role in this battle. See *Akty, otnosiashchiesia k istorii zapadnoi Rossii,* 5 vols. (St. Petersburg, 1846–53), IV, no. 183, DCCLXVIII–DCCLXIX; Hellie, *Enserfment,* p. 329 n.47; Zhordaniia, *Ocherki,* I, pp. 270–79; Bussov, *Khronika,* pp. 186–87.

48. These charges may be found in Ustrialov, *Skazaniia sovremennikov,* I, p. 238, and in Zhordaniia, *Ocherki,* I, p. 280. While Margeret did play a major role in the battle, it appears that the Polish commander Gosiewski was responsible for the decision to burn the outer city. See Stanislas Zolkiewski, *Expedition to Moscow* (London: Polonica Publications, 1959), pp. 123–24.

49. These charges may be found in Zhordaniia, *Ocherki,* I, pp. 282–83, 293. See Margeret's relevant correspondence in Purchas, *Hakluytus Posthumus,* XIV, pp. 225–26.

50. On this charge see Zhordaniia, *Ocherki,* I, p. 269; SGGD, II, pp. 605–06. Kremlin records do indicate that Margeret periodically withdrew money from the treasury to pay his troops. He apparently also withdrew approximately 1800 rubles' worth of precious items for his own annual salary (September 1610–August 1611). See *Russkaia istoricheskaia biblioteka,* II, cols. 232–36, 243; Zhordaniia, *Ocherki,* I, pp. 283–90.

51. Margeret, *Estat* (1860), p. ix; SGGD, II, p. 606.

52. Purchas, *Hakluytus Posthumus,* XIV, pp. 225–26.

53. Zhordaniia, *Ocherki,* I, pp. 291–92, 302–04, 308–10, 319–23, 327–28, 353; Platonov, *Moscow and the West,* pp. 47–48.

54. SGGD, II, pp. 604–07; Zhordaniia, *Ocherki,* I, pp. 310–12, 328–29.

55. Zhordaniia, *Ocherki,* I, pp. 327–47, 355–57, 362–67.

56. Margeret's Soviet biographer (who took Pozharskii's opinion of the Frenchman at face value) completely misinterpreted Margeret's activities in this period, his correspondence, and his later association with Prince Janusz Radziwiłł. See Zhordaniia, *Ocherki,* I, pp. 293–379. Contradicting Zhordaniia completely or in part are Purchas, *Hakluytus Posthumus,* XIV, pp. 225–26; Waliszewski, *La Crise,* p. 425; Margeret, *Sostoianie* (1913), p. 7; Boldakov, *Sbornik,* pp. 91–98, 123; and Ustrialov, *Skazaniia sovremennikov,* I, pp. 240–41.

57. Margeret, *Estat* (1860), pp. xix–xxvi; Pirling, *Iz Smutnago Vremeni*, pp. 182–88; Boldakov, *Sbornik*, pp. 91–94, 124–25; Zhordaniia, *Ocherki*, I, p. 347.

58. Koretskii incorrectly indicated that Margeret might have died in 1618. See *Great Soviet Encyclopedia* (New York, 1977–), XV, p. 463.

59. Margeret, *Estat* (1860), pp. 125–26; *Mercure de France*, February 1738, pp. 371–72.

60. *Biographie Universelle Ancienne et Moderne*, 45 vols. (Paris, 1842–65), III, p. 391. Sébastien de Pontault, sieur de Beaulieu, is best remembered for his monumental *Les Glorieuses Conquêtes de Louis le Grand*, published in Paris between 1676 and 1694.

61. Cook, "Image of Russia," pp. 155–56; Mansuy, *Le Monde*, p. 426; Ruffman, *Das Russlandbild*, p. 176; Mongault, "Mérimée," pp. 194–95; Margeret, *Estat* (1860), pp. i–ii, viii, xxx.

62. Atkinson, *Nouveaux horizons*, pp. xi, 52–53; Wade, *Origins*, pp. 363–65; Rouillard, *Turk*, pp. 178–79; Martino, *L'Orient*, p. 51.

63. Wade, *Origins*, pp. xi, 16, 52–53, 361–62, 366; Atkinson, *Extraordinary Voyage*, p. 1; Atkinson, *Nouveaux horizons*, pp. 22–30, 44–45, 52–53, 102, 359, 365; Rouillard, *Turk*, p. 393; Waugh, *Defiance*, p. 10; Bodin, *Method*, p. 44.

64. Atkinson, *Nouveaux horizons*, pp. 74–75; Rouillard, *Turk*, pp. 363–64; Wade, *Origins*, p. 367; McFarlane, *History*, pp. 487–90.

65. Margeret, *Estat* (1607), pp. Aii–Aiii.

66. Bodin, *Method*, p. 44; Wade, *Origins*, p. 366; Atkinson, *Nouveaux horizons*, p. 365; Church, *Constitutional Thought*, pp. 215–16.

67. Bodin, *Method*, pp. xxxvii, 43–51; Atkinson, *Nouveaux horizons*, p. 31; Brown, "*Methodus*," pp. 40, 63, 86–87, 109, 170–71; Margeret, *Estat* (1607), pp. Aii(v)–Aiii.

68. Atkinson, *Nouveaux horizons*, pp. 10–12.

69. Wade, *Origins*, pp. 363, 366; Rouillard, *Turk*, pp. 178–79, 185–88, 292–93, 376–406.

70. Rouillard, *Turk*, pp. 189, 217, 230–31, 359–60; Waugh, *Defiance*, p. 189.

71. George Clark, *The Seventeenth Century* (New York, 1961), pp. xi–xix; Rouillard, *Turk*, p. 289; Waugh, *Defiance*, pp. 10, 189.

72. Rouillard, *Turk,* pp. 363, 377, 388, 393; Brown, *"Methodus,"* pp. 133, 142.

73. Rouillard, *Turk,* pp. 178–79, 182, 388–90; Waugh, *Defiance,* p. 23; Alpatov, *Russkaia mysl',* p. 32; Church, *Constitutional Thought,* pp. 217–18; Bodin, *Method,* p. 93; Bodin, *Commonwealth,* pp. 149, 201, 222, 507, 550, 614; Margeret, *Estat* (1607),p. Aii(v).

74. Charles J. Halperin, "Sixteenth-Century Foreign Travel Accounts of Muscovy: A Methodological Excursus," *The Sixteenth Century Journal* 6 (1975), 103–07; Szeftel, "Monarchie absolue," pp. 732–33; Ruffman, *Das Russlandbild,* pp. 126–27, 176; Seredonin, *Sochinenie,* pp. 6–8, 178–79; Kappeler, *Ivan Groznyi,* p. 14; BC, pp. x, 105; Anderson, *Britain's Discovery,* pp. 24–25; Martino, *L'Orient,* p. 308; Kliuchevskii, *Skazaniia inostrantsev,* p. 6.

75. Vernadsky, *Tsardom,* I, p. 117; Kliuchevskii, *Skazaniia inostrantsev,* p. 86; Kappeler, *Ivan Groznyi,* pp. 154, 230; Cook, "Image of Russia," pp. 115–16; Anderson, *Britain's Discovery,* p. 30; Kirchner, *Rise of the Baltic Question,* pp. 33–34, 39; Polosin, *Istoriia,* pp. 193, 215, 224.

76. Before Margeret's book was published, some French writers had made use of *Tractatus de duabus Sarmatiis* by Maciej z Miechowa. Herberstein's *Rerum Moscoviticarum Commentarii* was probably the most influential work on Russia in the sixteenth century, and it was often used by French writers. Latin accounts of Ivan IV's Livonian War, as well as Antonio Possevino's *Moscovia,* were also available to some French scholars by the end of the sixteenth century. The French themselves produced several cosmographies in the sixteenth century in which items of information about Russia (usually taken from Herberstein) could be found. Of particular note are the works of André Thevet, who even produced a rudimentary glossary of Russian words based upon sources available to him in France. See Zantuan, "Discovery," pp. 328–33; Limonov, *Kul'turnye sviazi,* pp. 97–109, 230; Leitsch, "Herberstein's Impact," pp. 8–9; Bodin, *Commonwealth,* p 548; Fournol, *Bodin,* p. 24; Bodin, *Method,* p. 378; Possevino, *Moscovia,* pp. ix, xxix–xxx; Atkinson, *Nouveaux horizons,* p. 462; Martino, *L'Orient,* p. 38; Atkinson, *Extraordinary Voyage,* pp. 1–3, 8; Kirchner, *Commercial Relations,* pp. 274–75.

77. Mansuy, *Le Monde,* pp. 10–15; Montaigne, *Complete Works,* passim.

78. Atkinson, *Nouveaux horizons*, p. 408; Brown, "*Methodus*," pp. 70, 83; Fournol, *Bodin*, p. 42; Franklin, *Bodin*, pp. 36–37; Church, *Constitutional Thought*, pp. 214–17; Bodin, *Method*, pp. 24, 90–94, 97–102, 110–12, 128, 216, 272–73, 292–93; Bodin, *Commonwealth*, pp. 23, 149, 201, 222, 507, 550, 555, 596, 605, 614, 719, 722, 780.

79. Limonov, *Kul'turnye sviazi*, pp. 199–230; Kinser, *Works of de Thou*, pp. 1–2, 7–10.

80. De Thou, *Histoire*, XIV, pp. 450–67, 490–504; Ustrialov, *Skazaniia sovremennikov*, I, p. 323; Kinser, *Works of de Thou*, pp. 83–85. Access to Margeret's wealth of information on Russia and Eastern Europe may well have helped convince de Thou to extend his *Universal History* to cover the period up to 1607.

81. Maximilien de Béthune, duc de Sully, *Memoires*, VIII (London, 1778), pp. 321–22, 325; Charles Corbet, *L'Opinion française face à l'inconnue russe, 1799–1894* (Paris: Didier, 1967), p. 15.

82. Zhordaniia, *Ocherki*, I, pp. 211, 214–17, 242–43; Ikonnikov, *Snosheniia*, pp. 7–8.

83. Pirling, *Iz Smutnago Vremeni*, pp. 182–88, 190–93; Zhordaniia, *Ocherki*, I, pp. 245, 260, 375; Waliszewski, *La Crise*, p. 231.

84. Pirling, *Iz Smutnago Vremeni*, pp. 193–94; Zhordaniia, *Ocherki*, I, pp. 242–43, 260; Pierling, *Dimitri et Possevino*, pp. 4–6.

85. Rouillard, *Turk*, p. 361; Ikonnikov, *Snosheniia*, pp. 9–10.

86. Kirchner, *Commercial Relations*, p. 108; Mansuy, *Le Monde,* p. 424; David Buisseret, *Sully* (London: Eyre and Spottiswoode, 1968), p. 19.

87. Margeret, *Estat* (1607), pp. Aii–Aii(v); Alpatov, *Russkaia mysl'*, p. 30.

88. Zhordaniia, *Ocherki*, I, pp. 238, 374–75.

89. Pirling, *Iz Smutnago Vremeni*, pp. 190–93; Platonov, *Boris Godunov*, pp. 52–53; Rambaud, *History*, I, p. 330.

90. Alpatov, *Russkaia mysl'*, p. 30.

91. Margeret, *Sostoianie* (1830), pp. xvii–xviii; Pirling, *Iz Smutnago Vremeni*, pp. 193–94.

92. Bodin, *Method*, pp. xxxvii, 42–43; Polybius, *Histories*, I, pp. xi–xiv, 35–36; Margeret, *Estat* (1607), p. Aiii.

93. Bodin, *Method*, pp. 43–44, 50–51; Atkinson, *Nouveaux horizons*, pp. 35–37; Polybius, *Histories*, I, pp. xii–xiv; Alpatov, *Russkaia*

mysl', pp. 29, 33; Margeret, *Estat* (1607), pp. Aii–Aiii.

94. Margeret, *Sostoianie* (1913), pp. 3–7; Alpatov, *Russkaia mysl'*, p. 29; Zhordaniia, *Ocherki,* I, p. 295; Mongault, "Mérimée," pp. 194–95; Ustrialov, *Skazaniia sovremennikov,* I, p. 241; Adelung, *Kritisch-literärische Übersicht,* II, p. 45; Platonov, *Moscow and the West,* p. 37; Seredonin, *Sochinenie,* p. 342; Koretskii, *Formirovanie,* pp. 231, 253–54; Smirnov, *Vosstanie,* p. 368.

95. See Alpatov, *Russkaia mysl'*, pp. 28–32; Dolinin, "K izucheniiu," p. 490; Kopanev and Man'kov, *Vosstanie,* p. 35; Koretskii, *Formirovanie,* ch. 6, esp. pp. 249–57; Hellie, *Enserfment,* pp. 107–09. Cf. Smirnov, *Vosstanie,* pp. 88, 365–70. Theories that Tsar Dmitrii faced a growing popular revolt in the spring of 1606 are actually dependent upon a highly selective and questionable use of evidence. See nn. 259, 275 below.

96. Margeret, *Sostoianie* (1830), pp. xxi–xxii; Ustrialov, *Skazaniia sovremennikov,* I, p. 241; Margeret, *Sostoianie* (1913), pp. 3, 10; Paris, *Chronique,* I, p. 425; Pierling, *La Russie,* III, pp. 397–429; Pirling, *Iz Smutnago Vremeni,* pp. 182, 193–94, 229; Barbour, *Dimitry,* p. 325.

97. Scholars wishing to use Margeret's French text should consult the 1607 edition if at all possible. An excellent copy is located in the Houghton Library, Harvard University. This copy was formerly in Tsar Nikolai II's library and was apparently a gift from Prince Aleksei Lobanov-Rostovskii, a noted diplomat and historian. Another copy, acquired in the seventeenth century from the library of John Morris for inclusion in the Old Royal Library, is now in the British Library. A very good copy (the original copy belonging to Henri IV) is located in the Bibliothèque Nationale in Paris. A beautiful copy is located in the M. E. Saltykov-Shchedrin State Public Library in Leningrad. A fair copy, incorrectly catalogued as a 1669 edition in the *National Union Catalogue,* is located in the rare book collection of the University of Minnesota. A copy missing its title page and also incorrectly catalogued as a 1669 edition is in the rare book collection of the University of Michigan. No doubt there are others.

Problems with the later French editions are discussed in my dissertation, "Jacques Margeret's *State of the Russian Empire and Grand*

Duchy of Muscovy: A translation" (Boston College, 1976). There is no evidence whatsoever for the existence of a 1721 edition, as claimed by Adelung; nor is there any evidence for the existence of a 1769 edition, as claimed by Tatishchev. Kordt's reference to a 1754 edition was a misprinted reference to Henri Chevreul's 1855 edition. See Adelung, *Kritisch-literärische Übersicht*, II, p. 21; V. N. Tatishchev, *Istoriia Rossiiskaia*, 7 vols. (Moscow-Leningrad, 1962–68), VII, p. 449; V. Kordt, *Chuzhozemni podorozhni po skhidnii Evropi do 1700 r.* (Kiev, 1926), p. 67.

98. Ustrialov made many errors in translation. For example, in one passage Margeret wrote that Boris Godunov "even appeared to refuse to see those from the Empress's Council who came before his door." Ustrialov translated this to indicate that Boris feigned refusal even when offered the throne in the Duma. See Margeret, *Estat* (1607), p. 7; Margeret, *Sostoianie* (1830), p. 15. In another passage, referring to an estimate of the size of the Muscovite army in 1598, Margeret wrote, "I say there were at least this many, for Russia has never had greater power than at that time." Ustrialov translated this as "I say less than that many, for Russia has never been more disturbed than at that time." See Margeret, *Estat* (1607), p. 8; Margeret, *Sostoianie* (1830), p. 17. More insidious is Ustrialov's occasional "doctoring" of the text so that it conformed to official imperial Russian views of Boris Godunov. For example, in describing Boris's activities in 1598 in the matter of choosing a new tsar, Margeret wrote that Boris wished "to convoke in due course the Estates of the country." Ustrialov translated this to read that Boris wished to convoke a "fake" Assembly. See Margeret, *Estat* (1607), p. 7(v); Margeret, *Sostoianie* (1830), p. 16. The error is repeated in Cherepnin, *Zemskie sobory*, p. 146.

STATE OF THE RUSSIAN EMPIRE AND GRAND DUCHY OF MUSCOVY

1. The image of Russia for most early modern Europeans was largely based upon classical sources. Ancient Scythia and the Scythians were well known to Herodotus, Plato, and Aristotle. Classical references to these supposed descendants of Herakles emphasized their

great abilities as warriors and horsemen. European writers of the sixteenth century often confused the ancient Scythians with the Mongol horsemen who conquered Russia in the thirteenth century. It was also not uncommon to attribute Scythian traits to the Russians themselves.

2. The Russians had actually paid homage to the khan of Kypchak (or the Golden Horde). The khanate of Crimea (1430–1783) was merely one of the successor states of the Golden Horde.

3. Margeret was trying to provide an accurate response to prevailing European notions about the meaning of the word "Russia." In the sixteenth century most European writers distinguished between Muscovy and Russia, often using "Russia" to mean the Ukraine or Lithuania and regarding Muscovy as a country located east of Russia. See Cook, "Image," p. 236; Herberstein, *Notes,* I, p. 6; Mansuy, *Le Monde,* pp. 10, 21–25, 37–38.

4. *Rusak* is a colloquial term meaning "Russian."

5. There is no evidence that the term "White Russia" was used before the Russian victory over the Mongols in 1380. In the mid-fifteenth century, the word *belyi* ("white") seems to have been applied to the ruler of Muscovy rather than to the country itself, perhaps in conscious imitation of the title of the khan of Kypchak. This khanate was originally known as the White Horde, white being the Mongol and Chinese symbol for west. The assertion of Muscovy's position as a successor to this Mongol khanate may have led to a transfer of the name "white khan" (*belyi tsar'* in Russian) to the grand prince of Moscow. It is interesting to note that this transfer coincided with Muscovy's claim to be an Orthodox successor to the defunct Byzantine Empire. Since the khan had assumed the imperial status of the Byzantine emperor in the minds of many Russians during the period of Mongol domination, the title may have represented a double assertion of Muscovy's independence and sovereignty. See Szeftel, "Title," pp. 70–74; Cherniavsky, "Khan or Basileus"; Vernadsky, *Mongols,* pp. 138–40, 235–36, 388–89; Prawdin, *Mongol Empire,* p. 518; Vakar, "Name"; Uroff, "Kotoshikhin," pp. 90, 388–89; V. V. Bartol'd, *Istoriia izucheniia Vostoka v Evrope i Rossii* (Leningrad, 1925), p. 172; Keenan, "Muscovy and Kazan."

6. The origin and significance of the term "Black Russia" is not

known. As early as the thirteenth century it was applied to the upper Nieman River area which came under the domination of the grand prince of Lithuania during the Mongol conquest of Russia. While it may have been called Black Russia because of its heavy tax burden as part of the Lithuanian state, the term may have merely distinguished this area from White Russia, the Russian lands under the domination of the "white khan" of Kypchak. By the seventeenth century the term applied to a large region of western Russia stretching far south from the original area. Margeret is certainly one of the first Western European authors to identify and locate Black Russia, although it became fairly well known in the West during the seventeenth century. See John Seldon, *Titles of Honor* (London, 1614), p. 84; Mercator and Hondius, *Atlas*, I, p. 105; Vakar, "Name," p. 202; Hrushevsky, *History*, pp. 268–69.

Podolia was a wooded-steppe province of Poland-Lithuania located near Muscovy's southwestern border. Margeret, however, uses the word in a general sense to mean the Ukraine.

7. The *versta* is slightly longer than a kilometer. The "league" Margeret refers to is approximately two and a half miles. Margeret's distances are not accurate, but estimates of distance in Muscovy varied greatly depending upon routes taken. His overall estimate of the size of the state (very roughly 4,000,000 sq. kilometers) is not unreasonable.

8. Here Margeret confuses Tsar Simeon Bekbulatovich, a Tatar prince in Russian service, with Tsar Simeon, khan of Kazan at the time Ivan IV conquered that country. The latter, known as Khan Yadigar before his conversion to Christianity, lived in Muscovy until his death in 1565.

9. The Cheremissians (Mari), a group of the middle-Volga peoples of Finnish origin, caused many problems for the Muscovite government as the Russians extended their domain eastward. Zimin, "Osnovnye etapy," p. 51.

10. Although Margeret was one of the first western authors to note the fertility of the Astrakhan region, he merely echoes common European beliefs about the barometz plant, one of the many fabled monsters of "Tartary." Known in Europe since at least the early fifteenth century, the "Scythian lamb" or "vegetable lamb" was described in scientific works of the sixteenth and seventeenth centuries,

including a work published in Paris in 1605. Many Western Europeans continued to believe in the creature until the eighteenth century. See BC, p. 121; Herberstein, *Notes,* II, pp. 74–75; Olearius, *Travels,* p. 122; Collins, *Present State of Russia,* p. 85; Miege, *Relation,* p. 32; Atkinson, *Nouveaux horizons,* pp. 277–78; Mansuy, *Le Monde,* p. 427; Zantuan, "Discovery," p. 329.

The *brasse,* a French measure of length, was either five or six feet long.

11. Margeret was one of the few western writers before the eighteenth century to call this region "Siberia." Although Herberstein had referred to Siberia in passing, the area was customarily called Tartary in the sixteenth and even the late seventeenth century. Purchas, *Hakluytus Posthumus,* XIII, pp. 171–93; Olearius, *Travels,* pp. 105–06; Herberstein, *Notes,* I, p. 115, II, p. 27; Mercator and Hondius, *Atlas,* I, p. 105.

12. The Ob River was associated with European attempts to find a northeast passage to Cathay. Some outstanding sixteenth-century geographers believed that it was very near the northeastern "edge" of Asia and that the Asian continent sloped sharply to the south just beyond the river, providing a short-cut to Cathay. Others maintained that the elusive Cathay could only be reached by sailing up the Ob itself. A not uncommon view was that the Ob marked the northeastern boundary between Europe and Asia. See Cook, "Image," pp. 239–40, 251–52; Miege, *Relation,* p. 27; Purchas, *Hakluytus Posthumus,* XIII, pp. 202–04, XIV, pp. 292–97.

13. More than four Russian forts or "towns" were constructed in Siberia by the time Margeret wrote his account. Although the Russians were dominant, strong native resistance to Russian exploitation at the end of the sixteenth century had to be suppressed in 1604. Kerner, *Urge to the Sea,* pp. 68–88; Lantzeff, *Siberia,* pp. 87–115.

14. The battle of Mezö Keresztés was fought not in 1595 but in October 1596 near the Hungarian fort of Erlau (or Agria). The Turks were greatly aided in that battle and in the Hungarian War in general by the Crimean Tatars.

15. Livny, built in 1585 by the Muscovite government, was one of the most important new military outposts of the southern defense line. While it did represent a significant advance against the Tatars, it

was actually less than five hundred versts from the capital. This region was very sparsely populated, although perhaps less so than has been maintained by some historians. See Tikhomirov, *Rossiia,* p. 422; Struys, *Voyages,* p. 167. Tsarev-Borisov, on the lower Oskol River, was about seven hundred versts south of Moscow and only about two hundred fifty versts northwest of the important Tatar fortress of Azov. It was a very important first line of defense against the Tatars, as well as a possible forward base for Russian attacks against the Crimea.

16. This passage has been cited by many Russian historians. The Muscovite government actively promoted the growth of these new towns by transferring garrisons and encouraging volunteer settlers. Merchants and artisans gradually followed, and peasants settled in the vicinity where they tilled for themselves and were required to provide grain for the garrisons. See Kliuchevskii, *Skazaniia inostrantsev,* pp. 202–03; Platonov, *Ocherki,* p. 86; Tikhomirov, *Rossiia,* pp. 422–29.

17. As noted earlier, Margeret uses the term "Podolia" to mean the Ukraine. Overall, his geographic description of Russia is more accurate than that found in the works of most other western writers of the period.

18. When Margeret uses the term *denga* (plural *dengi*), he refers to *kopeinye dengi,* Russian coins first minted in 1534–35 and later known simply as *kopeiki* (kopeks). The French coin sol (sou) Margeret refers to is probably the sol tournois, then equal to one-tenth of an English shilling. The denier and denier tournois were French pennies worth one-tenth of a sol tournois.

19. The arpent is the French acre, equal to about one and a half English acres.

20. The Russian *Primary Chronicle* is indeed the source of the tradition that the Scandinavian Varangians or Normans were invited "from over the sea" by the native Slavs to rule over them sometime around the year 860 A.D., but it appears that Riurik and his brothers Sineus and Truvor came from Ladoga, located on the Volkhov River only some two hundred kilometers from Novgorod. Margeret may have consulted manuscripts of the Russian chronicles himself, although he does not specifically claim to have done so. He may also have been influenced by the French historian de Thou, who had written about the

Varangians and the Russian chronicles (without having seen them). Other travelers who learned Russian, including Herberstein and Jerome Horsey, apparently did consult the chronicles. See Herberstein, *Notes*, I, pp. 8–9; Cook, "Image," p. 421; Alpatov, *Russkaia mysl'*, p. 30; Limonov, *Kul'turnye sviazi*, pp. 204–06, 230.

21. Riurik became prince of Novgorod, not Vladimir, which was founded only in the twelfth century; the first person to be called grand prince of Vladimir was apparently Vsevolod III of the Large Nest (r. 1176–1212). The princes of Moscow were descended from Riurik in the male line, although they actually represented a junior branch of the family. The Holy Roman Emperor Maximilian II (r. 1564–76) was not the first to call the grand prince of Moscow emperor. In fact, the Holy Roman Emperor Maximilian I (r. 1493–1519) addressed Vasilii III as emperor in 1514, long before the conquest of Kazan, Astrakhan, and Siberia—a fact known by some sixteenth-century Western European writers, including de Thou. The king of Denmark used the title emperor in addressing Ivan III in 1493; the duke of Milan used it as early as 1463. Despite the confusion, Margeret's association of the title with the conquest of the Tatar khanates is very interesting and has considerable support from contemporary travelers and even the Russian government. Ivan IV justified his "imperial" title by his conquests of the Tatar khanates, and popular opinion held that the title was derived from Ivan's victories over the Tatars. See Cherniavsky, "Khan or Basileus," pp. 72–73; Szeftel, "Title," pp. 70–75; D'iakonov, *Vlast'*, pp. 142–43; Uroff, "Kotoshikhin," pp. 30, 308–09; Herberstein, *Notes*, I, pp. 37–38; Mayerberg, *Relation*, II, p. 34; Bodin, *Commonwealth*, p. 149; Massa, *Kratkoe izvestie*, p. 23; BC, pp. 264–65; Vernadsky, *Mongols*, p. 387; Limonov, *Kul'turnye sviazi*, p. 220; Pelenski, *Russia and Kazan*, pp. 208–09, 298–301.

22. The Russian word for king, *korol'*, need not be considered an imitation of the Polish word for king. The Russian term is easily derived directly from Germanic, e.g., Old High German *Karl* (after Charlemagne, Karl der Grosse, Carolus Magnus).

23. This was a common name for the shah of Persia in this period. *Kizilbasha* ("red-head") is derived from Turkish; although there is

some dispute concerning the origin of the word, it was corrupted into the Muscovite *Kizilbashets,* which referred to Persians in general and not just the shah. See Herberstein, *Notes,* I, p. 34; Szeftel, "Title," p. 72 n.41; Allen, *Russian Embassies,* I, pp. 237 – 38; Pushkarev, *Dictionary,* p. 38.

24. The belief that *tsar'* was derived from Hebrew was not uncommon in Muscovy at this time. The Slavonic Bible did equate the terms "tsar" and "king." It should also be pointed out that in this period Russian writers often compared the grand prince or tsar with Moses (a common device of Byzantine imperial oratory since Constantine the Great) or with other kings of the Old Testament. The current scholarly view is that *tsar'* was actually derived from *Caesar,* either by way of the Gothic *kaisar* or directly from Byzantine Greek (as a translation of *basileus*). Several writers in the sixteenth and seventeenth centuries noted the connection between "tsar" and "king," pointing out that it was a mistake to translate *tsar'* as "emperor." This was important because of a widely held view in Europe that the tsars wished to claim the imperial legacy of the defunct Byzantine Empire. See Olearius, *Travels,* p. 174; Herberstein, *Notes,* I, pp. 33-34; Collins, *Present State of Russia,* p. 54; Mayerberg, *Relation,* II, pp. 34-35; Szeftel, "Title," pp. 70-81; Rowland, "Problem of Advice," pp. 277–82.

25. Starting in 1590 the Muscovites attempted to dislodge the Swedes from Narva, which they had held since 1581. Indecisive campaigns led to an armistice in 1593 and to a formal peace treaty in 1595 which recognized Sweden's retention of that important Baltic port. Tsar Fedor did occasionally refer to himself as emperor in diplomatic correspondence. Szeftel, "Title," p. 79 n.59.

26. Although the Holy Roman Emperor Maximilian I had addressed Vasilii III as emperor in 1514, this was an exception based upon diplomatic needs of the time. After 1514 the Holy Roman emperors did not recognize this title until the eighteenth century, although they did recognize the title "tsar." (See DRV, XVI, pp. 138–49; Szeftel, "Title," p. 75.) The English were fairly consistent in recognizing the tsar as an emperor. (See DRV, XVI, pp. 157–64; Evans, "Queen Elizabeth and Tsar Boris"; Szeftel, "Title," p. 76.) As noted earlier, the king of Denmark had used the title emperor as early as 1493. (See DRV, XVI, pp. 164–67.)

27. Ivan IV actually had five sons: three by his first wife, Anastasiia Romanovna; one by his second wife, Mariia Temriukovna; and one by his last wife, Mariia Nagaia. Only Anastasiia's youngest son, Fedor, and Mariia Nagaia's son, Dmitrii, survived Ivan. Since Dmitrii was not the offspring of one of Ivan's first three marriages, he could technically be regarded as illegitimate under Orthodox law.

28. Margeret is wrong. Ivan IV did indeed mortally wound his son Ivan Ivanovich when he struck him with the imperial staff in November 1581. It was his first-born son, Dmitrii (1552–53), who died during Ivan's pilgrimage to Kirillov Monastery in June 1553. There is no evidence that the staff in question was given as a sign of submission; the Crimean Tatars were in fact allies of the Ottoman Turks.

29. In using the word "tyrant" (Russian *muchitel'*) Margeret is probably repeating the view of the Muscovite lords. In Western Europe, however, where the term had a very specific meaning, the question of tyranny was being fiercely debated. That Margeret was aware of these debates is suggested by his care in distinguishing between *tyranny* and *absolutism* as applied to various Muscovite rulers; hence his use of "tyrant" may also reflect non-Russian views. Throughout Europe during the Livonian War and on into the seventeenth century Ivan was constantly vilified as a bloodthirsty and cruel tyrant. The French historian de Thou was strongly influenced by such attitudes, and he consulted with Margeret. See Collins, *Present State of Russia*, p.47; Olearius, *Travels*, pp. 181–82; Uroff, "Kotoshikhin," p. 30; Korb, *Diary*, I, p. 289; BC, p. 361; Bodin, *Method*, pp. 219–20; Bodin, *Commonwealth*, p. 555; Polosin, *Istoriia*, p. 215; Franklin, *Bodin*, pp. 49–50; Limonov, *Kul'turnye sviazi*, p. 223.

30. Grand Prince of Moscow.

31. At least one Russian mentioned in the *Piskarev Chronicle* agreed with Margeret that the purpose of this episode was to test the loyalty of Ivan's subjects. Simeon Bekbulatovich was a Tatar prince of royal blood, a descendant of Jenghiz Khan. Known as Sain-Bulat before his conversion to Christianity in 1573, Simeon was a loyal servant of Ivan IV and was appointed tsar of the khanate of Kasimov (dependent upon Muscovy since the fifteenth century) in 1567. He played an active part in the Livonian War and married into the

Mstislavskii family, one of Muscovy's foremost princely clans. He was apparently chosen by Ivan in 1575 as a temporary successor because of his high birth, his unquestionable loyalty, and because he was not close to any of the troublesome native Muscovite boiar clans. He reigned for about eleven months, conducting domestic and possibly foreign affairs, although Vernadsky states that Ivan tried to hide the whole episode from all foreigners except the English. Whatever duties Simeon performed as head of state, he did so only at Ivan's pleasure. After resuming the throne in 1576, Ivan proclaimed him grand prince of Tver, granting him that principality and a large measure of independence which later worried some of Tsar Fedor's regents. They forced Simeon to call himself a "slave" of Fedor and to renounce the principality. See *Materialy po istorii SSSR*, pp. 81–82; BC, p. 275; Vernadsky, *Tsardom*, I, pp. 141–45, 186–88; Jack M. Culpepper, "The Kremlin Executions of 1575 and the Enthronement of Simeon Bekbulatovich," *Slavic Review* 24 (1965), 503–06.

32. There is some confusion here. Fedor married Boris Godunov's sister, not his daughter. Margeret knew this and hereafter identifies Irina correctly. The traditional date for their wedding is 1580, but there is evidence that it took place as early as 1574. This marriage certainly furthered Boris Godunov's career. However, the Godunov family were certainly not *moskovskie dvoriane*, who were merely a select group of gentry settled on lands near Moscow that acted as a kind of guards detachment for the tsar and performed minor governmental functions. Margeret also knew this and his subsequent references to this group are correct. Platonov, *Boris Godunov*, pp. 6–8; Vernadsky, *Tsardom*, I, p. 155.

33. Boris Godunov has traditionally been regarded as one of Fedor's regents, although he was not so named by Ivan. Many historians believe that for all practical purposes he ruled from the very beginning of Fedor's reign. Boris was at least able to use his position as the tsar's brother-in-law to outmaneuver his opposition and to clear a path for his own complete ascendancy by the late 1580s. Skrynnikov, "Boris i Dmitrii," pp. 184–86; Skrynnikov, "Boris Godunov's Struggle," p. 325.

34. Almost immediately upon the death of Ivan IV some members of the Nagoi clan (relatives of Ivan's last wife, Mariia) contested Fedor's

accession to power because of his simple-mindedness. However, nothing came of this, and the leader of the clan, A. F. Nagoi, was quickly arrested and banished from the capital. By 1587 there was no one left who could openly challenge Boris's position. He became the sole ruler of Russia. He obtained the right to conduct correspondence with foreign governments, and by 1591 he had obtained an elaborate title from Tsar Fedor and held his own court, which was as impressive as the tsar's. See Vernadsky, *Tsardom,* I, pp. 184–85; Skrynnikov, "Boris i Dmitrii," p. 183; Platonov, *Boris Godunov,* pp. 40–43.

35. Fedor's daughter Feodosia (1592–94) died before she was two years old. Margeret, like most western writers of the period, believed that Boris aspired to the throne from the beginning. This was the "official" view of Boris's successors (including Dmitrii Ivanovich), and of most Russian historians in the nineteenth century; it still has supporters today. The Soviet scholar Skrynnikov, however, believes that Boris was satisfied with his position as regent until the mid-1590s, when it became obvious that Fedor might die without an heir. Skrynnikov, "Politicheskaia bor'ba."

36. There was a sharp struggle for power in the early years of Fedor's reign. One after another of Boris's opponents were removed from positions at court, usually after unsuccessful efforts to oust the tsar's brother-in-law. On the other hand, Boris adopted many policies to win the support of the important gentry service class in the 1590s. For example, he may have completed the process of enserfing the Russian peasants in an effort to win gentry support for his bid for the throne. See Massa, *Histoire,* II, pp. 53, 118; Skrynnikov, "Politicheskaia bor'ba"; Skrynnikov, "Boris i Dmitrii," pp. 183–88.

37. In 1584 Boris was not yet in a position to exile Mariia and Dmitrii. This decision was made by the Muscovite high officials collectively, shortly after Ivan's death and probably in the context of A. F. Nagoi's unsuccessful bid for power. Uglich was granted to Dmitrii as his inheritance. That town had served a similar function for Ivan IV's younger brother Iurii Vasil'evich and temporarily for Ivan IV's younger son Fedor. Mariia Nagaia was not pleased with her removal from Moscow and exile to "shabby" Uglich. See Vernadsky, "Death," p. 2; Rudakov, "Razvitie legendy," p. 262; Skrynnikov, "Boris i Dmitrii," pp. 183–84, 188; Platonov, *Boris Godunov,* p. 130.

38. There are innumerable stories of Boris's plots to remove his rivals, most of them lacking any substantiation. By 1589 the English were aware of the Nagoi clan's rumors about Boris's plots and how "unsafe" Tsarevich Dmitrii was in Uglich. These rumors included stories of attempted poisonings. There is, however, some evidence that Boris was relatively mild in his treatment of banished lords. See BC, pp. 128, 140–42, 330; Zimin, "Osnovnye etapy," p. 50; Kleimola, "Up Through Servitude," p. 225; Vernadsky, "Death," p. 3.

39. No doubt the mysterious deaths of the princes I. P. and A. I. Shuiskii in 1588 and 1589 helped to convince the Nagoi clan that Dmitrii was in immediate peril. That Dmitrii was hidden and another child put in his place was, of course, the "official" version of Dmitrii's escape from Boris Godunov's assassins—a story Margeret may have heard from Dmitrii himself. The idea of hiding a vulnerable young prince in disguise was not new to the Russians in the 1590s. One of the Shuiskii princes had resorted to this expedient many years earlier. See Tikhomirov, "Samozvanshchina," p. 116; Solov'ev, *Istoriia,* IV, pp. 413–14, 424; Thompson, "Legend," p. 55; Chistov, *Russkie legendy,* pp. 43–46; Platonov, *Boris Godunov,* p. 192; Skrynnikov, "Boris i Dmitrii," pp. 186–87.

40. Tsarevich Dmitrii's death occurred in the spring of 1591. Although the official investigation held immediately after the incident determined that the death was accidental, Boris's guilt was accepted by nearly all contemporary European writers, who were merely repeating Russian rumors. Most Russian sources not only accepted Boris's guilt but considered the "murder" in Uglich to be the main cause of the Time of Troubles—God's punishment of Boris's sin. Tsar Dmitrii Ivanovich and Tsar Vasilii Shuiskii both claimed that Boris was guilty, and under the Romanovs the Russian Orthodox church and the state officially condemned Boris for the "murder." Most nineteenth-century Russian historians agreed. Once the sources were subjected to careful study, some historians (including Sergei Platonov) concluded that Boris was innocent, that indeed no murder took place in Uglich. Many scholars today also reject Boris's complicity, although recently some Soviet historians have again reasserted the traditional view. R. G. Skrynnikov, a leading Soviet authority in this field, does exonerate Boris of at least this one "murder" and accepts the verdict of accidental death.

The reference to a secretary in this passage is to the *d'iak* Mikhail Bitiagovskii, who was the supervisor of the Uglich district financial administration and controller of the Uglich palace estates from 1590 to 1591. He was not a mere secretary, and he was responsible to Moscow, not to Mariia Nagaia. The Nagoi clan regarded him as Godunov's spy. In fact, Bitiagovskii's background did include watching over other "disgraced" officials in Kazan.

Thompson, "Legend," p. 48; Cook, "Image," p. 435; Palitsyn, *Skazanie,* p. 251; RIB, XIII, cols. 151, 837–59; Tikhomirov, "Samozvanshchina," p. 117; Koretskii and Stanislavskii, "Amerikanskii istorik," pp. 241–42; Chistov, *Russkie legendy,* p. 35; Polosin, *Istoriia,* pp. 218–45; Platonov, *Boris Godunov,* p. 155; Vernadsky, "Death," pp. 3, 14, 18–19; Skrynnikov, "Boris i Dmitrii," pp. 182–83, 188–91, 195–97; Skrynnikov, *Boris Godunov,* pp. 67–84; Kashtanov, "Diplomatika," pp. 43–44.

41. Before the investigating commission could arrive in Uglich, the Nagoi clan planted evidence to implicate Mikhail Bitiagovskii, whom they had killed, and through him Boris Godunov. Some Uglich townspeople were also tortured in order to force them to swear that Dmitrii had been murdered by Bitiagovskii. The child's body was buried very simply and somewhat mysteriously in Uglich. No effort was made, even by his family, to honor his grave, and the body was unrecognizable by the time the commission arrived, only a few days after the incident. Boris Godunov has even been accused of complicity in Dmitrii's "murder" because of a decision not to bury Dmitrii in Archangel Cathedral in Moscow; but there is little evidence that Boris was ever called upon to make such a decision. The Nagois had taken care of their own "martyred" child, and according to Patriarch Iov there was certainly no precedent for placing an illegitimate boy (who had technically committed suicide) in the tomb of the tsars. See Thompson, "Legend," p. 55; Barbour, *Dimitry,* p. 324; Platonov, *Boris Godunov,* pp. 148–50; Vernadsky, "Death," p. 14; Solov'ev, *Istoriia,* IV, pp. 413–14.

42. Most sources that implicate Boris in Dmitrii's death also claim that he set the fire that burned much of Moscow up to the Neglinnaia River. Many claim that he also invited a Crimean Tatar attack on the

capital to divert people's attention from the Uglich incident. Even to-day, a few historians blame Boris for the fire. Skrynnikov has demon-strated, however, that the fire was extremely disadvantageous for Boris and was very likely set by agents of the Nagoi clan. See Massa, *Kratkoe izvestie,* pp. 39–41; Bussov, *Khronika,* p. 204; Purchas, *Hakluytus Posthumus,* XIV, p. 147; PSRL, XIV, pt. 2, p. 42; Solov'ev, *Istoriia,* IV, pp. 413–14; BC, p. 358; Rudakov, "Razvitie legendy," pp. 272–73; Thompson, "Legend," p. 56; Skrynnikov, "Boris i Dmitrii," pp. 190–93; Hellie, *Enserfment,* p. 99; Planonov, *Boris Godunov,* p. 150; Koretskii, "Iz istorii," p. 121.

43. The death of Fedor, which brought an end to the ancient rul-ing dynasty of Muscovy, is traditionally regarded as the beginning of Russia's Time of Troubles. There is little evidence to link Boris to Fedor's death, but in the power struggle which followed, Boris's en-emies spread rumors that he had poisoned the tsar in order to gain power for himself. Speculation about Boris's involvement lasted for many years. See Timofeev, *Vremennik,* p. 218; Massa, *Kratkoe izvestie,* p. 45; Paris, *Chronique,* I, p. 405; Crull, *State of Muscovy,* II, p. 4; Skrynnikov, "Boris Godunov's Struggle," pp. 329–35; Platonov, *Boris Godunov,* pp. 155–56; Platonov, *Time of Troubles,* pp. 43–44.

44. Although Russian customs usually condemned upper-class women to a life of seclusion, there was some precedent for Irina to rule. After the death of Vasilii III in 1533, Elena Glinskaia ruled Muscovy for several years until her son, Ivan IV, was old enough to as-sume power (it is not clear whether she ruled formally or informally). Boris worked hard during the 1590s to reinforce Irina's claim to the throne, and the day after Fedor's death she issued her first decree, a general amnesty for all prisoners which was apparently designed to win popularity for the new ruler. Irina soon renounced her authority, however, and retired to Novodevichii Monastery. It is doubtful that there existed any historical precedent which would have forced Irina to enter a monastery, although she did so within six weeks of Fedor's death. There is considerable disagreement about her exact position, some sources claiming that Fedor gave all power to Irina and that the boiar duma swore an oath of loyalty to her, others claiming that before

his death Fedor ordered Irina to enter a convent. See Kashtanov, "Diplomatika," pp. 43–44; Platonov, *Boris Godunov*, pp. 153–54; Massa, *Kratkoe izvestie*, p. 47; PSRL, XIV, pt. 1, pp. 19–20, 49; BC, pp. 129, 315–17; *Materialy po istorii SSSR*, p. 78; Solov'ev, *Istoriia*, IV, pp. 345–46; Skrynnikov, "Boris Godunov's Struggle," pp. 329–31, 334.

45. Boris did stop attending the boiar duma and joined his sister at the Novodevichii Monastery, where several large processions organized by Patriarch Iov went to try to convince him that he had popular support for becoming tsar. The crowds cheered loudly and spontaneously, but because of strong opposition to his candidacy by members of the boiar duma, he hesitated before accepting the throne.

The phrase "empress's council" may be a reference to the boiar duma; but since that body was reluctant to recognize Irina's right to the throne, this is somewhat doubtful. It may simply be a reference to Irina's advisors, who were apparently sent by the patriarch to "order" Boris to leave the monastery, return to the Kremlin, and mount the throne. Or indeed it may be a direct reference to the "consecrated council" headed by Iov which attempted to "elect" Boris as tsar without the approval of the boiar duma. See Timofeev, *Vremennik*, pp. 52–53; Vernadsky, *Tsardom*, I, pp. 206–07; Skrynnikov, "Boris Godunov's Struggle."

46. Boris may at first have refused the throne in an effort to still the charge of having poisoned Fedor. A rumor that he was planning to become a monk may have helped to demonstrate that he was not power-hungry and may have pushed his supporters into taking action. It appears that Boris did accept the throne in February, only to reject it again in light of continued opposition from the boiar duma. Skrynnikov, "Boris Godunov's Struggle," pp. 334–38.

47. The *zemskii sobor*, or assembly of the land, was convened only for extraordinary purposes and thus met rather infrequently. The *zemskii sobor* called after Fedor's death was the first one ever assembled to "elect" a tsar. Ustrialov [Margeret, *Sostoianie* (1830), p. 16] badly mistranslated this passage so that in Russian it confirmed the official imperial Russian view of Boris Godunov as a usurper who wished to convene a "sham" *zemskii sobor*. Skrynnikov has demonstrated that the "election" of Boris may well have been a sham, but Margeret certainly did not make this assertion.

There is some evidence that Boris deliberately delayed the convocation to allow him time to neutralize his opponents. According to Skrynnikov, the *zemskii sobor* did not meet until 1599, and then only to confirm Boris as tsar several months after his coronation. Documents were then forged to make it appear that Boris had been elected in 1598. Margeret does not actually indicate an election in early 1598, the traditional view, and his discussion of how Boris because tsar is not substantially different from Skrynnikov's.

See Solov'ev, *Istoriia*, IV, pp. 348, 692; Cherepnin, *Zemskie sobory*, pp. 51, 146 n.53; Skrynnikov, "Boris Godunov's Struggle." Cf. Platonov, *Stat'i*, pp. 279–338.

48. By April 1, 1598, Moscow was buzzing with reports from the Don Cossacks that the Crimean Tatars were preparing a major raid against Muscovy. There is little evidence, however, that Boris contrived this threat as a means to gain support for his election. The charge has been rejected by many scholars as just one more false report spread by Boris's enemies. In fact, since the terrible invasion of 1571 the Russians had good reason to fear a return by the Crimean Tatars. As late as 1591 the Tatars reached the suburbs of Moscow, and in 1592 they again raided Muscovy in force. In 1591 Boris's enemies also falsely claimed that he had "invited" the Tatar attack on Moscow in order to divert attention from the "murder" of Tsarevich Dmitrii. Like Margeret, Skrynnikov regards the 1598 charges as true, claiming that Boris was well aware that the Crimean Tatars were too busy helping the Turkish sultan in the Hungarian War to attack Moscow. Skrynnikov states that the rumor of a Tatar attack, which conveniently allowed Boris to appear as the savior of his country, was the cleverest move Boris made in his struggle to win recognition as tsar. Skrynnikov, "Boris Godunov's Struggle," p. 346; Vernadsky, *Tsardom*, I, pp. 197–98, 207–09; Platonov, *Boris Godunov*, pp. 71–72.

49. Boris was proclaimed tsar for the second time by Patriarch Iov on April 1, 1598. His decision to lead the Muscovite forces personally against the Crimean Tatars was made after April 20, when Don Cossack reports arrived in Moscow stating that squadrons of Tatars were already attacking Russian border guards. Three weeks later news that the khan himself was leading the invasion force was again received in Moscow. The acceptance of Boris's military leadership by his opponents

virtually decided his election. On the campaign he was able to play the part of the generous ruler while his opponents quarreled over rank and precedence. When they appealed to Boris for rulings, they were clearly acknowledging him as tsar. Skrynnikov, "Boris Godunov's Struggle," pp. 337–38, 346–47; Platonov, *Boris Godunov,* p. 162; Vernadsky, *Tsardom,* I, pp. 207–09.

50. Boris left Moscow for Serpukhov on May 2. Irina had entered Novodevichii Monastery months earlier, upon her abdication, when she became the nun Aleksandra.

51. This figure, based on hearsay, is almost invariably considered "an epic exaggeration." Nonetheless, most writers of the sixteenth and seventeenth centuries had a healthy respect for Muscovy's real or potential military strength and estimated that the Muscovite ruler could put into the field between two and three hundred thousand soldiers in time of war (a figure accepted by Kliuchevskii, although he has since been criticized for his "uncritical" acceptance of Margeret's estimates as well as those of other foreigners). Seredonin subjected foreign estimates to careful scrutiny and concluded that the Muscovite army at the end of the sixteenth century was about one hundred ten thousand strong, a figure not dissimilar to Margeret's own estimate of the size of the usual standing forces (found below in his lengthy discussion of the military). This figure has been accepted by Soviet and western military historians, although it does not seem to take into account the extraordinary levies made in times of emergency when virtually the whole state was mobilized. Contemporaries such as the Swedish King Gustavus Adolphus (r. 1611–32) believed that Boris Godunov had been able to field an army of 1.5 million. Margeret's figure may have been influenced by sixteenth-century French estimates of Muscovy's military might. Rabelais, many years earlier, had estimated the Russian army to contain up to four hundred fifty thousand elite troops; and Professor Louis Le Roy's very influential sixteenth-century published works cited a figure of seven hundred thousand. Kliuchevskii, *Skazaniia inostrantsev,* pp. 89–96; Nechkina, *Kliuchevskii,* p. 116; Seredonin, *Sochinenie,* pp. 335–46; Chernov, *Vooruzhennye sily,* p. 95; Hellie, *Enserfment,* pp. 164, 267; Limonov, *Kul'turnye sviazi,* p. 222; Mansuy, *Le Monde,* p. 14;

Hakluyt, *Principal Navigations*, II, pp. 229–32, 258, 424; Konovalov, "Chamberlayne's Description," p. 113; Herberstein, *Notes*, II, pp. 196–97, 254; Olearius, *Travels*, p. 153; Milton, *History*, p. 56; Mercator and Hondius, *Atlas*, I, p. 105.

52. According to Skrynnikov, Boris was still having difficulty getting the boiar duma to recognize him as tsar. He again retired to the Novodevichii Monastery, and on September 1, 1598, received a huge procession there of clergy, boiars, merchants, bureaucrats, and other townspeople from Moscow. Boris then acceded to this new entreaty and was crowned two days later in the *Uspenskii Sobor* in the Kremlin according to the ancient customs. See Skrynnikov, "Boris Godunov's Struggle," pp. 348–49.

Margeret was inconsistent in his style of dating, sometimes using the New Style (or Gregorian) calendar and sometimes using the Old Style (or Julian) calendar. I have retained his original dates in the translation.

53. The reference is to ikons. Hereafter, the French *image*, which is ambiguous in English, will be translated as "ikon" in brackets when this aids in clarifying the text.

54. A reference to *Our Lady of Vladimir*, a famous Byzantine ikon transported from Kiev by Prince Andrei Bogoliubskii in the twelfth century. This ikon was often attributed to St. Luke and was supposedly responsible for many military victories of the principality of Vladimir-Suzdal, and later of Moscow. See G. P. Fedotov, *The Russian Religious Mind* (New York, 1960), pp. 296–97.

55. This is not true: the Russians venerated the Greek female saints. Margeret probably meant Russian females.

56. The Russian patriarchate was actually established in 1589, during the reign of Ivan IV's son Fedor. At that time there were six archbishoprics (Vologda, Suzdal, Nizhnii Novgorod, Smolensk, Riazan, and Tver), eight bishoprics (Kolomna, Pskov, Rzhev, Ustiug Velikii, Beloozero, Briansk, Dmitrov, and Chernigov) and many monasteries. Boris Godunov established a new bishopric (Karelia) in 1599. Margeret neglected to mention the metropolitans, who held the highest position in the Russian church until the establishment of the patriarchate. When Margeret was in Russia there were four metropolitans (Novgorod, Kazan, Rostov, and Krutitsa). SGGD, II, pp. 98–99; Skrynnikov, "Boris Godunov's Struggle," p. 328.

57. During the reign of Ivan IV a policy of rebaptizing Protestants was adopted in Muscovy. Catholics were exempt from this. During the Time of Troubles, however, anti-Catholic feelings in Muscovy were intensified and Catholics lost their exemption. Although Patriarch Macarius of Antioch succeeded in gaining the abrogation of this requirement for Catholics in the mid-seventeenth century, Catholics were not free to practice their faith openly in Muscovy until the late seventeenth century. According to one seventeenth-century western writer, Catholics had to be baptised three times before being accepted into the Russian Orthodox church. See Mayerberg, *Relation*, I, p. 127; Korb, *Diary*, II, p. 175; Tsvetaev, *Protestantstvo*, pp. 338–90.

58. The first printing press was set up in Moscow during Ivan IV's reign. A regular printing office was temporarily established in 1563 under Ivan Fedorov, who produced its first book in 1564. Although Fedorov's press was destroyed by a mob in 1565 and he was forced to flee to Lithuania, a printing office was reestablished a few years later by the tsar. Very few books were produced in Muscovy before the seventeenth century, however, and it is not surprising that Margeret saw more imported ones. See Possevino, *Moscovia*, p. 51; Miege, *Relation*, p. 66.

59. Margeret is describing the ceremony of blessing the running waters during the feast of Epiphany. This is a very ancient ceremony in the Greek Orthodox church, similar to the much later Latin Adoration of the Magi. Waters were also blessed before the Assumption of the Virgin Mary. See BC, pp. 233–34; Possevino, *Moscovia*, p. 55.

60. Jerusalem Church was the name given by foreigners to the *Pokrovskii Sobor* or *Sobor Vasiliia Blazhennogo*, properly known as the Cathedral of the Shroud. The correct name for the chapel facing Red Square was The Entry into Jerusalem. The Church of Our Lady is the *Uspenskii Sobor* (Cathedral of the Assumption).

61. Although this was generally true, there were a few exceptions. For example, Herberstein visited several Russian churches. See Herberstein, *Notes*, I, p. 90; Olearius, *Travels*, pp. 50–51; Korb, *Diary*, II, p. 175.

62. Many western travelers, especially Protestants, noted the religious toleration in Muscovy, a contrast with most of the rest of Europe

at the time. Because Catholics were not permitted to worship publicly in Muscovy until the late seventeenth century, they tended to be less impressed. Montaigne, *Complete Works*, pp. 506–09; Avril, *Travels*, p. 130; Crull, *State of Muscovy*, I, p. 11; Korb, *Diary*, I, pp. 129–30.

63. Anti-Semitism characterized the Russian Orthodox church from the Middle Ages. The Muscovite clergy warned against contact with Jews, the "killers of Christ." Few, if any, Jews lived Muscovy before the fifteenth century, although Grand Prince Ivan III retained a Jewish doctor for a few years. Anti-Semitism reached a very high level during the reign of Ivan IV, leading to some forcible conversions and even death. In 1563, after capturing the Lithuanian town of Polotsk, Ivan supposedly ordered all local Jews to convert to Orthodoxy; some three hundred who resisted were thrown into the river. See Staden, *Land and Government*, pp. 61, 65; Cook, "Image," p. 350; Olearius, *Travels*, p. 277.

64. During the early stages of the Livonian War, and especially in 1565, thousands of Livonians were forcibly relocated in Vladimir, Nizhnii Novgorod, Kostroma, and Uglich. Some were sent to the southern frontier to help defend Muscovy from Tatar incursions and were still there when Margeret arrived in Russia. The first Lutheran minister in Moscow appears to have been captured in Livonia in 1559. The first Lutheran church was built in a Moscow suburb in 1575/6. News of the kind treatment of these Livonian Lutherans even reached the Holy Roman emperor. Cook, "Image," p. 54; Platonov, *Moscow and the West*, pp. 15–17; BC, p. 288.

65. This incident, which occurred in 1578, was apparently the one deviation from Ivan IV's general policy of showing kindness to the Livonians. Historians have often cited Margeret's testimony, although it may be somewhat exaggerated. See Platonov, *Moscow and the West*, p. 29.

66. Skilled Livonian captives were made employees of the Muscovite state, and many received great privileges. The right to sell liquor gave them a status similar to top-ranking Russian merchants. Apparently, this disturbed some Russians who criticized Livonian drunkenness as well as pride. Platonov concluded from this passage that the Livonians were profiting from illicit traffic in spirits. See

Platonov, *Moscow and the West*, pp. 14–17, 29; Uroff, "Kotoshikhin," pp. 254, 582.

67. The Mordvinians were people of Finnish origin who had settled between Nizhnii Novgorod and Kazan. Anti-Islamic fanaticism was not unknown in Muscovy during this period, although religious toleration generally characterized Muscovy's relations with its Moslem neighbors. After the conquest of Kazan, strenuous efforts were made to convert the natives to Orthodoxy. These efforts were only marginally successful, and many Tatar "Christians" in the 1590s were Christian in name only. Moslem religious activity was increasing, despite Muscovite attempts to eliminate Moslem influences in Kazan. The Mordvinians were restive, perhaps in connection with this. See Keenan, "Muscovy and Kazan," pp. 548–58; Hellie, *Enserfment*, p. 99; Pelenski, *Russia and Kazan*, pp. 251–75.

68. *Maslenitsa* is actually closer in meaning to *Mardi gras* or carnival than to *semaine grasse* or shrovetide. Hereafter, Margeret's *semaine grasse* will be translated as *Maslenitsa* (in brackets).

69. *Bog tebia prostit* actually means "God will pardon you."

70. "Retzes" may be a reference to the Rhaeto-Romanians or Rumanians, derived from Raetia, an ancient Roman province which did extend to the Danube at one time. Cf. Bodin, *Method*, p. 140.

71. The reference here is to Stephen Bathory (prince of Transylvania, 1571–75) and to Sigismund Bathory (prince of Transylvania, 1581–1601). Margeret's "Arians" are Unitarians.

72. The tsars valued foreign soldiers highly and made it difficult for them to leave. Margeret was not the first, but the procedure he went through to obtain permission was elaborate. See de Thou, *Histoire*, XIV, p. 504; Staden, *Land and Government*, p. 69; Hakluyt, *Principal Navigations*, II, p. 289; Massa, *Kratkoe izvestie*, p. 154; Anderson, *Britain's Discovery*, p. 15; Paris, *Chronique*, I, pp. 404–22; Morgan and Coote, *Early Voyages*, II, p. 331; Possevino, *Moscovia*, p. 17; Zhordaniia, *Ocherki*, I, pp. 258–60.

73. It was a common practice of the Muscovite government to use European captives and mercenaries on the southern frontier and Tatar recruits and mercenaries against the Europeans. See BC, pp. 180, 286–87; Kliuchevskii, *Skazaniia inostrantsev*, pp. 93–94; Platonov, *Moscow and the West*, p. 15.

74. Margeret neglected to mention the stone walls of Serpukhov, Nizhnii Novgorod, Pskov, Mozhaisk, Vologda, and a few others. Tikhomirov, *Rossiia,* p. 24.

75. Although there are varying estimates of its size and population, Moscow was at this time the largest city in Russia. Estimates of its circumference—anywhere from twelve to thirty-two miles—vary because much of the city burned in 1571, 1611, and again in 1626. In the early sixteenth century Moscow was said to be twice the size of Cologne or Prague. Several Englishmen claimed it was about the same size as London. At the time Margeret was in Muscovy, Moscow's outer wooden wall enclosed a little more than forty-six hundred acres, making the circumference of the city about nine and one-half miles. It was burned in 1611 by the Poles, who were then occupying the Kremlin. The inner wall was the White Stone Wall, constructed on Boris Godunov's orders, that enclosed approximately thirteen hundred acres and was about five miles in circumference. See Avity, *Description,* III, pp. 1157–58; Konovalov, "Chamberlayne's Description," p. 112; Struys, *Voyages,* p. 117; BC, p. 124; Hakluyt, *Principal Navigations,* II, p. 226; Herberstein, *Notes,* II, pp. 196, 202; *Istoriia Moskvy,* I, pp. 173, 334–39.

76. This section of Moscow, enclosed in 1534–35, was called Kitaigorod.

77. More than one Italian architect had been involved in construction of the Kremlin. The towers and walls were built during the reign of Ivan III, Vasilii III's father; but some work continued under Vasilii III. See Pierling, *La Russie,* I, pp. 204–05.

78. The *kniaz'ia* were the princes whose families, once independent, had either joined or been forced into Muscovite service. They represented the social summit of the Russian nobility, although they had no special political advantage at this time. Just below the princes were the *boiare* (boiars), the highest ranking members of the service aristocracy. Margeret's reference to these nobles as *dumnye boiare* is somewhat redundant since all boiars by right served in the boiar duma. Below the boiars were the *okol'nichie,* who also served in the boiar duma. They also served as military commanders, ambassadors, judges, and administrators. The *dumnye dvoriane* were courtiers who were granted membership in the boiar duma. They followed the

okol'nichie in rank. The *moskovskie dvoriane* served in Moscow, but usually not at court. However, they often served in lower capacities in the same jobs as did members of the boiar duma. Few western writers discussed the various gradations of the Muscovite nobility, and among those who did Margeret stands out for his accuracy and detail. Kliuchevskii, *Sochineniia*, VI, pp. 353–55; Kliuchevskii, *Boiarskaia duma*, pp. 258–63.

79. There is considerable debate about the council or boiar duma. Although some historians regard this institution as an informal consultative body with no real power, the consensus now seems to be that is was a permanent organization which played a vital role in the legislative process. Contemporary western writers, however, emphasized the tsar's domination of his government and counselors. See Kliuchevskii, *Boiarskaia duma*, pp. 448–506, 528; Seredonin, *Sochinenie*, pp. 214–26; Hellie, *Enserfment*, p. 41. Cf. Crull, *State of Muscovy*, I, pp. 169, 180; Olearius, *Travels*, p. 177; Herberstein, *Notes*, I, p. 32; BC, pp. 136, 156.

80. In describing the nature of the Muscovite government, some historians have emphasized the limitations and institutional restraints upon Russian "absolutism," while others regard Muscovy as a truly autocratic state. Most foreigners in the early modern period regarded the Muscovite ruler as an autocratic, "oriental" despot, and the fact that his subjects (like those of the Turkish sultan) referred to themselves as his slaves was often cited as evidence of Muscovite "tyranny." Margeret was an exception: his positive portrayal of Russian absolutism and his unwillingness to place Muscovy outside the arena of European-style absolute governments have earned him praise from Russian and Soviet scholars. Margeret was probably influenced by Henri IV, Jean Bodin, and by the changing French attitude toward monarchy itself. See Herberstein, *Notes*, I, pp. 30, 32, 54, 95; BC, pp. 132–33, 177; Bond, *Russia*, p. 207; Hakluyt, *Principal Navigations*, II, p. 439; Olearius, *Travels*, pp. 147, 151, 177; Staden, *Land and Government*, pp. 55–56; Miege, *Relation*, p. 60; Crull, *State of Muscovy*, I, pp. 6, 170; Avity, *Description*, III, p. 1146; Massa, *Histoire*, II, p. 238; Kliuchevskii, *Boiarskaia duma*, pp. 66, 243–49, 356–72; Sergeevich, *Russkie drevnosti*, II, pp. 606–16; D'iakonov, *Vlast'*,

p. 415; Szeftel, "Title," pp. 67-69; Szeftel, "Monarchie Absolue," pp. 733-40; Kleimola, "Up Through Servitude," pp. 210-13, 220, 223; Rowland, "Problem of Advice," pp. 260-66, 270; Rouillard, *Turk*, pp. 182, 388-89; Alpatov, *Russkaia mysl'*, p. 32; Church, *Constitutional Thought*, pp. 32-38, 43-71, 77, 222-31, 239; Atkinson, *Nouveaux horizons*, pp. 364-65.

81. The *dumnye d'iaki*, or state secretaries, were the most powerful secretaries in Russian service since they determined which petitions would be considered by the boiar duma and they were responsible for drafting the decisions of the council. Because the functions of the boiar duma are not well known, the actual position of the *dumnye d'iaki* is difficult to determine. Margeret was not alone in underrating their importance; even native Russian sources did so, no doubt because of the vastly different social positions of the boiars and the *d'iaki*. The *dumnye d'iaki* apparently stood during boiar duma meetings while their superiors sat. See Kliuchevskii, *Boiarskaia duma*, pp. 263-69, 411-20; Platonov, *Stat'i*, pp. 195-200; Uroff, "Kotoshikhin," pp. 67, 372; BC, p. 157; Possevino, *Moscovia*, p. 143.

82. The *Posol'skii Prikaz*.

83. The *Razriadnyi Prikaz*. Kliuchevskii claimed that there were other *prikazy* which dispatched governors also. By "lieutenant general" Margeret means an assistant to a military governor. (That is how the term was then used in France.) The *strel'tsy* (see n. 126) carried harquebuses similar to muskets. Kliuchevskii, *Skazaniia inostrantsev*, p. 154 n.186.

84. The *pravezh*, a system of forcible exaction of a debt or damages, is discussed in n. 89.

85. These exiles contributed to the colonization of Siberia. See Vernadsky, *Tsardom*, I, pp. 196-97; Olearius, *Travels*, p. 176.

86. The gifts at Easter were quite legal and were related to maintenance fees. Zlotnik, "Fiscal Policy," pp. 250-51. Successful or not, the Muscovite government in this period did make strenuous efforts to weed out corruption. Margeret has been praised by Soviet scholars for his observations on this subject. Alpatov, *Russkaia mysl'*, pp. 31-32.

87. The *gubnoi starosta*, an elected elder with the duties of a district criminal judge, was under the direct supervision of the

Razboinyi Prikaz (brigandage chancellery), the highest court for criminal affairs and the police office.

88. There were exceptions to this rule. See BC, p. 149 n.11; Uroff, "Kotoshikhin," p. 550.

89. Margeret misunderstood the meaning of *pravezh*. It was not a place of punishment, but rather the punishment itself—daily beatings for failure to pay a debt or damages awarded by court action. Despite his confusion, Margeret's evidence concerning this punishment is important and has been used by several historians. *Nedel'shchik* is the Muscovite term for central-court bailiff or constable, a key figure in the Muscovite state apparatus. See Seredonin, *Sochinenie*, p. 302; BC, p. 175; Olearius, *Travels*, pp. 229–30; Kliuchevskii, *Skazaniia inostrantsev*, p. 140; Kliuchevskii, *Sochineniia*, VI, pp. 226–30; Kavelin, *Sobranie sochinenii*, IV, p. 280; Solov'ev, *Istoriia*, IV, pp. 390, 695; Staden, *Land and Government*, pp. 11, 127; Scott Seregny, "The *Nedel'shchik*: Law and Order in Muscovite Russia," *Canadian-American Slavic Studies* 9 (1975), 168–78.

90. Some sources say that the punishment would continue at a rate of one month for each one hundred rubles of debt. Others claim that the full term of punishment was one month, after which time the debtor was turned over to his creditor to work off the debt. Kliuchevskii, *Sochineniia*, VII, p. 259; Kavelin, *Sobranie sochinenii*, IV, pp. 328–35; Horace W. Dewey and Ann M. Kleimola, "Coercion by Righter (*Pravezh*) in Old Russian Administration," *Canadian-American Slavic Studies* 9 (1975), 156–67.

91. Margeret's equation of nobility with the possession of service land grants (by implication, *pomest'ia*) and salary from the tsar is quite interesting. Like most foreign observers, he ignored the so-called independent landholdings (or *votchiny*) because by the end of the sixteenth century service was required from owners of *votchiny* as well as holders of *pomest'ia*. By 1604 failure to serve the tsar could result in confiscation of a *votchina* estate. To a westerner in this period, the most striking aspect of the Muscovite nobility was its obligation to serve the state. See Herberstein, *Notes*, I, p. 95; Hakluyt, *Principal Navigations*, II, p. 239; BC, p. 152; Milton, *History*, p. 57; Kliuchevskii, *Skazaniia inostrantsev*, pp. 115–16; Hellie, *Enserfment*, pp.

26-27, 37-40, 55-56; SGGD, II, p. 605; Limonov, *Kul'turnye sviazi,* p. 222.

92. Margeret provides unique information on the daily life of the lords and on meetings of the boiar duma, information often cited by Russian and Soviet historians. There is some question, however, about whether he is describing informal meetings between the tsar and his advisors or formal boiar duma sessions. Both Fletcher and Margeret imply daily meetings of the council, a view that is accepted by some historians. (Fletcher may have been talking about something very different from a boiar duma, however.) Kliuchevskii maintained that these daily meetings were only informal sessions. See Kliuchevskii, *Skazaniia inostrantsev,* p. 80; Kliuchevskii, *Boiarskaia duma,* pp. 403-09; Seredonin, *Sochinenie,* pp. 228-33; BC, pp. 157, 237; Nechkina, *Kliuchevskii,* p. 186; Zagoskin, *Istoriia,* I, pp. 99-101, II, pp. 104-05.

In this passage Margeret used the Muscovite system of hours, calculated from sunrise to sunset and varying from season to season. I have used the western system in this translation. See Zabelin, *Domashnii byt,* I, p. 106.

93. More accurately, "stout person."

94. Approximately one meter.

95. The reference is to Genesis 24:65.

96. This passage has been cited by various Russian historians. Whereas income was important in the mid-sixteenth century, by the mid-seventeenth century it was insignificant in determining social status. See Kliuchevskii, *Skazaniia inostrantsev,* p. 236; Kleimola, "Up Through Servitude," p. 225.

97. Margeret appears to be confusing two Muscovite institutions, slavery and serfdom, whose origins and relationship are still not completely understood. There seems to be general agreement that the position of most Russian peasants was close to that of serfs by the end of the sixteenth century. Some historians see little difference between peasants and slaves in this period, while others maintain that slaves were actually in a more advantageous position. Slaves and peasants were treated differently under Moscovite law, but the juridical status of the peasant was so degraded by the end of the sixteenth century

that for a time the two groups were treated almost identically. As early as 1598 Russian lords regarded their peasants as slaves and, according to M. A. D'iakonov, had even devised ways of selling them. In official documents of 1606–07 the Shuiskii government virtually equated slaves and peasants. The widespread use of slaves may have slowed down the process of enserfing the Russian peasants, although it also provided a grim model for the treatment of peasants-becoming-serfs. It is clear from contemporary accounts that Muscovy was a rigidly stratified society with slaves and serfs bearing the main burden of support for the gentry service class. Most foreigners did not distinguish between slaves and serfs, but instead saw all members of the lower class as living in complete subjection and intolerable servitude. While Soviet historians claim that western travelers did not really understand the position of the Russian peasant, it is clear that westerners did notice the misery of the Muscovite lower classes. Hellie, *Enserfment,* pp. 1–18, 48–49, 95–103, 116–17, 335 n.128; Platonov, *Time of Troubles,* pp. 28–30; Alpatov, *Russkaia mysl',* pp. 28–32; Bussov, *Khronika,* p. 206; Herberstein, *Notes,* I, pp. 95, 106; Hakluyt, *Principal Navigations,* II, p. 233; BC, pp. 129, 152, 169–70; Olearius, *Travels,* pp. 147, 151; Morgan and Coote, *Early Voyages,* I, p. 376; Miege, *Relation,* p. 49; Massa, *Histoire,* II, p. 238; Crull, *State of Muscovy,* I, p. 170; Struys, *Voyages,* p. 123; Richard Hellie, "Recent Soviet Historiography on Medieval and Early Modern Russian Slavery," *Russian Review* 35 (1976), 26–29; V. I. Koretskii, *Zakreposhchenie krest'ian i klassovaia bor'ba v Rossii vo vtoroi polovine XVI v.* (Moscow, 1970), pp. 9, 189.

98. The Biblical quote actually begins with Ezekiel 2:9 and continues to 3:3.

99. Also called the *Prikaz Bol'shogo Dvortsa* or *Bol'shoi Dvorets* (great palace). This office managed the vast complex of palace buildings and lands and the numerous servants and peasants who served the needs of the tsar's extensive household. See BC, pp. 148, 158–59; Lappo-Danilevskii, *Organizatsiia,* pp. 444–53.

100. *Chetvert'* (or *chet'*) is the general term for any one of the several fiscal departments that collected taxes from certain districts of the state in order to pay salaries to military servicemen. There appears to

be some confusion about their number and function. Some historians claim that there were three; others, four. Margeret is probably correct in mentioning five of them. These were the *Vladimirskaia, Galitskaia, Kostromskaia, Novgorodskaia,* and *Ustiuzhskaia Chetverti.* See BC, pp. 146–48, 159–60; Seredonin, *Sochinenie,* pp. 257–58; Lappo-Danilevskii, *Organizatsiia,* pp. 457–69; Eaton, "Early Russian Censuses," pp. 72–73.

101. The *Bol'shoi Prikhod* (great revenue) was the central Muscovite fiscal office, a kind of finance ministry. It is unclear, however, whether or not it had jurisdiction over the *chetverti.* If it did so at this time, it lost that jurisdiction later in the seventeenth century. See Lappo-Danilevskii, *Organizatsiia,* p. 475; BC, pp. 160–63.

102. Crown peasants paid rent *(obrok)* in cash or kind for the use of the tsar's lands. Crown lands were taxed at a considerably higher rate than lands held by the Russian lords and provided a handsome income to the tsar's treasury. Eaton, "Early Russian Censuses," pp. 42, 86–87.

103. *Vyt'* was the term for a taxable plot of land. It was in use on state and palace *(dvortsovye)* lands and varied in size depending upon the quality of the soil. The *desiatina* was equal to approximately 2.7 acres. A *vyt'* could vary from three to fifteen *desiatiny,* but was commonly about five to six *desiatiny.* Margeret's figure suggests a calculation based upon average soil. See Kliuchevskii, *Skazaniia inostrantsev,* p. 162; Smith, *Peasant Farming,* pp. 107–08; Kamentseva and Ustiugov, *Russkaia metrologiia,* p. 87; Veselovskii, *Soshnoe pis'mo,* II, p. 452.

104. Here the term *chetvert'* is used as a dry measurement for grain, being equal to somewhere between 180 and 324 pounds (usually about 216 pounds). Kamentseva and Ustiugov, *Russkaia metrologiia,* pp. 88–114.

105. *Chetvert'* was also a land measurement equal to approximately 1.35 acres—about the same size as the French arpent. It was the amount of land sown by one *chetvert'* of grain. See Pushkarev, *Dictionary,* pp. 7–8.

106. Margeret's figures on peasant *obrok* payments have been cited by several Russian historians, who generally regard his estimate of tax rates as too high. Total tax obligations did grow at a very rapid rate in

Muscovy during this period, however, and exact figures are not available. See Kliuchevskii, *Skazaniia inostrantsev,* pp. 161–62, 306–07; Nechkina, *Kliuchevskii,* p. 117; BC, p. 159; Zlotnik, "Fiscal Policy," pp. 252–54.

The ruble *(rubl'),* which contained one hundred *dengi kopeinye* or *kopeiki* (kopeks), was worth approximately 13.3 English shillings at this time. The livre Margeret refers to is probably the livre tournois, worth about two English shillings sterling. Margeret's figures have been used by historians to estimate the value of the ruble at the end of the sixteenth century. Cf. Bushkovitch, *Merchants,* p.52.

107. While there may be some difficulties with Margeret's estimate of *Dvorets* income, his figure is far more believable than that of Fletcher (230,000 rubles). A similar figure to Margeret's is given by Kotoshikhin later in the seventeenth century, but it has been questioned by some historians. See BC, pp. 158–59; Seredonin, *Sochinenie,* pp. 325–39; Kliuchevskii, *Skazaniia inostrantsev,* p. 161; Uroff, "Kotoshikhin," pp. 166–67, 444–45.

108. Earlier, Margeret referred to five *chetverti,* the regional fiscal departments from which military servicemen were paid. Since the *Kazanskii Dvorets* and the *Novaia Chetvert'* existed in addition to the other five *chetverti,* Margeret may have forgotten some of the *chetverti* in his earlier reference. The *Novaia Chetvert'* collected revenues from alcoholic beverage sales and from customs duties. The *Kazanskii Dvorets* had charge of the territories of Kazan and Astrakhan (and from 1599, of Siberia as well). The incomes of these departments varied considerably from year to year. Margeret's figure has been accepted by some historians, and it does not appear to be out of line with later seventeenth-century estimates. While it makes somewhat more plausible Fletcher's estimate of the total income from all *chetverti* (400,000 rubles), this has been rejected by historians as too high. Seredonin placed the total annual revenue of the Muscovite government at about 400,000 rubles. See BC, pp. 148, 159–60; Seredonin, *Sochinenie,* pp. 331–35; Kliuchevskii, *Skazaniia inostrantsev,* p. 162; Uroff, "Kotoshikhin," pp. 174, 502; Boris Nolde, *La Formation de l'empire russe: Études, notes et documents* (Paris, 1952–53), vol. I, pp. 40–47.

109. *Kazna* refers to both the state treasury and the storehouse of that fiscal office. See S. O. Shmidt, "K istorii Tsarskogo arkhiva serediny XVI v.," *Trudy Moskovskogo istoriko-arkhivnogo instituta* 11 (1958), 374–78.

110. The *Pomestnyi Prikaz* registered, granted, and redistributed *pomest'ia* (fiefs granted on condition of military service). It also decided claims and litigation concerning landed property.

111. The *Koniushennyi Prikaz* was the department of the tsar's stables and horse breeding.

112. It appears that the devastation of Muscovy during Ivan IV's later years had peaked by the 1580s. There is, however, a sharp debate over the "recovery" in the 1590s. Some historians accept contemporary reports of the wealth of Muscovy at the end of the sixteenth century. Others maintain that recovery was uneven at best, usually citing the extent of abandoned arable or the development of serfdom and an impending social crisis as evidence of continuing economic disruption. Margeret's evidence is far more believable than that provided by Fletcher or Chamberlayne. See Veselovskii, *Feodal'noe zemlevladenie*, p. 35; Zimin, "Osnovnye etapy," p. 50; Bond, *Russia*, pp. xi–xii, 223–24, 277; Hellie, *Enserfment*, pp. 96–97; BC, p. 163; Konovalov, "Chamberlayne's Description," p. 113; Possevino, *Moscovia*, p. 8; Platonov, *Boris Godunov*, p. 115; Samuel Purchas, *Purchas his Pilgrimage* (London, 1626), p. 985; Iu. V. Got'e, *Zamoskovnyi krai v XVII veke* (Moscow, 1937), pp. 138–48; Tikhomirov, "Monastyr'," pp. 159–60.

113. Literally, treasury for expenditures.

114. Margeret uses the word *bordée* ("bordered") ambiguously. Since wealthy Russians often had their clothing embroidered with pearls, it is possible that he really meant *brodée* ("embroidered").

115. It was in fact made of narwhal tusk. The existence of unicorns was widely accepted at this time, and references to them appeared in many scientific, geographical, and literary works throughout the sixteenth century and as late as 1674. It was a common heraldic symbol, even in Muscovy (Ivan IV's shield had a unicorn on it), and the unicorn was a symbol of power in Muscovite literature.

The staff Margeret describes was adorned with diamonds and other precious stones by Ivan IV. It was stolen by the Poles in 1611, who removed the stones and cut up the "unicorn horn" into small pieces to distribute to mercenary soldiers. Many years later the Russians were still complaining about the loss of this precious staff. See Purchas, *Hakluytus Posthumus*, XIV, p. 117; Olearius, *Travels*, p. 190; Atkinson, *Nouveaux horizons*, pp. 50, 278–79; Atkinson, *Extraordinary Voyage*, pp. 2, 16; McFarlane, *History*, p. 230; Polosin, *Istoriia*, p. 268; Timofeev, *Vremennik*, p. 10.

116. *Muid* here refers either to a French liquid measure equal to about sixty-three gallons or to a vessel of that capacity.

117. An écu was a French coin equivalent to an English crown.

118. Most foreigners in this period doubted the existence of mineral deposits. Although silver mining was well known in Russia up to the fourteenth century, for a variety of reasons it ceased by the fifteenth century. Toward the end of the fifteenth century Grand Prince Ivan III requested foreign technical assistance in mining minerals, with one result being a working copper mine in northern Russia. Ivan IV made similar requests for foreign silver miners, as did Fedor's government in 1597. In the seventeenth century Kotoshikhin wrote a passage very similar to Margeret's, and the Romanov government continued to seek foreign technical assistance to mine for gold and silver. See Alpatov, *Russkaia mysl'*, p. 29; Kliuchevskii, *Skazaniia inostrantsev*, p. 189; Seredonin, *Sochinenie*, pp. 125–26; Uroff, "Kotoshikhin," pp. 186–87, 475; SGGD, III, no. 76 and no. 83; Chaudoir, *Aperçu*, pp. 5, 90; *Ocherki istorii SSSR*, p. 52.

119. The *moskovskaia denga*, an older Russian coin, was worth one half of a newer *denga kopeinaia* (kopek). The minting of *moskovskie dengi* tapered off in the sixteenth century before it was finally abandoned altogether. A *polushka* was a fairly rare quarter-kopek coin. *Real de ocho* was a Spanish coin widely known in English as a "piece of eight." The *grivna* and the *altyn* were old Russian monetary units even in the sixteenth century.

120. The *Reichstaler* was a large silver coin, the official coin of the Holy Roman empire. Called *efimki*, they were valued in Muscovy which had no native sources of silver for coinage and other uses. Due to a favorable balance of trade, these coins flooded into Muscovy. In 1604, for example, nearly forty thousand rubles worth were imported,

accounting for about 25 percent of the value of all imports that year. See Bushkovitch, *Merchants,* pp. 62–63; Chaudoir, *Aperçu,* I, pp. 50–79, 144; Hakluyt, *Principal Navigations,* II, p. 439; Mayerberg, *Relation,* II, p. 128.

121. Russian merchants, especially the privileged *gosti,* made a good profit from the sale of *efimki* and other foreign coins to the mint. By the mid-seventeenth century, however, this privilege was abolished and became a government monopoly. The actual rate of exchange for *efimki* and other coins varied throughout this period, changing the rate of profit to be made in this trade. Margeret's estimate of a profit of about 15 percent (minus a service charge at the mint) is quite believable. See Bushkovitch, *Merchants,* pp. 62–63; Kliuchevskii, *Skazaniia inostrantsev,* p. 307; Olearius, *Travels,* p. 178; A. S. Mel'nikova, "Osobennosti russkogo denezhnogo obrashcheniia v XVII v.," *Istoriia SSSR* 10, no. 5 (1966), 103–04, 110; Uroff, "Kotoshikhin," pp. 185–86.

122. "Ducat" here probably refers to a Hungarian or Genoese silver coin, although there were several types of European coins with this name.

123. It is not clear that the office of "master of the stable" was the greatest office before Boris Godunov assumed the title after 1584. It did become the preeminent position at court under Fedor. D. I. Godunov held the position under Boris; M. F. Nagoi, under Dmitrii Ivanovich; and F. I, Mstislavskii, in 1610–11. The office was abolished in the seventeenth century, apparently because of its association with the "usurper" Boris Godunov. There is no way to confirm Kotoshikhin's claim that in the absence of an heir to the throne the master of the stable would automatically become tsar (even without an election). See BC, pp. 144, 239–40; Olearius, *Travels,* 219–20; Uroff, "Kotoshikhin," p. 158; Sergeevich, *Russkie drevnosti,* I, pp. 441–48.

124. The master of the household *(dvoretskii)* apparently replaced the defunct master of the stable as the highest court official in the seventeenth century. The "tasters" also held a very important position of trust. These were usually sons of members of the high nobility who could look forward to membership in the boiar duma later in life. See BC, p. 237; Olearius, *Travels,* pp. 219–20; Sergeevich, *Russkie drevnosti,* I, pp. 449–52.

125. The *stol'niki* were high-ranking court officials who served the tsar and his guests at gala dinners. However, their chief function was to assist the *boiare* and *okol'nichie* in military, civil, and diplomatic affairs. The *chashnik* was a court official who served drinks to the tsar and his guests during court feasts. *Striapchie* were courtiers who attended to food, clothing, and other household matters of the tsar. See Hellie, *Enserfment*, p. 23; Kliuchevskii, *Sochineniia*, VI, pp. 353–55, 389–92; Sergeevich, *Russkie drevnosti*, I, pp. 500–21; Zabelin, *Domashnii byt*, II, pp. 365–72.

126. The *strel'tsy*—singular *strelets* ("shooter"), derived from *strela* ("arrow")—were established in 1550 by Ivan IV as a permanent Muscovite standing infantry unit capable of fighting against European powers. (The gentry cavalry force was only effective in steppe warfare.) Originally composed of three thousand soldiers, the *strel'tsy* proved so useful that their numbers steadily grew, reaching about ten thousand stationed in the capital by 1600. Other units performed garrison duty on the frontier, so that overall there may have been twenty to twenty-five thousand *strel'tsy* by 1600. Margeret's figure of ten thousand serving in Moscow has been accepted by many historians. See Esper, "Military Self-Sufficiency," p. 193; Collins, *Preent State of Russia*, p. 111; Korb, *Diary*, II, pp. 136–38; Morgan and Coote, *Early Voyages*, II, pp. 360–62; Bond, *Russia*, p. 197; BC, pp. 162, 241; Solov'ev, *Istoriia*, IV, p. 379; Hellie, *Enserfment*, pp. 161–63; L. G. Beskrovnyi, *Russkaia armiia i flot v XVIII veke (Ocherki)* (Moscow, 1958), p. 20; S. L. Margolin, "Vooruzhenie streletskogo voiska," *Trudy Gosudarstvennogo istoricheskogo muzeia* 20 (1948), 94.

Prikaz here means "military unit," not to be confused with *prikaz* meaning "office" or "department." *Golova* literally means "head" or "chief." The commanders were usually drawn from upper-service class *stol'niki* or from the middle service class.

127. Margeret's figures on *strel'tsy* pay have often been cited by Russian historians and are preferred to estimates such as Fletcher's. Although the *chetvert'* varied throughout this period, making comparisons difficult (see n. 104), the annual ration of oats and rye probably

declined in the seventeenth century. See Solov'ev, *Istoriia*, IV, pp. 379, 694; Hellie, *Enserfment*, p. 163.

128. The number of *strel'tsy* accompanying the tsar varied considerably, but Margeret's estimate may be accurate for the very early seventeenth century. Ordinarily, some two thousand were selected to act as a "mounted infantry" guard for the tsar. See BC, pp. 180, 240; Uroff, "Kotoshikhin," pp. 78–79, 375–76.

129. The permanent presence of elite gentry cavalry in Moscow dates from the reign of Ivan IV. Margeret has already mentioned the *moskovskie dvoriane*, elite troops who were settled near Moscow and who performed minor tasks in government. Ranking below the *moskovskie dvoriane*, the *dvoriane vybornye* were the top group of provincial gentry sometimes chosen for service in Moscow. See Zimin, *Reformy*, pp. 366–75; Hellie, *Enserfment*, p. 36; Veselovskii, *Feodal'noe zemlevladenie*, pp. 314–26.

130. About three hundred were chosen annually from the *vybornye dvoriane* to serve in Moscow for three years. These were known as *zhil'tsy*, a group which also included sons of *moskovskie dvoriane*. In this period there were perhaps one thousand to twelve hundred *zhil'tsy* who often acted as waiters at state banquets and functioned as an honorary cavalry guard for the tsar. While some stayed in Moscow and eventually became permanent members of the *moskovskie dvoriane*, most returned to their provinces after three years. See Hellie, *Enserfment*, p. 23; Uroff, "Kotoshikhin," pp. 360–61; Kliuchevskii, *Skazaniia inostrantsev*, p. 94.

131. This figure has been questioned by some historians. It should be pointed out that Margeret's reference is not just to *zhil'tsy*, but is to the tsar's entire traveling retinue, including *strel'tsy* and other serving men (along with support personnel). Fletcher cited a figure of fifteen thousand, which Russian historians have found credible. Hellie, *Enserfment*, pp. 23, 267; BC, p. 178; Seredonin, *Sochinenie*, p. 344.

132. *Tsvetnoe plat'e* literally means "colored clothes." *Tabis* is a type of watered silk fabric. Camlet, a fine fabric from Angora, may have been mohair. *Chistoe plat'e* simply means clean, neat, or best clothing.

133. *Korm* literally means "feeding." The Muscovites always provided food and transportation for foreign ambassadors. See Herberstein, *Notes*,

II, pp. 120–21; Hakluyt, *Principal Navigations,* III, pp. 105, 322; Olearius, *Travels,* pp. 40–42.

134. *Nabat* means "tocsin." The shawm was an early woodwind instrument, a forerunner of the modern oboe.

135. These well-traveled routes, known as *shliakhi,* were watched very closely by the Russians.

136. The Muscovites did not trust the Tatars to stay on the *shliakhi,* so the entire southern frontier had to be patrolled in order to avoid a surprise attack.

137. This passage is a unique description of the early warning system *(zasechnaia cherta* or *zaseka)* used to protect Muscovy's southern flank. Organized after the devastating Crimean Tatar raid on Moscow in 1571, the system was apparently working effectively at the end of the sixteenth century. While it was a capital offense to leave one's post, there were no penalties for errors such as reporting a herd of wild horses. See Hellie, *Enserfment,* pp. 174–77. Cf. Zlotnik, "Fiscal Policy," pp. 247–48; Zagorovskii, *Cherta,* pp. 54–64.

138. Some historians claim that the grass was burnt in the fall. Citing this passage from Margeret, Hellie disputed Margolin's claim that the rapid growth of towns on the southern frontier at the end of the sixteenth century made it difficult or impossible for the Muscovites to continue the practice of burning the tall grass. Although Hellie is incorrect in claiming that Margeret witnessed these burnings in the 1590s, his point is still a good one: Margeret did observe the practice in the early seventeenth century. The Tatars would also burn the tall grass near Muscovite fortified lines, endangering the Russians unless precautions were taken. See Hellie, *Enserfment,* pp. 176, 353 n.77; Esper, "Military Self-Sufficiency," p. 192; S. L. Margolin, "Oborona russkogo gosudarstva ot tatarskikh nabegov v kontse XVI veka," *Trudy Gosudarstvennogo istoricheskogo muzeia* 20 (1948), 15.

139. These terms date from the fifteenth century. *Gorodovye dvoriane* were the most numerous group of the *dvoriane* (or middle service class) and ranked below the *vybornye dvoriane*—the top group of provincial gentry. *Deti boiarskie* were petty gentry who in this period ranked below and *dvoriane.* They were the most

numerous group of the tsar's military servicemen. (In this sentence Margeret also listed *syn boiarskii,* which is simply the singular form of *deti boiarskie.*) Hellie, *Enserfment,* pp. 24–25, 28; Sergeevich, *Russkie drevnosti,* I, pp. 362–63, 560–70; Kliuchevskii, *Sochineniia,* VI, pp. 160–61, 402–03; Veselovskii, *Feodal'noe zemlevladenie,* pp. 203–16; Chernov, *Vooruzhennye sily,* p. 78; Makovskii, *Razvitie,* p. 286.

140. By a decree of 1576 military servicemen were to receive land grants *(pomest'ia)* only in the districts of the towns from which they served. This benefited the servicemen as well as the state, making it easier and more efficient to organize companies for a campaign. Hellie, *Enserfment,* p. 46.

141. According to Ivan IV's 1556 decree on service, one armed horseman was to be provided for each 100 *chetverti* of good land in one field (altogether, for each 300 *chetverti* of land held under the prevailing three-field system of agriculture). Probably because this was too great a burden in the period of famine at the beginning of the seventeenth century, Boris Godunov temporarily lowered the service requirement in 1604. I have found no other source which mentions the requirement for an additional foot soldier in times of necessity. However, military service from all able-bodied Muscovite citizens could be required for major campaigns (such as the Smolensk campaign in 1512 or the Kazan campaign in 1547), and this may be what Margeret was thinking of when he wrote this passage. Routine provision of additional soldiers would have been beyond the means of most holders of *pomest'e* estates in this period. See Kliuchevskii, *Sochineniia,* VI, p. 155; Veselovskii, *Soshnoe pis'mo,* II, pp. 347–57; Veselovskii, *Feodal'noe zemlevladenie,* pp. 89, 308–09; Zimin, *Reformy,* pp. 438–40; Zlotnik, "Fiscal Policy," pp. 247–48; N. E. Nosov, *Ocherki po istorii mestnogo upravleniia russkogo gosudarstva pervoi poloviny XVI veka* (Moscow-Leningrad, 1957), pp. 117, 121–22. Cf. Hellie, *Enserfment,* pp. 37–39, 48–50; Lappo-Danilevskii, *Organizatsiia,* pp. 400–01; Chernov, *Vooruzhennye sily,* pp. 93–94, 125; Makovskii, *Razvitie,* p. 183.

142. There is some disagreement on compensation received by members of the boiar duma. Seredonin estimated that the usual

range was 400 to 700 rubles; but there is evidence that those members of the council with seniority commanded salaries of 1000 or even 1200 rubles. See BC, p. 143; Seredonin, *Sochinenie,* p. 190; Solov'ev, *Istoriia,* IV, p. 379; Zagoskin, *Istoriia,* II, pp. 63–64. Cf. Stashevskii, "Sluzhiloe soslovie," p. 19.

143. Prince F. I. Mstislavskii was the son of I. F. Mstislavskii (a great-grandson of Ivan III), who had been an outstanding general during Ivan IV's reign and had even been appointed as one of Tsar Fedor's regents. Although he lost out in the subsequent struggle for power with Boris Godunov and was exiled in 1586, this did not adversely affect the career of his son Fedor. Fedor Mstislavskii became a boiar in 1576 and was several times appointed commander of the Muscovite army during campaigns under Ivan IV, Fedor, and Boris Godunov. He was a serious candidate for tsar and a leading figure in government throughout the Time of Troubles. He died in 1622. See Skrynnikov, "Boris Godunov i Dmitrii," p. 185. Cf. BC, p. 142.

144. Margeret's information on the income of the lords appears substantially correct. See Hellie, *Enserfment,* p. 36; Chernov, *Vooruzhennye sily,* pp. 78–79; Zagoskin, *Istoriia,* II, pp. 63–64; Stashevskii, "Sluzhiloe soslovie," p. 19; Seredonin, *Sochinenie,* p. 356; Kliuchevskii, *Skazaniia inostrantsev,* pp. 117–23.

145. See n.141. The usual requirement was for only one mounted soldier for every one hundred *chetverti* of land.

146. This is an interesting statement. According to several historians, the Muscovite government was so short of funds that often no payment was made to servicemen for several years at a time. Pay seems to have been irregular throughout this period, although Margeret's information may be correct for the early seventeenth century when Muscovy was "prosperous." His figures on the pay for *deti boiarskie* are accurate. See Hellie, *Enserfment,* pp. 36–37; Chernov, *Vooruzhennye sily,* pp. 78–79, 159. Cf. BC, pp. 178–79.

147. Some historians regard these figures as too high. Seredonin argued that the combined cavalry forces of Muscovy's Tatar, Cheremissian, and Mordvinian "allies" amounted to only some ten thousand. However, it should be pointed out that Seredonin's comparative

figures are from an earlier period. Contemporary estimates of twenty-five to thirty thousand for these auxiliary forces were not uncommon. Apparently, by the end of the sixteenth century the disturbances among these various groups had subsided, allowing the Muscovite government to make active use of them in patroling the southern frontier or even in bolstering the forces facing Europe. See Seredonin, *Sochinenie,* pp. 346–47; Esper, "Military Self-Sufficiency," pp. 193–94; Kliuchevskii, *Skazaniia inostrantsev,* pp. 93–94; Hellie, *Enserfment,* pp. 99, 177, 267, 353 n.81; Zimin, "Osnovnye etapy," p. 51; Solov'ev, *Istoriia,* IV, pp. 379–80.

148. *Cherkasy* (an old Russian name for Circassians) was from the late fifteenth century a Muscovite name applied to Ukrainian Cossacks, derived from their headquarters at Cherkasy, on the Dnieper River. In the seventeenth century *Cherkasy* came to apply specifically to Ukrainian Cossacks settled along the southern frontier to help protect Muscovy from the Crimean Tatars. Margeret's estimate is probably quite accurate. (For Cossacks, see n.155.) See Vernadsky, *Mongols,* pp. 289–92; Vernadsky, *Russia at the Dawn,* p. 250; Allen, *Ukraine,* pp. 69–70; Allen, *Russian Embassies,* I, pp. 24–26; BC, p. 180; Chernov, *Vooruzhennye sily,* pp. 165–67.

149. Margeret must be considered one of the leading authorities on the subject of foreign mercenaries in Muscovite service at this time, especially since he became the co-commander of these troops under Boris Godunov (and not under Fedor, as maintained by Hellie). In addition to Germans, Poles, and Greeks, contemporary sources mention English, Scots, French, Danish, Flemish, Dutch, Austrian, and Swedish soldiers in Russian service. Their numbers increased rapidly in the late sixteenth century, although the total is in dispute. Ustrialov accepted Margeret's figure of twenty-five hundred, but some historians place the figure at forty-three hundred or even nine thousand by the end of the sixteenth century. In my opinion, Margeret's figure is to be preferred. See Hellie, *Enserfment,* p. 169; Purchas, *Hakluytus Posthumus,* XIV, p. 148; BC, pp. 286–89; Kliuchevskii, *Skazaniia inostrantsev,* pp. 93–94; N. G. Ustrialov, *Istoriia tsarstvovaniia Petra Velikago,* vol. I (St. Petersburg, 1858), p. 179.

150. *Datochnye liudi* were recruits. On these recruits and the ecclesiastical contributions to the Muscovite military, see Hellie, *Enserfment*, pp. 43–44; Staden, *Land and Government*, p. 40; Makovskii, *Razvitie*, p. 275; Veselovskii, *Feodal'noe zemlevladenie*, pp. 231–43.

151. *Kon'* (plural *koni*) simply means "horse."

152. This is an important point to keep in mind in attempting to reconstruct "typical" Muscovite peasant activity. Much of the time peasants could not afford to feed oats to horses; yet it is known that the typical Muscovite peasant household did own a horse. See Herberstein, *Notes*, I, p. cl; Smith, *Peasant Farming*, pp. 43, 90–93, 136–37.

153. A fine Asiatic horse, commonly called "Turkish" in Europe at this time, and often given as gifts to the tsars and Chinese emperors. See Morgan and Coote, *Early Voyages*, I, p. 89; Herberstein, *Notes*, II, p. 135; Allen, *Russian Embassies*, I, pp. 227, 322–24.

154. *Merin* (plural *merina*) literally means "gelding."

155. The name "Cossack" (Russian *kazak*) is derived from Turkish *quazaq*, meaning "free adventurer." Originally Tatar freebooters, in the fourteenth century some Cossacks served the Tatar khan as an advance guard. Tatar Cossacks were sometimes used by the Muscovite government to bolster its military forces. They were first mentioned as a light cavalry force in the Muscovite army in 1444, and their numbers rose quickly under Grand Prince Vasilii II and his successors. Gradually the Tatar Cossacks came to be greatly outnumbered by Slavs, especially Ukrainians, many of whom were simply peasants seeking a better life as frontiersmen. Many Cossacks were settled near the Oka River to give early warning of Tatar attacks. These were the ancestors of the "fortress" or "service" Cossacks *(sluzhilye kazaki)* Margeret is referring to in this passage. For this service they were granted land, cash, and eventually even weapons by the Muscovite government. How many service Cossacks there were at the end of the sixteenth century is a subject of some dispute. Margeret's figures are probably fairly accurate. There were still about five thousand of them in the mid-seventeenth century. See Hellie, *Enserfment*, pp. 94, 106, 175, 177, 208, 353 n.81; Vernadsky, *Russia at the Dawn*, pp. 112–13, 249–52; Vernadsky, *Mongols*, pp. 289–91, 316; Zagorovskii, *Cherta*, p. 29; Seredonin, *Sochinenie*, p. 348.

156. Margeret's reference to eight to ten thousand Cossacks willing to join the Muscovite army was generally true, but it did not always apply during the reign of Boris Godunov. Boris was hated by many Cossacks for his efforts to bring them under Muscovite control. His attempts to enlist Cossack support against the pretender Dmitrii failed completely. Alpatov, *Russkaia mysl'*, p. 32; Platonov, *Boris Godunov*, pp. 197–201.

157. Margeret here refers to Ukrainian Cossacks, using "Podolia" to mean the Ukraine in general.

158. Military service could be required from all able-bodied Muscovites (see n.141). Units levied from the peasantry were known by the end of the fifteenth century, although these reinforcements usually acted in support capacities rather than in actual combat. Dressing those peasants like the feared Cossacks was a good use of psychological warfare. See Hellie, *Enserfment*, p. 25; Zlotnik, "Fiscal Policy," pp. 247–48; BC, p. 180; Staden, *Land and Government*, pp. 88–89; Chernov, *Vooruzhennye sily*, pp. 93–94; Razin, *Istoriia*, II, pp. 303–05, 313.

159. Townsmen were recruited in times of need, but they seldom participated in actual combat until the time of Peter the Great. See Razin, *Istoriia*, II, pp. 303–13; Zlotnik, "Fiscal Policy," pp. 247–48; Hellie, *Enserfment*, pp. 25, 232, 267.

On the basis of Margeret's various estimates of the strength of Muscovy's military forces at the beginning of the seventeenth century, an overall picture emerges which is not dissimilar to modern Soviet and western estimates of an army of about one hundred ten thousand. In times of need this force could be augmented by "shadow" forces—extra troops levied from service lands, the Russian Orthodox church estates, and among peasants and townspeople. If one includes slaves and support personnel, it is possible to imagine a fully mobilized Muscovy fielding over two hundred thousand men.

160. Under normal conditions, half the army was on call from about the first of April for springtime service on the southern frontier, with the other half taking up position in mid-summer and staying until late fall. In times of emergency, however, the entire army would be called up in the spring. Soldiers supplied their own provisions

which were shipped to the front ahead of them; the soldiers were also supposed to arrive ahead of time. See Hellie, *Enserfment,* pp. 29, 31, 176–77; Staden, *Land and Government,* pp. 60, 73; Hakluyt, *Principal Navigations,* II, pp. 230–31; BC, p. 184; Korb, *Diary,* II, p. 139.

161. In their campaign against Astrakhan in 1569–70, the Turks were aided by Circassians, Nogai Tatars, and Crimean Tatars. Diplomatic contact between Muscovy and the Ottoman Empire was in fact severely limited during this period, with the last Muscovite ambassador to the Sublime Porte being held captive in 1595 by the Turks.

The Piatigorskie Cherkasy were groups of Circassians (Cherkesses) living in the northern Caucasus. Margeret is incorrect in calling them Georgians. The word *piatigorskie* refers to the five mountains of the northern Caucasus which commanded the way west to the Crimea, northeast to Astrakhan, southeast to Persia, and south to Orthodox Christian Georgia. See Allen, *Russian Embassies,* I, pp. xvi, 9, 14, 19, 24–26, II, pp. 526–27; Kusheva, *Narody,* pp. 145–46; Allen, *Problems,* pp. 35–37.

162. Margeret is referring only to fighting in the south; he earlier mentioned the confrontation with the Swedes during this period. Once again, Margeret confuses the Circassians and other Caucasian peoples with the Georgians.

163. In 1563 the Russians constructed a town on the Terek River, which flows from the north Caucasus to the Caspian Sea, ostensibly to protect Temriuk of Kabarda, a Circassian prince whose daughter Mariia married Ivan IV in 1561. The fate of this town is not known. A second Russian town was built there in 1567. The existence of this town was a major source of concern to the Crimean Tatars and the Turks and may have influenced Sultan Selim II's decision to launch a major offensive (unsuccessfully) against Astrakhan in 1569–70. The fate of this second town is not clear, either. By 1588 a new or restored town, called Terek, was constructed by the Russians. The Russian town of Samara was built along the lower Volga in 1586, at about the same time that (under the influence of the Kabardians) the ruler of the Georgian kingdom of Kakhetia applied to Moscow for protection against the Turks. No doubt all this activity alarmed the Crimean

Tatars as well as many Caucasian peoples who found themselves coming under increasing pressure from the Muscovites. In 1593 the Turks complained to the Russian ambassador at Istanbul about the Russian forts on the Terek River. See Allen, *Russian Embassies*, I, pp. 20–26, 281; Allen, "Marriage Projects," p. 70; Allen, *Problems*, pp. 37, 60; Kusheva, *Narody*, pp. 133–54, 268–75, 315–23.

164. Once again Margeret is confusing Georgians with another Caucasian people. In addition to the Russian presence in Kabarda, the extension of Muscovite protection to the Orthodox Georgian kingdom of Kakhetia provoked a serious conflict with the Turkish-oriented Moslem state of Tarki (located on the west coast of the Caspian Sea). By 1604–05, the Russians had succeeded in capturing and fortifying the town of Tarki, and another Georgian kingdom (Kartlia) seemed to be coming under Muscovy's control. However, in June 1605 the Russians suffered a disastrous defeat at Tarki. This defeat, combined with Boris Godunov's death and the collapse of his planned dynastic alliance with Christian Kartlia, caused the Russians to retreat to their base at Terek and abandon even their commitment to Georgian Kakhetia. Panic and fear of an imminent Turkish assault reigned in Terek for some time, and it was many years before the Russians were able to resume their penetration of the Caucasus. See Allen, *Russian Embassies*, II, pp. 434–53, 549–50; Allen, "Marriage Projects," pp. 71–78; Platonov, *Boris Godunov*, pp. 73–75; Kusheva, *Narody*, pp. 268–88.

165. Margeret is once again referring to the Circassians, who were noted horse-breeders and brilliant guerrilla warriors. Circassian soldiers were celebrated in the Byzantine and Islamic worlds. They even composed a sizeable part of the powerful Mamluk corps which dominated Egypt in this period. Conversely, Mamluk military skills (learned from the Mongols), may also have influenced these fierce warriors, who had themselves in an earlier period impressed the Mongols. See Allen, *Russian Embassies*, I, pp. 24–25, 270–71; Prawdin, *Mongol Empire*, pp. 212–13, 361. Pontus Euxinus was the ancient name for the Black Sea.

166. Once again, Margeret emphasizes that Muscovy at the end of the sixteenth century was a wealthy country. See n. 112.

167. Fedor Borisovich (1589?–1605) was a youth of considerable intelligence and promise. Kseniia Borisovna (1582–1622) was also praised as a youth for her intelligence, education, and beauty. See Allen, *Russian Embassies,* II, pp. 547–49, 571–73.

168. Boris became involved in many complex negotiations seeking foreign marriages for both Kseniia and Fedor, but nothing came of them until it was too late. See Evans, "Queen Elizabeth and Tsar Boris," pp. 60–65; Allen, "Marriage Projects," pp. 69–79; Tsvetaev, *Protestantstvo,* pp. 417–511.

169. Boris guaranteed that there would be no executions for five years after his coronation. To rid himself of dangerous or potentially dangerous rivals he resorted to the less severe punishment of exile. See Massa, *Histoire,* II, pp. 53, 118; Hakluyt, *Principal Navigations,* III, pp. 343–44; Skrynnikov, "Boris Godunov's Struggle," pp. 349–50; Kleimola, "Up Through Servitude," p. 225.

170. Prince F. I. Mstislavskii was married at least twice during his life, although he was probably still single at the end of the sixteenth century. According to some sources, Boris offered him the hand of his daughter Kseniia at least three times. He refused the offer and was therefore not allowed to marry during Boris's reign. Mstislavskii's sister Anastasiia married Simeon shortly after his conversion to Christianity, making Simeon a potentially powerful rival to Boris. Forcing members of powerful families to enter monasteries or convents removed them from active political life and contributed to the extinction of those rival clans. This tactic had been used by Grand Prince Ivan III and became more frequent in the sixteenth century. Boris was thus merely continuing an already existing Muscovite practice. See A. B. Lobanov-Rostovskii, *Russkaia rodoslovnaia kniga,* vol. I (St. Petersburg, 1895), p. 402; BC, pp. 140–41; Kleimola, "Up Through Servitude," p. 214.

171. The Shuiskii family traced its ancestors back to the elder brother of Aleksandr Nevskii. Although they had one of the strongest claims to the throne upon the death of Fedor in 1598, the Shuiskiis refrained from an open struggle with Godunov. At that time the family was led by four Shuiskii brothers, sons of the boiar I. A.

Shuiskii (d. 1573): Vasilii, Dmitrii, Aleksandr, and Ivan. One brother, Aleksandr, died in 1601—hence Margeret's reference to only
three. Dmitrii married Princess Ekaterina, daughter of Ivan IV's no-
torious henchman Maliuta Skuratov. Ekaterina showed herself to be a
true representative of the Skuratov family—she is accused of poisoning her godson in 1610. One reason for Boris favoring Dmitrii
Shuiskii was that Shuiskii had attempted to mediate between Boris
and his opponents in 1598, even to the point of urging the boiar
duma to take no action behind Boris's back. See Vernadsky, *Tsardom*,
I, p. 251; Tikhomirov, "Samozvanshchina," p. 121; Skrynnikov,
"Boris Godunov's Struggle," p. 344; Platonov, *Ocherki*, p. 218;
Platonov, *Boris Godunov*, p. 162; BC, p. 142 n. 14.

172. See n.31. Tsar Simeon Bekbulatovich actually fell from favor
and was exiled many years earlier, in the context of his father-in-law's
unsuccessful bid for power upon the death of Ivan IV. In 1585 Simeon
was still the "sovereign" grand prince of Tver; as such, he represented
a very serious potential challenge to the upstart Boris Godunov.
Fedor's government abolished Simeon's title to Tver and exiled him
to his remote estate at Kushalov. Margeret probably mentions
Simeon's exile at this point because he was aware that Simeon represented as great a potential rival to Boris as the princes Mstislavskii and
Shuiskii. Simeon had actually been the compromise candidate for tsar
of those lords opposed to Godunov in 1598, leading Boris to force all
the lords to swear an oath not to recognize Simeon as tsar or to join
with him in any conspiracy. Simeon actually went blind in 1595,
before Boris became tsar. However, this incident occurred at about
the time Skrynnikov claims that Boris may have begun to contemplate taking the throne himself. In any event, many contemporary
Russian sources, including Tsar Dmitrii Ivanovich, blamed Boris for
Simeon's blindness. After Boris's death, Dmitrii brought Simeon out
of exile and restored him to a position of honor. Margeret thus had
ample opportunity to hear Simeon's story in Moscow. In the spring of
1606 Dmitrii apparently forced Simeon to enter a monastery where (as
the monk Stefan) he lived until 1616. See Solov'ev, *Istoriia*, IV, p. 413;
Platonov, *Boris Godunov*, pp. 172–74; Vernadsky, *Tsardom*, I, pp.

186-88, 210-11; Skrynnikov, *Boris Godunov,* pp. 87-90; Skrynnikov, "Boris Godunov's Struggle," pp. 345-49.

173. Gustavus (1568-1607), the son of the deposed "mad" King Erik XIV of Sweden, lived in Poland from 1575, where he became a Catholic and was educated by the Jesuits. He mastered many languages, including Russian. He also became an excellent chemist and was known as the "second Paracelsus." In 1585 the government of Tsar Fedor unsuccessfully invited Gustavus to live in Muscovy. Tsar Boris once again extended the invitation in 1599, and this time the prince accepted. Vernadsky, *Tsardom,* I, p. 212.

174. One reason for Boris's generosity was that the prince was quite poor and did not have the means to set up a household worthy of Kseniia Godunova.

175. Gustavus's "disgraceful behavior" which abruptly terminated the proposed marriage included his refusal to give up the Catholic faith and to rid himself of his mistress. Despite this, Uglich was given to him as his appanage. He remained in Uglich practising chemistry for several years. After Boris's death, he was removed to Iaroslavl, and he died in northern Russia in 1607. See Massa, *Histoire,* II, pp. 57-58; Vernadsky, *Tsardom,* I, p. 212.

176. Margeret's dates here appear to be incorrect. According to several historians, Sapieha's embassy did not arrive in Moscow until mid-October 1600. The ambassador and his party were shut up in their quarters for over six weeks before even being allowed to greet Tsar Boris. It appears that negotiations were finally concluded only in August 1601. See Solov'ev *Istoriia,* IV, pp. 359-63. Cf. Morgan and Coote, *Early Voyages,* I, p. 247.

177. Although some writers have claimed that Boris's illness in 1600-01 was largely feigned in an effort to delay negotiations with the Poles, others point out that he was chronically in poor health. In 1600 his health was so poor that rumors of his imminent death were widely circulated and believed. See Solov'ev, *Istoriia,* IV, pp. 403-05; Pirling, *Iz Smutnago Vremeni,* p. 155; Skrynnikov, *Boris Godunov,* pp. 137-38.

178. These guards (usually two on each side of the tsar) were called *ryndy.* Many westerners were struck by their awesome appearance.

The *ryndy* were similar to the ancient Roman lictors. See Hakluyt, *Principal Navigations*, III, p. 319; Purchas, *Hakluytus Posthumus*, XIV, pp. 118–19, 138; Konovalov, "Chamberlayne's Description," p. 112.

179. Although Margeret translates *tsar'* as "king" in the Note to the Reader, in his text he consistently translates it as "emperor." He variously translates *vseia Rusi* ("of all Rus'") as "of all Russia" or "of all the Russians."

180. Although Margeret's use of the word "claret" probably means simply light red wine, chances are that it was French. French wine, especially from Gascony and Poitou, was imported into Muscovy from at least the 1560s. The heavier and more expensive wines from Burgundy were especially prized by the Russians and were used in Russian religious services. See Kirchner, *Commercial Relations*, pp. 93, 98; Zhordaniia, *Ocherki*, I, pp. 155–69; Haumant, *La Culture française*, pp. 3–4.

181. *Podacha* means "presenting" or "feeding." On this custom see Zabelin, *Domashnii byt*, I, pp. 370–72, II, p. 738; Herberstein, *Notes*, II, p. 129.

182. The original text here uses *chopine*, which (to avoid confusion) I have translated as "pint." A *chopine* is a Parisian half-pint, about equal to an English pint.

183. Margeret's account contains important evidence concerning grain prices during the famine years. Profiteering was apparently commonplace, leading Boris unsuccessfully to attempt to end grain speculation. Some historians have estimated that grain prices rose as much as 80 to 120 (even up to 360) times the prefamine prices. R. E. F. Smith has recently challenged many of these high figures, suggesting a multiplier closer to 15. Margeret's figure of a price rise on the order of 26 times the prefamine level is much closer to Smith's than to those of Kliuchevskii or even V. I. Koretskii. However, his use of the term *mesure* somewhat complicates the analysis. A *mesure* was a French unit for measuring grain, containing about a bushel and a half. If this term is strictly interpreted, then Margeret's figures are somewhat higher than those found in native Russian sources; if he used the term in a general sense as a "unit" of grain and in this instance actually referred to a typical Russian "unit" of grain (a *chet'*),

then his prices are very similar to those found in Russian sources for rye, oats, and barley in the years 1600 and 1602. See Hellie, *Enserfment*, pp. 106–07; Alpatov, *Russkaia mysl'*, p. 33; Billington, *Icon and Axe* p. 675; Kostomarov, *Smutnoe vremia*, p. 40; Koretskii, *Formirovanie*, pp. 129, 145, 231–32; Smirnov, *Vosstanie*, pp. 64–65; Platonov, *Boris Godunov*, p. 191; Vernadsky, *Tsardom*, I, pp. 216–17; Kopanev and Man'kov, *Vosstanie*, pp. 68–73; Bussov, *Khronika*, pp. 97–98; Smith, *Peasant Farming*, pp. 143–46; Kliuchevskii, *Sochineniia*, VII, pp. 187, 216, 471–72.

184. Margeret may be using the word *poisle* (i.e., *poêle)* here to refer not to a dwelling but merely to a "heated room" or "room with a stove." Cf. Mayerberg, *Relation*, I, p. 129.

185. Although some estimates placed the number of famine-related deaths in Moscow at five hundred thousand, historians have generally accepted the much more conservative figure cited by Margeret—which is very close to a contemporary Russian estimate of one hundred twenty-seven thousand. See Bussov, *Khronika*, pp. 97–98, 346–47; Palitsyn, *Skazanie*, pp. 105–06; Billington, *Icon and Axe*, p. 675; Koretskii, *Formirovanie*, p. 129; Koretskii, "Iz istorii," p. 122.

186. The reference is to a *kopeinaia denga* or kopek.

187. Boris was indeed very generous to the Russian Orthodox church and had the strong support of most of the clergy—including Patriarch Iov. He encountered some opposition from such clergymen as Germogen of Kazan, the future patriarch. See Platonov, *Boris Godunov*, p. 110; Hakluyt, *Principal Navigations*, III, p. 449; Timofeev, *Vremennik*, p. 65; Palitsyn, *Skazanie*, p. 252; Skrynnikov, "Boris Godunov's Struggle," p. 342.

188. After the failure of the marriage project involving Prince Gustavus, Boris sought other foreign consorts for his children. Johan, son of Fredrik II of Denmark (who died in 1588) and the youngest brother of Kristian IV, was about the same age as Kseniia. Kristian and Boris agreed that the two should be betrothed in 1601. The following year Johan traveled to Moscow. See Solov'ev, *Istoriia*, IV, pp. 366–67.

189. Johan died on October 28, 1602. Both the tsar and the Danish government suspected that he was poisoned by one of Boris's

enemies. See Tsvetaev, *Protestantstvo*, pp. 215–18, 443–54; Solov'ev, *Istoriia*, IV, p. 367; Barbour, *Dimitry*, p. 61; Rambaud, *History*, I, p. 319.

190. The Lutheran church located in the Livonian-German suburb of Moscow.

191. Tsaritsa Irina, known as the nun Aleksandra after her "abdication" in early 1598, was buried at Novodevichii Convent on September 27, 1603.

192. Skrynnikov has shown that Boris continued to face opposition even after his "election" in 1598. Especially during his illness in 1600, his enemies appear to have been quite active—Boris's response was to take action against his real or perceived opponents and to protect himself and his family. No doubt his suspicions grew with the mysterious death of Duke Johan. Although Boris apparently did not suspect that his sister had been murdered, her death (along with the famine years) helped to put him in a very grim mood. According to some historians, like Anastasiia's legendary influence over Ivan IV, Irina's devotion to Boris helped to keep him on a steady course. With her death the tsar came increasingly under the influence of his suspicious and cruel wife Mariia. No doubt this changed the tone of Boris's reign. See Skrynnikov, *Boris Godunov*, pp. 103–42; Barbour, *Dimitry*, p. 63.

193. A reference to Dmitrii Shuiskii, who had married Ekaterina Skuratova. This passage is of considerable interest. While many seventeenth-century documents speak of the persecution of the Shuiskiis by Boris Godunov, it has been generally argued that these were written merely for propaganda purposes. Platonov even claimed that the Shuiskiis had not suffered under Godunov, at least after their unsuccessful bid for power during Fedor's reign. In reality, of course, the Shuiskiis did represent a threat to the position of Boris Godunov (although they did not take an active role against him in his 1598 "election"). There is some evidence, even beyond Margeret's testimony, that the Shuiskiis were kept under very close scrutiny by a suspicious Tsar Boris. See Platonov, *Boris Godunov*, pp. 4, 35–38, 162, 194; Platonov, *Ocherki*, pp. 218, 559 n.64; Solov'ev, *Istoriia*, IV, pp. 398, 696 n.52; Skrynnikov, *Boris Godunov*, pp. 131–32; Skrynnikov, "Boris Godunov's Struggle," p. 344.

194. While there were some garbled rumors circulating by 1598 concerning a "substitute" Dmitrii, the legend that Dmitrii had actually escaped death in Uglich in 1591 did not take its final shape until about 1600. Platonov used Margeret's unique testimony (here and at n.306) to link these rumors in 1600 with the Romanov clan—something no native Russian source was able to establish clearly. The Romanovs, as cousins of the late Tsar Fedor, had a strong claim to the throne and opposed Boris's "election" in 1598. Skrynnikov believes that rumors about Dmitrii were circulated by the Romanovs and others during Boris's illness in 1600. By the time the pretender Dmitrii Ivanovich actually invaded Muscovy in 1604, these rumors had prepared a sizeable portion of the Muscovite population to accept him and to champion his cause against the "usurper" Boris Godunov. See Solov'ev, *Istoriia*, IV, pp. 403–05; Platonov, *Boris Godunov*, pp. 166–68, 181–86, 193–94; Chistov, *Russkie legendy*, pp. 35–37, 41; Kostomarov, *Smutnoe vremia*, pp. 30–31; Koretskii, *Formirovanie*, p. 232; Skrynnikov, *Boris Godunov*, pp. 131–42, 155–61; Thompson, "Legend," pp. 48, 58; Palitsyn, *Skazanie*, pp. 252–53; Skrynnikov, "Boris Godunov's Struggle," p. 350; Pirling, *Iz Smutnago Vremeni*, p. 155; Margeret, *Sostoianie* (3rd ed.), pp. 216–17.

195. Several other sources also speak of Boris "setting servants against their masters." The Romanovs were prime targets: a servant of A. N. Romanov was suborned by the Godunov government, resulting in that prince's exile for witchcraft. It should be noted, however, that surveillance of a suspect lord's servants and the requirement that they report any disloyal words or conduct to the government was a characteristic of the Muscovite system in general, and not just of Boris's regime. See Kleimola, "Up Through Servitude," pp. 217–22; Palitsyn, *Skazanie*, pp. 252–53; RIB, XIII, cols, 563, 1283–84; Solov'ev *Istoriia*, IV, pp. 394–95; Skrynnikov, *Boris Godunov*, pp. 137–38; Tikhomirov, "Samozvanshchina," pp. 120–21. Cf. Peter Heylyn, *Cosmography in Four Books* (London, 1682), II, p. 128.

196. Mariia Nagaia (known as the nun Marfa since she was forced to take the veil in 1591) was exiled to a monastery near Vologda, far to the north.

197. According to V. I. Koretskii, the "thieves" referred to in this passage may have been Khlopko's band of discontented slaves and

servants who rebelled against the Godunov regime in 1603. These miserable souls, most of whom had been forced onto the road during the famine years by desperate or unscrupulous lords, posed a real threat to the government. A regular Muscovite army led by the able commander I. F. Basmanov defeated Khlopko's forces, although in the battle Basmanov himself was killed. Khlopko was captured and later hanged. His rebellion is considered by Soviet historians to have been the dress rehearsal for the Bolotnikov rebellion which broke out in 1606. See Koretskii, "Iz istorii," pp. 119–22, 129, 134; Koretskii, *Formirovanie*, pp. 195–235, esp. pp. 231–32; PSRL, XIV, pt. 1, p. 58; Vernadsky, *Tsardom*, I, pp. 218–19; Avrich, *Russian Rebels*, p.15.

198. Prior to his invasion of Muscovy in October 1604, the pretender Dmitrii Ivanovich had assembled about four thousand troops, consisting mostly of Ukrainian Cossacks and volunteers raised by the opportunistic Pan Jerzy Mniszech, palatine of Sandomierz. These forces were joined by thousands of volunteers (primarily Cossacks) as the invasion progressed. Crossing Podolia (Margeret again means the Ukraine), Dmitrii invaded the Muscovite province of Severia where he found that his strength lay less in his small army than in the hostile attitude of many Russians toward the Godunov government. For many reasons, primarily related to Boris's policy of enserfment, Dmitrii was welcomed as a potential savior by many peasants, slaves, and townspeople as well as by Don Cossacks. The town of Moravsk surrendered to Dmitrii without a shot. Soon thereafter the townspeople of Chernigov overpowered their garrison and opened their gates to Dmitrii's forces. See Platonov, *Boris Godunov*, pp. 106–07, 196–201; Platonov, *Time of Troubles*, pp. 34, 38–39, 71–74; Avrich, *Russian Rebels*, pp. 16, 46; Barbour, *Dimitry*, pp. 71–81; Troitskii, "Samozvantsy," p. 134.

199. From Chernigov, Dmitrii's army went to Novgorod Severskii, which did not surrender to him. While testing the defenses of Novgorod Severskii, Dmitrii received word of the surrender of the very important town of Putivl, as well as several other towns in the area, including Ryl'sk, Kromy, and Karachev. Some historians have maintained that it was not so much social protest or love of the "true tsar" on the part of the townspeople which led to such gains for Dmitrii as it was the hostility of the commanders of these towns

toward Boris Godunov. While this was probably true of some (e.g., the *voevoda* of Putivl, Prince V. M. Mosal'skii-Rubets), the power of lower-class protest against Godunov in southwestern and southern Muscovy should not be underestimated, nor should the influence of the ubiquitous Cossacks, who championed Dmitrii's cause as far east as the Urals. See Solov'ev, *Istoriia*, IV, p. 417; Avrich, *Russian Rebels*, p. 24; Barbour, *Dimitry*, pp. 85–86, 106; Platonov, *Time of Troubles*, p. 75; Allen, *Ukraine*, p. 92.

200. Dmitrii's forces actually went directly from Chernigov to the well-fortified and strategically located Novgorod Severskii. The march took about a week, and by the time Dmitrii arrived there his forces numbered well over ten thousand. See Barbour, *Dimitry*, pp. 80–81; Platonov, *Boris Godunov*, p. 197; Tikhomirov, *Rossiia*, p. 413.

201. Petr F. Basmanov, one of Boris's chief military commanders, was sent to stop Dmitrii at Chernigov, but that town fell before Basmanov arrived. Along with his senior commander Prince N. R. Trubetskoi, Basmanov then retired to Novgorod Severskii where he was determined to resist Dmitrii and to block his access to the road to Moscow. Basmanov had the outskirts of the town burned and with about six hundred men held out in the fort proper. Since the Russians were excellent defensive fighters, Novgorod Severskii proved to be too hard a nut for Dmitrii to crack. The pretender's forces made several halfhearted efforts to take the fort by storm but broke off the siege in mid-December in order to face the tsar's army which was then taking up its position nearby. See Barbour, *Dimitry*, pp. 82–84; Purchas, *Hakluytus Posthumus*, XIV, p. 141; BC, p. 186; Olearius, *Travels*, pp. 43, 152; Avity, *Description*, III, p. 1143.

202. The arrival of a Muscovite relief army forced Dmitrii to turn his attention away from Novgorod Severskii itself. Although the Muscovites greatly outnumbered Dmitrii's forces, Mstislavskii had hoped for even more troops before engaging the enemy. After a bit of initial skirmishing, the two armies joined battle on December 21 (O.S.). By capturing the Muscovite army's standard and inflicting several thousand casualties, Dmitrii officially won the battle — although, as the professional military observer Captain Margeret relates, he failed to follow up his victory by decisively defeating the wavering

Muscovite forces. See Solov'ev, *Istoriia*, IV, p. 418; Barbour, *Dimitry*, pp. 86–89.

203. "One might have said the Russians had no arms to strike with" is one of the most famous phrases in Margeret's book. In various forms it found its way into the writings of historians such as Karamzin and Solov'ev and of playwrights and poets such as Alexander Pushkin. The line was embellished by Karamzin and Pushkin so that not only did the tsar's troops have no arms to strike with, they had only legs to run away. In composing his play *Boris Godunov*, Pushkin carefully consulted Karamzin's history of Russia, which is where he first encountered this famous passage. But he may also have read Margeret's book, for the brave captain personally speaks these lines (in French) in the play. As for the strength of the Muscovite army facing Dmitrii, Margeret's estimate of forty or fifty thousand is generally accepted by historians, who prefer his conservative figure to the much higher figures found in several other foreign accounts. See Pushkin, *Boris Godunov*, pp. 7–9, 86–87; Solov'ev, *Istoriia*, IV, p. 418; Massa, *Kratkoe izvestie*, p. 195; Rambaud, *History*, I, p. 325.

204. The Muscovite army retired north to Starodub, there to await reinforcements and a new general to aid the wounded Mstislavskii.

205. This is probably a reference to the same Pan Mateusz Domoracki who was later to occupy a prominent position in Tsar Dmitrii's court and who was imprisoned in 1606 by Tsar Vasilii Shuiskii. See Barbour, *Dimitry*, pp. 204, 290; Solov'ev, *Istoriia*, IV, p. 492; S. F. Platonov, *Sotsial'nyi krizis smutnogo vremeni* (Leningrad, 1924), p. 165.

206. Dmitrii was already in Severia (see n.198). It was at this point, after his victory, that he was confronted by the Polish volunteers in his army. These opportunistic knights demanded money, which Dmitrii did not have. Expecting the fighting in Muscovy to get worse in the days ahead, most of them decided to return immediately to Poland. Even Pan Mniszech, the organizer of the Polish volunteer force, deserted his future son-in-law (claiming poor health and an upcoming meeting of the Polish Diet in Warsaw). The fifteen hundred Poles who remained were very quickly joined by some twelve thousand Cossacks who (along with many disaffected Muscovites) were still

quite willing to fight for their "true tsar." See Barbour, *Dimitry*, pp. 89–90; Allen, *Ukraine*, p. 92; Solov'ev, *Istoriia*, IV, pp. 418–419.

207. The tsar's army received so many reinforcements that it reached perhaps seventy thousand before the end of January 1605. It also received a new commander to aid the wounded Mstislavskii, none other than Prince Vasilii I. Shuiskii. Probably to cover the Muscovite army's flank and to protect the roads to Moscow, a small force under the boiar F. I. Sheremetev was sent to invest Kromy (a town located to the east which had declared for Dmitrii). It has been pointed out that Shuiskii was no better a general than Mstislavskii, so it should be no surprise that the Muscovite forces did not press their advantage against Dmitrii. See Barbour, *Dimitry*, p. 91.

208. Even under the best of conditions, the Muscovite army could travel only about fifteen kilometers per day. Margeret's implication that the army was purposely delayed in its pursuit of Dmitrii is interesting. Several historians have maintained that many of the Muscovite commanders only halfheartedly supported Boris Godunov and were not particularly interested in defeating his foes. Some even claimed that Dmitrii would be difficult to beat because he was "the inborn tsar." See Razin, *Istoriia*, II, p. 349; Vernadsky, *Tsardom*, I, p. 227; Solov'ev, *Istoriia*, IV, pp. 419–20. Cf. Platonov, *Boris Godunov*, pp. 194–96.

209. The Muscovite army set up camp in the village of Dobrynichi. Despite misgivings voiced by his Polish officers, Dmitrii was urged by his Cossack commanders to attack the cramped Muscovite position immediately. Barbour, *Dimitry*, pp. 91–92.

210. During the battle of Dobrynichi, Dmitrii's Polish volunteers formed his main cavalry force. The Cossacks were on the right wing and his new Muscovite forces on the left.

211. The reference to "ledit Polonois" I have translated as "Poles" because there is no mention of any *one* leader except Dmitrii, whom Margeret would never call a Pole.

212. Although he does not say so, Margeret was a major participant in this battle. According to reliable testimony, it was the foreigners under Margeret and Von Rosen (a German captain) who saved the day for the wavering Muscovite army; Margeret was profusely thanked

and rewarded by Boris. Dmitrii and his Polish officers blamed their defeat on the "flight" of the Cossacks during the battle. He hastily retreated first to Ryl'sk, where he rested for two days, and then to the stronghold of Putivl, arriving there five days after the disaster at Dobrynichi. At Putivl (which was strongly committed to Dmitrii's cause) another four thousand Don Cossacks joined his decimated forces. Pushkin immortalized Margeret's actions at Dobrynichi in *Boris Godunov*, although he shifts the action to Novgorod Severskii. See Bussov, *Khronika*, pp. 102, 186–87; Massa, *Histoire*, II, p. 103; Ustrialov, *Skazaniia sovremennikov*, I, p. 237; Alpatov, *Russkaia mysl'*, pp. 17, 33; Zhordaniia, *Ocherki*, I, pp. 250, 255, 273–76; Waliszewski, *La Crise*, p. 165; Pushkin, *Boris Godunov*, pp. 86–88; Hellie, *Enserfment*, pp. 162–68; Barbour, *Dimitry*, pp. 92–96; Solov'ev, *Istoriia*, IV, pp. 419–20.

213. Shuiskii and the other generals made no effort to crush Dmitrii. Instead, they turned to the task of "punishing" the Muscovites of Severia who had dared to champion Dmitrii's cause. Because the town of Ryl'sk had declared for Dmitrii and had temporarily sheltered him after his defeat at Dobrynichi, it was singled out for severe punishment. See Vernadsky, *Tsardom*, I, p. 228; Platonov, *Time of Troubles*, pp. 91–94; Solov'ev, *Istoriia*, IV, p. 420.

214. Several thousand Cossacks from Putivl broke through the Muscovite lines and were able to resupply besieged Ryl'sk. This so discouraged the Muscovite commanders that they soon broke off the siege. Platonov believed that the Muscovite commanders, seeing the entire southern and southwestern frontier so ardently supporting Dmitrii, withdrew northward in order to protect the roads to Moscow and to avoid being cut off from the capital. See Barbour, *Dimitry*, p. 104; Platonov, *Boris Godunov*, p. 201; Platonov, *Ocherki*, pp. 252–53.

215. That Boris's commanders failed to pursue Dmitrii vigorously and even contemplated temporarily disbanding the army while the entire south and southwest were still in rebellion suggests that there was treachery brewing among the Muscovite commanders, especially in light of the fact that some Muscovite lords were secretly involved in the conspiracy to replace Boris Godunov with Dmitrii. In any event,

Boris was able to stop the plans to dismiss his army. See Platonov, *Ocherki*, pp. 253–54; Platonov, *Boris Godunov*, p. 194; Vernadsky, *Tsardom*, I, p. 227; Crull, *State of Muscovy*, I, p. 147; BC, p. 181; Konovalov, "Chamberlayne's Description," p. 113.

216. Kromy, which occupied a strategically important road junction, had declared for Dmitrii and had been reinforced by several hundred Don Cossacks. A small Muscovite force commanded by the boiar F. I. Sheremetev had been sent to invest the town in December 1604. Two months later, the town was still holding out. The tsar's main army was then brought to Kromy to aid in the siege operations. See Platonov, *Boris Godunov*, p. 201; Barbour, *Dimitry*, pp. 101, 104.

217. This famous passage is often quoted or paraphrased. The tsar's army was unable to dislodge the Cossacks from Kromy. Although the Muscovite army was not usually very good at siege operations, several historians blame its failure upon treachery among the tsar's commanders, some of whom were either secret supporters of Dmitrii or at least very hostile toward Boris Godunov. According to some sources, at a decisive moment one of the Muscovite commanders, Mikhail G. Saltykov, even removed the cannon from action and sent them to the rear of the besieging forces, making capture of Kromy virtually impossible. Boris had long been in ill health, but his sudden death at this critical moment prompted many rumors of murder or suicide by poisoning. Skrynnikov rejects these rumors and prefers Margeret's testimony; he believes that Margeret was actually at court when Boris died. (He may have returned to Moscow in the triumphal procession of the heroes of the battle of Dobrynichi.) See Vernadsky, *Tsardom*, I, pp. 227–28; Solov'ev, *Istoriia*, IV, pp. 416, 421; Platonov, *Time of Troubles*, p. 76; Platonov, *Ocherki*, pp. 254–56; Skrynnikov, *Boris Godunov*, p. 179; Thompson, "Legend," p. 57; Bussov, *Khronika*, p. 230; BC, p. 363; Purchas, *Hakluytus Posthumus*, XIV, pp. 147, 160.

218. *Beschestie* meant either the offense itself (injury to honor) or the payment of a fine for the offense. Margeret's testimony is useful in trying to reconstruct this institution. See Kliuchevskii, *Sochineniia*, VI, pp. 449–51; H. W. Dewey, "Old Muscovite Concepts of Injured Honor *(Beschestie)*," *Slavic Review* 27 (1968), 594–603.

219. It is not clear that the guilty party was forced to pay this sum simply if the offended party was married. This was the amount expected if both the man and his wife had been dishonored. The normal fine for dishonoring a man's wife was twice his annual salary. See Uroff, "Kotoshikhin," pp. 224–25. *Batog* (plural *batoga*) is a Russian word for rod or cudgel.

220. Recalling Mstislavskii and Shuiskii was a precautionary measure. The Godunovs felt that leaving command of the army to these two princes with strong claims to the throne might spell trouble for the new dynasty. However, their recall probably harmed the Godunov cause because it left the army under the influence of the treacherous Princes Golitsyn.

221. The able Basmanov was well liked and trusted by Fedor Godunov, just as he had been a favorite of Boris. Because of *mestnichestvo* tradition, however, Basmanov could not be appointed commander-in-chief of the army, only deputy commander. Basmanov's supposedly "senior" officer was Prince Mikhail Petrovich Katyrev-Rostovskii. See Vernadsky, *Tsardom,* I, p. 228; Platonov, *Time of Troubles,* p. 77; Skrynnikov, *Boris Godunov,* p. 180.

222. The oath was administered to the army on April 17, 1605 (O.S.), by Basmanov and Metropolitan Isidor of Novgorod, almost immediately upon their arrival in camp.

223. According to some historians, when Basmanov arrived at Kromy he discovered that the other senior commanders were leaning toward support of Dmitrii; he was won over by the arguments of his half-brothers, the very prestigious Princes Vasilii and Ivan Vasil'evich Golitsyn. Other sources claim that on May 7 (O.S.) Basmanov himself, looking for advancement, led the move to join Dmitrii. See Skrynnikov, *Boris Godunov,* pp. 179–80; Solov'ev, *Istoriia,* IV, p. 423; Barbour, *Dimitry,* pp. 114–17, 341; Purchas, *Hakluytus Posthumus,* XIV, pp. 147–48, 161; Platonov, *Ocherki,* pp. 262–64; Platonov, *Time of Troubles,* pp. 76–78.

224. Ivan Godunov (Boris's grandnephew) was indeed captured, tied up, and taken to the pretender by Ivan Golitsyn, who was to announce to Dmitrii (then still in Putivl) the transfer of allegiance of the

tsar's army. There is, however, some evidence that Mikhail G. Saltykov had joined the conspiracy to recognize Dmitrii as tsar. According to some sources, Saltykov had regarded the pretender as the "inborn tsar" for some time and had sabotaged the siege of Kromy (see n.217). He also supposedly helped the Golitsyns convince Basmanov to recognize Dmitrii. Why, then, does Margeret say that Saltykov was taken prisoner? Since Margeret was in Moscow at the time, his evidence concerning events at Kromy is only second-hand, perhaps learned from the foreign mercenaries who fled from Kromy to Moscow. It is possible that Margeret was simply misinformed. It is also possible that Saltykov later lied to Margeret about the incident, and Margeret never questioned the word of a man he had served with for several years. It is even remotely possible that Margeret was covering for Saltykov by avoiding any reference to the cannon at Kromy and by lying about Saltykov's involvement in the treachery of the Muscovite commanders, but this would be very much out of character for Margeret, who would have had little motive for concealing the truth in a book printed in France in 1607. One explanation may be that most of the sources indicting Saltykov were composed in later years by writers influenced by the hostility of the Shuiskii government toward Saltykov (a relative of the Romanovs) or by Saltykov's "treason" in supporting a Polish candidate to the Muscovite throne in 1610–11. For many Russians, Saltykov became a hated figure as a Tushinite lord and as one of the leading collaborators in Polish-occupied Moscow. This hatred may have resulted in distorted accounts of his earlier activities. See Platonov, *Time of Troubles,* p. 114; Platonov, *Ocherki,* p. 264; Vernadsky, *Tsardom,* I, pp. 227–28, 249, 254–55; Solov'ev, *Istoriia,* IV, pp. 416–23; Skrynnikov, *Boris Godunov,* p. 179; Zhordaniia, *Ocherki,* I, pp. 250–51.

225. Prince Katyrev-Rostovskii and the prince-boiar Andrei Andreevich Teliatevskii fled to Moscow with the few troops still loyal to Fedor Godunov. See Skrynnikov, *Boris Godunov,* p. 180.

226. Riazan, Tula, Aleksin, and Kashira all declared for Dmitrii at this time. Dmitrii left Putivl on May 19 (O.S.). See Solov'ev, *Istoriia,* IV, pp. 423–24; *Ocherki istorii SSSR,* p. 497.

227. On his march toward the Muscovite army, now located at Orel, Dmitrii was greeted by several of the Muscovite commanders—notably P. F. Basmanov, V. V. Golitsyn, M. G. Saltykov, and F. I. Sheremetev—who pledged their loyalty to him. Dmitrii ordered the dismissal of part of the army and had the rest sent toward Moscow under the command of V. V. Golitsyn. He apparently wished to keep his forces separate from the Muscovite army, probably as a security measure. See Solov'ev, *Istoriia*, IV, pp. 423–24; Barbour, *Dimitry*, p. 120; *Ocherki istorii SSSR*, pp. 496–97.

228. Dmitrii's "seductive letters" proved to be an effective propaganda tool throughout his campaign. Although the first messengers he sent to Moscow were captured and tortured to death, others were able to read Dmitrii's message on June 1 (O.S.) to a crowd of merchants and townspeople at Krasnoe Selo, a suburb of Moscow known to be at best lukewarm in its support of the Godunovs. The response of the people was strong and favorable, and they immediately escorted the messengers to Red Square, there to read the letter to all the citizens of Moscow. See Troitskii, "Samozvantsy," p. 135; Purchas, *Hakluytus Posthumus*, XIV, pp. 148–50; PSRL, XIV, pt. 1, p. 65; Solov'ev, *Istoriia*, IV, p. 424; Barbour, *Dimitry*, pp. 120–22; Platonov, *Ocherki*, pp. 269–70.

229. In addition to summoning Mstislavskii and Shuiskii to Moscow, the government of Fedor Godunov had recalled from exile Bogdan Bel'skii, a favorite of Ivan IV who had been banished after an unsuccessful bid for power in 1584. Since none of them was loyal to the Godunovs, it is no surprise that they failed to calm the crowd, which then stormed the Kremlin in the name of the "true tsar" Dmitrii. Several sources claim that on that day Bel'skii was instrumental in stirring the people against the Godunovs. His connections with the plot to place the pretender Dmitrii on the throne have often been discussed, and he was later greatly honored (along with Golitsyn and Basmanov) by Tsar Dmitrii. Chances are that Bel'skii was indeed a leader of the revolt. See Platonov, *Boris Godunov*, pp. 177–83; Purchas, *Hakluytus Posthumus*, XIV, p. 151; Vernadsky, *Tsardom*, I, pp. 229–30; Solov'ev, *Istoriia*, IV, pp. 424–25; Platonov, *Ocherki*, pp. 269–74; Skrynnikov, *Boris Godunov*, pp. 181–82.

230. On June 3 (O.S.) a procession went from Moscow to Tula to offer a pledge of the capital's loyalty to the "true tsar" Dmitrii. In that procession were Prince I. M. Vorotynskii, Prince Andrei Teliatevskii, Petr Sheremetev, and the *d'iak* Afanasii Vlas'ev. According to Platonov, Prince V. I. Shuiskii later joined them. See Barbour, *Dimitry*, p. 124; Platonov, *Time of Troubles*, p. 78.

231. Princes Vasilii V. Golitsyn and V. M. Mosal'skii-Rubets, along with others, strangled Mariia and murdered Fedor Godunov. See Skrynnikov, *Boris Godunov*, pp. 181–82; Platonov, *Boris Godunov*, p. 204.

232. Apparently, during the palace coup most of the Godunov clan were simply arrested. Besides Mariia and Fedor, only the hated chief of Boris's secret police, Semen Godunov, was murdered. Legend has it that Dmitrii raped Kseniia Godunova before she was forced to take the veil as the nun Olga. See Vernadsky, *Tsardom*, I, p. 229; Barbour, *Dimitry*, pp. 126, 130, 164–65.

233. Boris's body was first removed from Archangel Cathedral and taken to the Varsonof'ev Monastery in Moscow. Later it was placed in the Trinity–St. Sergius Monastery where other members of the family were eventually buried. Platonov, *Boris Godunov*, p. 204.

234. Margeret appears to be in error here. The task of fetching the nun Marfa was entrusted to the very able cousin of V. I. Shuiskii, Prince Mikhail V. Skopin-Shuiskii, and to Semen Shapkin (one of Dmitrii's courtiers who was married to Marfa's cousin). In the meantime, Dmitrii issued several documents which included his mother's name alongside his own. He steadfastly refused to be crowned before her arrival in Moscow. Other members of the exiled Nagoi clan were also recalled to Moscow where they received great honors as Dmitrii's closest relatives. See Solov'ev, *Istoriia*, IV, pp. 426, 429; Troitskii, "Samozvantsy," pp. 135–36.

235. Marfa was greeted by Dmitrii in the village of Tainskoe on July 18 (O.S.). There she publicly "recognized" Dmitrii as her son. Whether she was merely anxious to end her fourteen-year confinement and to be treated once more like a tsaritsa or whether she truly believed Dmitrii to be her son no one will ever know for sure. Her later denial that he was her son should be viewed in the context of political events after Dmitrii's assassination in 1606. See Barbour,

Dimitry, pp. 147–52; Troitskii, "Samozvantsy," pp. 135–36; Tikhomirov, "Samozvanshchina," p. 121.

236. Quarters were prepared for Marfa at the Kirillov Monastery in the Kremlin.

237. Patriarch Ignatii, a Greek from Cyprus and former archbishop of Riazan, was appointed by Dmitrii to replace the deposed Iov. Margeret refers to Archangel Cathedral (*Arkhangel'skii Sobor*) simply as "Archangel." The Chuch of Our Lady is the *Uspenskii Sobor* (Cathedral of the Assumption).

238. Much to the dissatisfaction of some Orthodox Muscovites, Catholic Poles and even Jesuits attended this banquet. See Barbour, *Dimitry,* p. 155.

239. Margeret's chronology here is inaccurate, although his information is extremely valuable. While exact dating of this incident is difficult to determine, it is certain that Shuiskii was accused of spreading rumors that Dmitrii was a fraud almost immediately after Dmitrii's arrival in Moscow. Probably on June 23 or 24 (O.S.) Dmitrii submitted the matter to what might have been a *zemskii sobor* (Margeret's unique evidence is all too brief). Shuiskii was very quickly found guilty by those present. See Platonov, *Ocherki,* pp. 272–74; Platonov, *Stat'i,* pp. 299–300; Kliuchevskii, *Sochineniia,* VIII, p. 112; Solov'ev, *Istoriia,* IV, p. 428; Cherepnin, *Zemskie sobory,* p. 150.

240. Shuiskii was to have been beheaded on *lobnoe mesto,* a stone platform erected in Red Square in 1534 from which proclamations were often read. Who convinced Dmitrii to commute the sentence is not exactly clear. Although the nun Marfa had not yet arrived in Moscow, she could possibly have sent word to her "son" not to execute such a high-born prince at the outset of his reign. According to some sources, there was considerable sympathy for Shuiskii in Moscow, and for many this episode cast Dmitrii's reign in a bad light. On the other hand, some claim that Shuiskii had few adherents and many were glad to see him brought so low. The *d'iak* Afanasii Vlas'ev is sometimes mentioned as advising the new tsar against the execution. As for "a Pole named Buczyński," Dmitrii had two very close Protestant advisors (personal secretaries) named Buczyński, the brothers Jan and Stanisław. Some sources say that Jan Buczyński urged

clemency on this occasion; others maintain that he strongly opposed clemency. See Barbour, *Dimitry,* pp. 47, 142, 146–47, 165; Platonov, *Time of Troubles,* p. 79; RIB, XIII, col. 160; Purchas, *Hakluytus Posthumus,* XIV, p. 183;Treadgold, *West,* I, p. 49; Solov'ev, *Istoriia,* IV, p. 428; Thompson, "Legend," p. 57.

241. Shuiskii was pardoned even before reaching his place of exile, an act that has puzzled historians as well as Margeret. While Kliuchevskii declared that Tsar Boris would never have made such a mistake, Kleimola has argued that punishment for members of the Muscovite elite in this period was becoming generally less severe. Dmitrii may have wished to appear benevolent, or he might have wished to prove that he did not fear being called an impostor. It is even remotely possible that pardoning Shuiskii was a secret price Dmitrii had to pay for recognition of his claims by the Nagois or other great lords. See Kleimola, "Up Through Servitude," pp. 225–27; Kliuchevskii, *Course,* pp. 31–32; Howe, *False Dmitri,* p. 32; Margeret, *Sostoianie* (3rd ed.), p. 218.

242. Vlas'ev, former ambassador for Tsar Boris and head of the foreign office *(Posol'skii Prikaz)* since 1601, was greatly favored by Dmitrii. He left Moscow in September 1605. See Platonov, *Time of Troubles,* p. 80.

243. The infamous Pan Jerzy Mniszech was one of Dmitrii's earliest and strongest supporters in Poland, championing his cause and helping him gather troops. Dmitrii signed a contract with Mniszech agreeing (once Dmitrii became tsar) to pay him a large sum of money and to cede certain territories to him in return for his help. Money and land were also to be given to Mniszech's daughter Marina, who was to become Dmitrii's wife once he occupied the Muscovite throne. Although Mniszech soon deserted the campaign, Dmitrii was still very much interested in obtaining Marina's hand in marriage. Vlas'ev's mission to Poland was primarily concerned with completing the marriage agreement. He carried with him, along with elaborate gifts for King Sigismund, a huge sum of money for Mniszech. See Barbour, *Dimitry,* pp. 48–50, 118, 129, 177.

244. Vlas'ev arrived in Krakow in November 1605. There he was greeted by Mniszech and presented to King Sigismund. For many

reasons, the king was willing to show some favor toward Dmitrii. The young man was, after all, now tsar of Russia and no longer just an impoverished pretender stirring up trouble with Poland's neighbor to the east. Sigismund no doubt was anxious to enlist Dmitrii's aid in his own efforts to regain the Swedish throne; and even Pope Paul V was urging cooperation with Dmitrii. On November 12 (O.S.), with the participation of the king and the papal nuncio, the marriage between Dmitrii and Marina was solemnized — with Vlas'ev acting as Dmitrii's proxy. See Barbour, *Dimitry*, pp. 167–80; Pierling, *La Russie*, III, pp. 69–70.

245. Dmitrii's foreign guard received the highest pay in the Muscovite army and dressed the part, in red velvet and cloth-of-gold. Their weapons were also richly adorned. These privileged soldiers accompanied Dmitrii everywhere and provoked dissatisfaction among many Muscovites who resented this innovation as well as the favoritism shown to foreigners. Some writers have mistakenly believed that the first company of the guard, Margeret's archers, were primarily Frenchmen; most in fact were Swedes and Livonians, and German was their common language. Margeret's use of the word "Archer" has also confused several historians, primarily because of its similarity to the Russian *strelets* and *strelok*. Originally, archers in Western Europe had carried bows and arrows, but the term came to mean simply "a member of the king's guard." Despite the name, the first company of Dmitrii's guard actually carried partisans (or pole-axes) and pistols. See Barbour, *Dimitry*, pp. 204–08; Zhordaniia, *Ocherki*, I, pp. 250–55; de Thou, *Histoire*, XIV, p. 492; Purchas, *Hakluytus Posthumus*, XIV, pp. 162–63, 176; Howe, *False Dmitri*, p. 33; Massa, *Histoire*, II, p. 148; Bussov, *Khronika*, pp. 112, 118, 129; Platonov, *Time of Troubles*, p. 79.

246. In addition to recalling from exile many lords who had been out of favor with Boris (including the Nagois, Romanovs, and Bel'skii), Dmitrii took other measures to strengthen the position of the Nagoi clan and to demonstrate that his was to be a reign quite unlike that of the "tyrant" Boris. Just exactly which of Dmitrii's "cousins" Prince F. I. Mstislavskii married is not known. See Platonov, *Time of Troubles*, p. 80; Barsukov, *Rod*, II, pp. 114–15; BC, p. 140; Kleimola, "Up Through Servitude," p. 214.

247. Vasilii Shuiskii chose to marry Mariia Petrovna Buinosova-Rostovskaia, who was related by marriage to the Nagois. Their wedding was, however, delayed until 1608.

248. This is one of Margeret's few serious criticisms of Dmitrii. Many Muscovites, especially the great lords, were deeply offended by Dmitrii's deviation from the traditional and awesome reserve of an Orthodox Russian tsar. No doubt this helped to undermine respect for Dmitrii's authority in important circles, where fear was replaced by contempt. Margeret's comments about the traditional "subjection and fear" of the Muscovite lords is echoed in the writings of several westerners of this period. See Massa, *Histoire*, II, pp. 148, 238, 298; Olearius, *Travels*, p. 177; Crull, *State of Muscovy*, I, p. 170; Barbour, *Dimitry*, pp. 158–60; Troitskii, "Samozvantsy," p. 136.

249. Dmitrii tried to enlist the active assistance of members of the boiar duma in running his government, using that council somewhat along the lines of the Polish Senate. In this he had very little success. Dmitrii was often impatient with the ignorance of his Muscovite advisors, and they then had to listen to his lectures. He did know much about the art of government, and several sources mention him "tutoring the lords." See Massa, *Histoire*, II, p. 147; Bussov, *Khronika*, p. 110; Troitskii, "Samozvantsy," p. 136; Kliuchevskii, *Boiarskaia duma*, pp. 448–506.

250. It is difficult to know just which plots Margeret is describing. Rumors that Dmitrii was an impostor were widely circulated in Moscow by the beginning of 1606. In early January 1606 a bold attempt was made upon the tsar's life in the Kremlin. Shortly thereafter, a rumor that some members of the *strel'tsy* regarded Dmitrii as a fraud was reported to the tsar by Petr Basmanov. After personally delivering an impassioned defense of his identity, Dmitrii allowed seven of the "guilty" to be murdered by their companions, who thereupon reaffirmed their loyalty to the "true tsar." See Barbour, *Dimitry*, pp. 204–07; Platonov, *Time of Troubles*, p. 79; Troitskii, "Samozvantsy," p. 136; Massa, *Kratkoe izvestie*, p. 123.

251. Apparently, more than one would-be assassin was captured and tortured, but to no avail. It is possible that this *d'iak* was one Timofei Osipov, who supposedly told Dmitrii to his face that he was

an impostor and was later tortured and sent into exile. In any case, V. I. Shuiskii was indeed behind these plots. Almost as soon as he returned from exile he began conspiring to overthrow Dmitrii. A few months of Dmitrii's reign was enough to convince Shuiskii and others that Dmitrii would not favor the princely clans and allow them to run the government. In early 1606 Shuiskii and the Golitsyns even wrote secretly to King Sigismund of Poland complaining about the impostor who sat on the Muscovite throne and declaring their intention of somehow overthowing him. See Barbour, *Dimitry*, pp. 204, 242–43; Platonov, *Time of Troubles*, p. 80; Vernadsky, *Tsardom*, I, pp. 231–32; Solov'ev, *Istoriia*, IV, pp. 449–51; Palitsyn, *Skazanie*, p. 113.

252. Marina's entourage numbered about two thousand when she set out for Moscow at the end of February 1606. She was accompanied by her father, her brother Stanisław, her brother-in-law Prince Konstanty Wiśniowiecki, and several other notables. They arrived at the Muscovite frontier on April 8, 1606 (O.S.). Prince Konstanty, whose powerful family owned vast territories in the Ukraine, had been one of Dmitrii's earliest supporters. It was he who had first introduced Dmitrii to his future father-in-law. See Barbour, *Dimitry*, p. 221.

253. Tatishchev, an able and experienced Muscovite diplomat, had served Boris Godunov well in many places. He quickly won Dmitrii's favor and became a frequent guest at merry-making in the royal apartments, rivaling Petr Basmanov as Dmitrii's favorite. When Shuiskii criticized Dmitrii for eating veal at a public dinner during Lent, Tatishchev rudely spoke up for Shuiskii and was dismissed from the table by the tsar. Dmitrii was apparently unaware of just how offended some Muscovite lords were by his deviation from Orthodox customs. Margeret's account of this event has often been cited by historians. See Allen, "Marriage Projects," p. 71; Solov'ev, *Istoriia*, IV, p. 450; Kostomarov, *Smutnoe vremia*, p. 172; Alpatov, *Russkaia mysl'*, p. 34; Collins, *State of Russia*, p. 60.

254. Just why Basmanov had Tatishchev restored to favor was unclear to many at the time. It certainly proved to be a fatal error for both Basmanov and Dmitrii. See Howe, *False Dmitri*, p. 45.

255. Margeret underestimated the Cossacks who appeared in the south during the winter of 1605–06. Although service Cossacks from

Terek were included in the force, not all the Terek Cossacks were infantry. In fact, Don Cossacks also joined this force, and Margeret has already noted the military prowess of these horsemen. In this passage he is using the Ukrainian Cossacks, for whom he had considerable respect, as an example of "true Cossacks." See Vernadsky, *Tsardom*, I, p. 231; Allen, *Russian Embassies*, I, pp. 18–23; Smirnov, *Vosstanie*, p. 373.

256. The Terek and Don Cossacks in question were denied entry into Astrakhan and subsequently traveled up the Volga River robbing merchants. See Barbour, *Dimitry*, p. 241.

257. There was no real Tsarevich Petr: Fedor and Irina had only one child, a daughter. Margeret's description is the most significant evidence which has survived concerning this affair. See Smirnov, *Vosstanie*, pp. 368–69; Koretskii, *Formirovanie*, pp. 253–54; Alpatov, *Russkaia mysl'*, p. 34; Dolinin, "K izucheniiu," p. 469.

258. Dmitrii rewarded the Don Cossacks who had accompanied him on his campaign to win the Muscovite throne, but he quickly dismissed them from his army after his victory. Some of them wished for further rewards and favors, and they did not appreciate being shoved aside in favor of the despised *dvoriane*. The Terek Cossacks had missed out on Dmitrii's campaign and were consequently now looking for booty and rewards of their own. In 1605 they chose as their leader a very able young man named Ileika Muromets. Following the example of the pretender Dmitrii Ivanovich, Ileika assumed the identity of "Tsarevich Petr" and led his men on a campaign to seek adventure and fortune. See Koretskii, *Formirovanie*, p. 253; Kopanev and Man'kov, *Vosstanie*, pp. 223–26; Chistov, *Russkie legendy*, pp. 48–51; Solov'ev, *Istoriia*, IV, pp. 448–49; Platonov, *Ocherki*, pp. 311–13.

259. A great deal of nonsense has been written about Dmitrii's relationship with "Tsarevich Petr." Soviet historians have rejected the legend (based largely upon Shuiskii propaganda) that Dmitrii himself "invented" Petr to help in his own struggle against the boiars. Viewing the entire reign of Dmitrii as merely an episode in the developing social struggle which led to the First Peasant War, they now emphasize Dmitrii's untenable position in 1606—caught between a growing

popular movement against the boiars and a boiar conspiracy against himself. Thus, Tsarevich Petr's force is considered to be the beginning of a much greater social movement which had dangerous overtones for the ruling elite of Muscovy. One view, based upon very shaky evidence, is that Tsarevich Petr offered to help Dmitrii against the "evil boiars." Another, based primarily upon an extraordinary interpretation of Margeret's testimony, is that a desperate Dmitrii invited Petr and his Cossacks to Moscow in order to intimidate the boiars (if not to begin a class war against them). According to this theory, the boiars then murdered Dmitrii to prevent this from happening. A more realistic explanation for Dmitrii's letter to Petr is simply that the tsar wished to neutralize Petr's force before it was joined by more Cossacks, peasants, and slaves and became a serious threat to Dmitrii himself. After Petr received Dmitrii's letter he did not hurry from Samara to Moscow to help the tsar, but rather continued up the Volga toward Kazan, staying safely out of the way. See Troitskii, "Samozvantsy," p. 137; Koretskii, *Formirovanie*, pp. 252–57; Hellie, *Enserfment*, pp. 107–08; Smirnov, *Vosstanie*, pp. 366–70. Cf. Vernadsky, *Tsardom*, I, p. 232; de Thou, *Histoire*, XIV, p. 502.

260. These Cossacks reportedly robbed or extorted some three hundred thousand rubles in cash or merchandise. See Barbour, *Dimitry*, p. 241; Howe, *False Dmitri*, p. 59.

261. The information Margeret received at Archangel was misleading, allowing him to underestimate Tsarevich Petr and his Cossacks. After hearing that Dmitrii had been assassinated, Petr did turn back to the south and all was quiet along the Volga for awhile; but by the fall of 1606 Petr was deeply involved in the Peasant War. Before those opposing the new Tsar Vasilii Shuiskii could find a suitable person to play the part of a "resurrected" Tsar Dmitrii, Tsarevich Petr became the nominal head of that movement. Petr appointed the real leader of the Peasant War, Ivan Bolotnikov, as his boiar and first *voevoda* (commanding general). After waging an extremely serious military campaign against Tsar Vasilii, both Petr and Bolotnikov were captured by the tsar's army in 1607. Petr was then hanged.

If Margeret had not misjudged the type (and therefore the military prowess) of the Cossacks in Tsarevich Petr's force, he might have had a greater appreciation of their potential danger to the Muscovite government. As it was, Tsar Vasilii Shuiskii's government was certainly not very concerned about these Cossacks when Margeret was allowed to depart from Moscow for Archangel and France during the summer of 1606. The Soviet view that Margeret completely misunderstood the developing Peasant War should be weighed against this. See Vernadsky, *Tsardom*, I, pp. 236–40; Zhordaniia, *Ocherki*, I, pp. 258–60; Alpatov, *Russkaia mysl'*, pp. 30–31; Koretskii, *Formirovanie*, p. 254; Troitskii, "Samozvantsy," p. 137; Smirnov, *Vosstanie*, p. 370.

262. "Haiduks" here refers to beautifully dressed Polish foot soldiers who carried harquebuses and either scimitars or pole-axes. The term also referred to Hungarian foot soldiers.

263. The crowning of Marina was an anomaly in Muscovite history. Under normal circumstances tsaritsas were never crowned. According to Platonov, the coronation was an unsuccessful attempt to sidestep the explosive issue of her Catholicism. The ambassador from Poland was Mikołaj Oleśnicki, castellan of Małogoszcz, a relative by marriage of Mniszech. Although a Polish senator, Oleśnicki was not a particularly high ranking dignitary. See Skrynnikov, "Boris Godunov's Struggle," p. 330; Barbour, *Dimitry*, pp. 236, 262; Platonov, *Moscow and the West*, p. 40.

264. The church was the Cathedral of Dormition. Since the rules of *mestnichestvo* still governed the position and rank of members of the tsar's wedding party, V. I. Shuiskii had clearly been returned to favor and was being honored on this occasion. The participation of the staunchly conservative and Orthodox Mstislavskii and Shuiskii in Dmitrii's wedding celebration is often overlooked by historians who emphasize the unpopularity of the tsar's marriage and point to it as one of the most important reasons for Dmitrii's assassination. See Platonov, *Moscow and the West*, pp. 37–42; Uroff, "Kotoshikhin," pp. 322–23.

265. The separation of the Orthodox Russians and the Catholic Poles was necessary not just to satisfy Muscovite tradition. Dmitrii's marriage to a Catholic princess was regarded with horror by many Muscovites, and it was necessary not to upset Orthodox sentiment any further. As it was, the two thousand or so Polish wedding guests behaved

so arrogantly that they created serious unrest in the capital. Many Muscovites were also offended that the wedding was being (profanely) celebrated on an Orthodox holy day. See Vernadsky, *Tsardom,* I, p. 233; Platonov, *Time of Troubles,* pp. 80–81; Barbour, *Dimitry,* pp. 201, 262; Howe, *False Dmitri,* pp. 39–42, 60; RIB, XIII, col. 583.

266. It is true that Afanasii Vlas'ev had sat at Sigismund's table. This meant very little to the Muscovites, however, since the king of Poland was a mere elected monarch. Under no circumstances did that entitle the Polish ambassador to sit at the tsar's table. Zabelin, *Domashnii byt,* I, pp. 360–79; Barbour, *Dimitry,* pp. 180–81.

267. Dmitrii did indeed seem certain that his position was secure. Yet, as Soviet scholars point out, he was facing a serious revolt among the lords. Although there is considerable debate over which actions or policies of Dmitrii provoked this final conspiracy, it is clear that Dmitrii was foolish to ignore it. Curiously, after their initial warnings neither Mniszech nor Basmanov seems to have persisted in urging Dmitrii to take precautions. See Barbour, *Dimitry,* pp. 268, 271, 276; Koretskii, *Formirovanie,* pp. 238–57; Purchas, *Hakluytus Posthumus,* XIV, p. 149; Hellie, *Enserfment,* pp. 107–08.

268. At this point in his narrative Margeret finally notes that the Russians used the Old Style calendar. He also says that he gives dates in the New Style, which is true only part of the time. (See n.52.) There is some question about just when the assassination took place. See Vernadsky, *Tsardom,* I, p. 233; Massa, *Histoire,* II, p. 291.

269. To distract people from the murder of the tsar, Dmitrii's assassins had an alarm sounded throughout Moscow. The thousands who responded were falsely informed that it was the Poles who were planning to murder the tsar. The angry citizens then began a bloody massacre of the hated Polish wedding guests, most of whom had been housed in various places throughout the Kitaigorod district of the city. This made self-defense very difficult. Estimates of the number of Poles killed vary widely, from five hundred to thirty-five hundred. Margeret's figure is very close to that of several other sources. See Platonov, *Moscow and the West,* pp. 43, 148; Barbour, *Dimitry,* pp. 276–85; Smirnov, *Vosstanie,* p. 147; Massa, *Histoire,* II, pp. 175, 291; Howe, *False Dmitri,* pp. 34, 41.

270. There were only about thirty guards on duty at the time and no officers. Shuiskii had ordered most of the guards to return to their barracks the night before the assassination, an action which apparently went unnoticed by Dmitrii. See Barbour, *Dimitry*, p. 275; Howe, *False Dmitri*, p. 44.

271. Dmitrii had urged his assassins to ask his mother who he was if they did not believe that he was really Dmitrii Ivanovich. When she was later put to the question in public, Marfa responded by saying that they should have asked the question while Dmitrii was still alive. However, within days Marfa joined Shuiskii in a propaganda campaign to "prove" that Dmitrii had been an impostor. See Solov'ev, *Istoriia*, IV, pp. 454–55; Rudakov, "Razvitie legendy," p. 256.

272. Shuiskii was proclaimed tsar on May 19, 1606 (O.S.).

273. Rumor had it that Dmitrii had practised witchcraft and that the great frost was one of his spells. His body was cremated at Kotly, outside Moscow, and according to tradition, the ashes were fired from a cannon in the direction of Poland. Burning witches was the traditional remedy in Russia as it was in the rest of Europe. Fear of witchcraft in Muscovy had increased markedly during the Time of Troubles. Tsar Vasilii Shuiskii demanded, among other things, that those swearing the oath of loyalty to him renounce all witchcraft and other occult practises which might harm the tsar or his family. See Purchas, *Hakluytus Posthumus*, XIV, p. 186; Massa, *Histoire*, II, p. 298; Russell Zguta, "Witchcraft Trials in Seventeenth-Century Russia," *American Historical Review* 82 (1977), 1189–94.

274. The following passages contain unique and important observations about the serious unrest which developed after Dmitrii's assassination and caused Tsar Vasilii so many problems. See Alpatov, *Russkaia mysl'*, pp. 34–35; Platonov, *Ocherki*, pp. 292–97. Cf. BC, p. 365.

275. Here and in later passages Margeret is definitely relating the growing unrest in the country to Dmitrii's assassination and to Shuiskii's seizure of power, a point ignored by those Soviet historians who claim that the revolt was already spreading in the spring of 1606 while Dmitrii was still alive. Dmitrii fell victim to a revolt of the Muscovite lords; despite his problems with deviations from Orthodox customs, he remained fairly popular with the masses until his assassination.

It was Tsar Vasilii Shuiskii who faced the Peasant War. See Koretskii, *Formirovanie*, pp. 243–57; Alpatov, *Russkaia mysl'*, pp. 30–32; Smirnov, *Vosstanie*, pp. 88–91; Cherepnin, *Zemskie sobory*, pp. 151–52; Platonov, *Time of Troubles*, pp. 83–84, 91–92; Treadgold, *West*, I, p. 48; Massa, *Histoire*, II, p. 175; Palitsyn, *Skazanie*, pp. 114–15. The revolt (which was carried out in Tsar Dmitrii's name) spread from the southwestern and southern provinces which had been Dmitrii's stronghold in his campaign to win the Muscovite throne. This region had long been an area of social unrest and was to become a center for all-out class war against the Shuiskii government during the First Peasant War.

276. Because Shuiskii's claim to the throne was shaky, he felt the need to "prove" that the true tsarevich had died in 1591 and that Tsar Dmitrii was a shameless impostor. In addition to exhuming the remains of Tsarevich Dmitrii in Uglich, Shuiskii launched a major propaganda campaign to acquaint all Russians (and foreigners) with his version of the story. See Thompson, "Legend," pp. 48–49; Skrynnikov, *Boris Godunov*, pp. 67–68; Rudakov, "Razvitie legendy," pp. 254–57.

277. The convenient discovery of a well-preserved body "proved" that Tsar Dmitrii had been an impostor; the nuts found in his hand also "proved" that the tsarevich had been murdered by Boris Godunov's agents and had not killed himself accidentally with a knife—which had been the official verdict of the investigation conducted in 1591. (It should be noted that Shuiskii himself had been head of the 1591 investigation and had agreed at the time with the verdict of accidental death.) See Tikhomirov, "Samozvanshchina," p. 117; Thompson, "Legend," p. 49.

278. Bodies preserved intact and causing miracles were also mentioned by Possevino. Many Russians and all the foreigners in Moscow were convinced that Shuiskii fabricated the whole story and had even ordered the death of some innocent child who could then be passed off as the miraculously preserved remains of the tsarevich. See Possevino, *Moscovia*, p. 58; Rudakov, "Razvitie legendy," pp. 279–83; Thompson, "Legend," p. 58; Vernadsky, *Tsardom*, I, p. 235.

279. The patriarch at this time was Germogen, former metropolitan of Kazan. The Greek Ignatii had been deposed and incarcerated as a supporter of Tsar Dmitrii.

280. In the official biography of the new St. Dmitrii it was written that Boris Godunov had caused his death. This put the authority of the Orthodox church behind Shuiskii's claims about both Boris Godunov and the pretender Dmitrii. It was also designed to prevent any future pretenders, since by then rumors that Tsar Dmitrii had escaped from his assassins were circulating widely. See Platonov, *Boris Godunov,* p. 128; Vernadsky, *Tsardom,* I, p. 235; Howe, *False Dmitri,* pp. 90–91; Purchas, *Hakluytus Posthumus,* XIV, p. 198.

281. Shuiskii was actually crowned on June 1, 1606 (O.S.).

282. In order to insure that the Polish government did not seek immediate revenge for the massacre of so many Polish citizens, Shuiskii ordered the retention of the ambassador and other dignitaries until an agreement could be worked out with King Sigismund. Other sources indicate that Mniszech and his daughter were sent to Iaroslavl, downstream a few miles from Uglich. Not until July 1608 was a treaty signed which allowed the Poles to return home. See Barbour, *Dimitry,* pp. 293–96; de Thou, *Histoire,* XIV, p. 504; Vernadsky, *Tsardom,* I, pp. 242–43.

283. Although in the eighteenth century French historians understood this passage to mean that Dmitrii was planning to send an embassy to Henri IV, in the mid–nineteenth century Henri Chevreul claimed that Dmitrii himself was preparing to travel to France. There is no substance to this claim. Margeret clearly refers to Dmitrii's secretary, not to the tsar. The mistake was picked up and used by some later historians. (There were, however, rumors shortly after Dmitrii's death that he had escaped to England.) See Margeret, *Estat* (1860), p. vii; Waliszewski, *La Crise,* p. 231; Mansuy, *Le Monde,* p. 425; Troitskii, "Samozvantsy," pp. 136–37.

284. Dmitrii's lack of suspicion as well as his belief in himself have been noted by many historians, even by many of those who accuse him of being an impostor. Most historians agree that, whoever Tsar Dmitrii really was, he genuinely believed that he was the true Dmitrii Ivanovich. This may help to account for his unwillingness to take effective measures to protect himself from assassination. See Vernadsky, *Tsardom,* I, p. 226–27; Kliuchevskii, *Course,* pp. 31–32; Shmurlo, *Kurs,* II, pt. 2, pp. 182–91.

285. Margeret's belief that the rumor of Dmitrii's escape was merely part of a plot against Shuiskii was, of course, correct. Several important former supporters of Tsar Dmitrii were involved in the circulation of this rumor. See Vernadsky, *Tsardom*, I, pp. 235–36; Barbour, *Dimitry*, pp. 290–92; Dolinin, "K izucheniiu," pp. 476, 488.

286. Bertrand of Kazan (originally from La Rochelle) was a jewel merchant who had traded in Muscovy since the 1580s. He was at one time commissioned by Tsar Dmitrii to purchase 3000 rubles worth of precious objects in France. In the aftermath of Dmitrii's assassination, Bertrand (like many other foreign merchants in Moscow) lost much of his fortune to the mob. Upon his return to France, Margeret petitioned Henri IV on behalf of Bertrand, with the result being a royal letter to Tsar Vasilii Shuiskii in 1607 regarding the possible recovery of Bertrand's loss. See Barbour, *Dimitry*, p. 284; Ikonnikov, *Snosheniia*, p. 8; Haumant, *La Culture française*, p. 4; Zhordaniia, *Ocherki*, I, pp. 95–116, 372; Platonov, *Moscow and the West*, pp. 42–43.

287. Could this young nobleman have been Mikhail Molchanov? Molchanov had been greatly favored by Tsar Dmitrii. After Dmitrii's death he escaped to Poland, from which he circulated rumors that Dmitrii was still alive. For a time Molchanov appears to have contemplated assuming the role of Tsar Dmitrii. See Barbour, *Dimitry*, pp. 290–91; Platonov, *Time of Troubles*, p. 80; Rambaud, *History*, I, p. 332; Massa, *Histoire*, II, p. 183.

288. Other sources also indicate that the Mniszechs were informed of Dmitrii's escape from assassination. This French cook later founded a cooking school in Muscovy; apparently, his pastries were excellent. See Dolinin, "K izucheniiu," p. 476; Haumant, *La Culture française*, p. 4.

289. Following Shuiskii's seizure of power, rumors that Dmitrii had escaped assassination spread quickly to the southern provinces which had supported his invasion of Muscovy in 1604–05. Many towns along the southern frontier, including Astrakhan, joined in a growing rebellion against the Shuiskii government. In some cases the townspeople did overthrow their generals; in others, the garrisons freely joined the cause of Tsar Dmitrii. See Platonov, *Time of Troubles*, pp. 91–93; Smirnov, *Vosstanie*, pp. 88–91.

290. This is a curious statement. During the summer of 1606 most of the southern frontier continued to support the rebellion against Shuiskii, and just which towns might then have sought a pardon from Moscow is not known. Margeret's statement does show clearly that the rebellion, for all its class-war overtones, was initiated in the name of Tsar Dmitrii—supposedly still alive and preparing to seek his revenge against Shuiskii. The fact that Margeret was able to obtain permission to return home in July 1606 may indicate that the Shuiskii government felt it was gaining the upper hand against the rebels. Perhaps overly optimistic officials at Tsar Vasilii's court influenced Margeret's perceptions. In any case, Margeret left Muscovy without understanding the full scope of the developing Peasant War. See Zhordaniia, *Ocherki*, I, pp. 258–60; Massa, *Kratkoe izvestie*, p. 154; Alpatov, *Russkaia mysl'*, pp. 30–32.

291. Margeret is quite correct on this point. The middle and lower gentry, especially in Riazan province, were in turmoil—dissatisfied with the oligarchical government of the Muscovite prince-boiars, a government which snubbed all those of lesser birth. Many disgruntled gentry found themselves side by side with peasants and slaves in opposing the Shuiskii government. In Moscow, Tsar Vasilii also faced opposition from many quarters. See Platonov, *Time of Troubles*, pp. 94–95; Vernadsky, *Tsardom*, I, p. 236.

292. Actually, June 1, 1606 (O.S.).

293. Although at this point Margeret's chronology is not very accurate, the following passages provide unique evidence which has allowed historians to reconstruct some of the events of Shuiskii's first stormy days in power. See Alpatov, *Russkaia mysl'*, pp. 34–35; Smirnov, *Vosstanie*, p. 281.

294. Margeret's testimony linking P. N. Sheremetev to the Nagois is unique. Platonov, however, reconstructs the plot against Shuiskii somewhat differently. P. N. Sheremetev was also related to the Romanovs. According to Platonov, in return for supporting Shuiskii's coup the monk Filaret (Fedor Romanov) had been nominated patriarch after Tsar Dmitrii's assassination. Filaret and Sheremetev were then both sent to Uglich to fetch the remains of Tsarevich Dmitrii. During their absence from Moscow a movement against Shuiskii took

place in the capital, and Tsar Vasilii narrowly missed being over-thrown. Convinced that the Romanov circle was behind the plot, Shuiskii "demoted" Filaret to his old position as metropolitan of Rostov and exiled Sheremetev. The resulting bitterness felt by the Romanovs and others toward Tsar Vasilii never faded. Filaret himself eventually joined forces with the second pretender Dmitrii at Tushino where he was recognized as the rightful patriarch. See Vernadsky, *Tsardom*, I, pp. 280–81; Platonov, *Time of Troubles*, p. 89; Platonov, *Ocherki*, pp. 287–94; Barsukov, *Rod*, II, p. 114; Smirnov, *Vosstanie*, p. 226.

295. This passage has often been cited (or quoted) by historians. The Moscow rabble intervened or attempted to intervene in state pol-itics on several occasions after the death of Ivan IV. Shuiskii was able to use the crowd against the Polish wedding guests in his own coup, but he was not able to control it. His enemies, on the other hand, were able to incite the Moscow rabble against the new tsar within days of his seizure of power. See Platonov, *Ocherki*, pp. 292–97; Platonov, *Time of Troubles*, pp. 90–91; Skrynnikov, "Boris Godunov i Dmitrii," p. 189; Cherepnin, *Zemskie sobory*, p. 152; *Istoriia Moskvy*, I, pp. 304–05. Cf. Howe, *False Dmitri*, p. 62.

296. Platonov believed that this gathering of the Moscow rabble may have taken place on Sunday, May 25, 1606 (O.S.), even before Shuiskii's coronation. However, at least one other contemporary source placed this event on June 15 (O.S.), some time after the cor-onation. The Soviet scholar Smirnov rejected Platonov's chronology, preferring Margeret's. See Platonov, *Ocherki*, pp. 292–93; *The Reporte of a Bloudie and Terrible Massacre in the Cittie of Mosco* (London, 1607); Zhordaniia, *Ocherki*, I, p. 258; Smirnov, *Vosstanie*, p. 281; Howe, *False Dmitri*, p. 62.

297. Shuiskii believed that the Romanovs were behind this inci-dent. See Platonov, *Ocherki*, pp. 292–97.

298. This passage indicates that Shuiskii's attempt to use the canoniza-tion of the "murdered Tsarevich Dmitrii" to silence his opponents was unsuccessful from the outset. Whether the people were gathered by disaf-fected supporters of Filaret Romanov or because they believed Tsar Dmitrii still to be alive is, however, impossible to determine.

299. The province of Severia, which had strongly supported Dmitrii in 1604–05, became the center of the rebellion against the Shuiskii government. One of the leading figures of Tsar Dmitrii's court, Prince Grigorii Shakhovskoi, had been "exiled" by Shuiskii to the town of Putivl in Severia—there to serve as *voevoda* (military governor). This was a major blunder on Shuiskii's part. Shakhovskoi helped to spread rumors of Tsar Dmitrii's escape from assassination throughout the southern provinces. When he discovered that the citizens of Putivl were angrily opposed to the "boiar-tsar" Shuiskii, he openly proclaimed rebellion against the Shuiskii government in the name of Tsar Dmitrii. He was supported immediately by the *voevoda* of Chernigov, Prince Andrei Teliatevskii, and by townspeople and peasants throughout Severia. Although no one had yet been found to play the part of Tsar Dmitrii, Teliatevskii's former retainer Ivan Bolotnikov was sent to Shakhovskoi to act as commander-in-chief of the revolutionary army. Soon they were joined by Tsarevich Petr and his Cossacks, and Tsar Vasilii found himself with a very serious rebellion on his hands. See Smirnov, *Vosstanie,* pp. 101, 138–39; Vernadsky, *Tsardom,* I, pp. 236–37; Troitskii, "Samozvantsy," p. 137.

300. Margeret was misinformed at Archangel concerning the size of the forces involved as well as the outcome of this encounter. Shuiskii's army, led by Iurii N. Trubetskoi, was actually forced to retreat. The rebels, who were led by the brilliant commander Ivan Bolotnikov, were greatly aided by peasant uprisings which tied down Shuiskii's forces. See Vernadsky, *Tsardom,* I, pp. 237–38; Platonov, *Time of Troubles,* pp. 92–93; Solov'ev, *Istoriia,* IV, p. 468.

301. Again, Margeret's information is wrong. Putivl had not surrendered at this time and was in fact still the nerve center of the rebellion being carried out in Tsar Dmitrii's name. It was from Putivl that Bolotnikov launched his revolutionary army against Shuiskii, an army which was actually able to lay siege to Moscow in October 1606—just one month after Margeret's departure from Russia. The rebellion was not caused by Polish troops, nor did any Polish troops join Bolotnikov's army. However, the rumor that Dmitrii was alive in Poland was widely circulated. Some of his supporters had escaped to Poland, from which they attempted to aid the rebellion and to keep

alive the rumor that Dmitrii would soon return to Muscovy with a huge army. See Barbour, *Dimitry*, pp. 290–91; Alpatov, *Russkaia mysl'*, pp. 30–32; Smirnov, *Vosstanie*, pp. 88–91.

302. In the final pages of his book Margeret offers his own views on the subject of Tsar Dmitrii's true identity. This was of considerable interest not only to Henri IV, but to Europeans everywhere. Opinions varied widely, especially after Shuiskii launched his international propaganda campaign to discredit Dmitrii. Margeret's defense of Dmitrii's authenticity, which is still one of the most important sources on the subject, may strike a twentieth-century reader as somewhat naive, but it did respond forcefully to Shuiskii's allegations and posed some questions which historians have not yet been able to answer. For a long time Margeret's testimony dominated the debate among historians; so strong was his evidence that Karamzin and Ustrialov had to work very hard searching through native and foreign sources before they felt any degree of confidence in challenging his views. It is interesting to note that all attempts to identify Dmitrii as the true tsarevich have been based at least in part upon Margeret's testimony, and while Soviet scholars reject the view that he was the son of Ivan IV, they do acknowledge the great significance of Margeret's testimony. See Margeret, *Sostoianie* (3rd ed.), pp. 220–22; Ustrialov, *Skazaniia sovremennikov*, I, p. 241; Pierling, *La Russie*, III, pp. 397–429; Alpatov, *Russkaia mysl'*, pp. 33–34; Shmurlo, *Kurs*, II, pt. 2, pp. 224–55; Pirling, *Iz Smutnago Vremeni*, pp. 182, 193–94, 229; Barbour, *Dimitry*, p. 325; Platonov, *Stat'i*, pp. 275–77.

303. *Rasstriga* means "unfrocked monk." Ever since the reign of Boris Godunov the most popular theory has been that Dmitrii was actually the runaway monk Grishka Otrep'ev, the son of a petty Muscovite nobleman from Galich. Boris made this claim, as did Patriarch Iov, and after Dmitrii's assassination it was actively promoted by Tsar Vasilii Shuiskii. Many seventeenth-century Russian sources (often mere compilations of Shuiskii's propaganda materials) repeated it. With several exceptions, Russian historians from the time of Karamzin have usually preferred this view—although Margeret's evidence has often proven a stumbling block. Even Paul Pierling, who was very impressed by Margeret's testimony, came to believe that Tsar Dmitrii

was Otrep'ev. In the Soviet period only a few scholars have questioned this theory, and Skrynnikov (primarily relying upon Godunov and Shuiskii propaganda) has reaffirmed it in unequivocal terms. With some notable exceptions, it has been accepted by western scholars. See Pirling, *Iz Smutnago Vremeni*, pp. 20–28, 221–35; Troitskii, "Samozvantsy," p. 135; Tikhomirov, "Samozvanshchina," pp. 117–19; Koretskii and Stanislavskii, "Amerikanskii istorik," pp. 240–43; Chistov, *Russkie legendy*, pp. 33, 40–41; Margeret, *Sostoianie* (3rd ed.), pp. 220–22; Skrynnikov, *Boris Godunov*, pp. 155–75; Mérimée, *Épisode*, pp. 95–102; Mérimée, "Mémoires," pp. 178–81; Platonov, *Stat'i*, p. 276; Barbour, *Dimitry*, pp. 317–27; Massa, *Histoire*, II, pp. xx–xxi; Palitsyn, *Skazanie*, pp. 110–15; Vernadsky, *Tsardom*, I, p. 226.

304. Although Boris Godunov was sure that the pretender scheme had originated in Muscovy, the fact that Dmitrii launched his invasion from Poland-Lithuania and had many Polish supporters led some people immediately to suspect that he was not a Russian. Historians have argued at length over the question of Dmitrii's nationality, but most scholars today believe him to have been a Russian. See Bussov, *Khronika*, pp. 132–33; Pirling, *Iz Smutnago Vremeni*, pp. 12–20; Mérimée, "Mémoires," pp. 179–81; Koretskii and Stanislavskii, "Amerikanskii istorik," p. 244; Platonov, *Stat'i*, pp. 276–77; Pierling, *La Russie*, III, pp. 407–10; Skrynnikov, *Boris Godunov*, p. 171; Solov'ev, *Istoriia*, IV, p. 406; Howe, *False Dmitri*, p. 1; Platonov, *Boris Godunov*, p. 192; Barbour, *Dimitry*, pp. 244, 321–22; Tikhomirov, "Samozvanshchina," p. 119.

305. See n.37.

306. This is a very important statement linking the Romanov clan to Tsarevich Dmitrii's "escape" from Uglich. On the basis of this statement, an earlier passage in Margeret's book (at n.194), and other documents, historians now believe that the Romanovs were very probably involved in the pretender affair by the year 1600. Skrynnikov, however, has shown that in 1591 the Romanovs actually stood to profit from Tsarevich Dmitrii's death. See Platonov, *Ocherki*, pp. 234, 561 n.70; Platonov, *Boris Godunov*, pp. 193–96; Platonov, *Time of Troubles*, pp. 66–68; Vernadsky, *Tsardom*, I, pp. 221, 230; Tikhomirov,

"Samozvanshchina," pp. 120–21; Skrynnikov, "Boris Godunov i Dmitrii," p. 197; Skrynnikov, *Boris Godunov,* pp. 72, 155–61.

307. Here Margeret repeats Tsar Dmitrii's official version of the events in Uglich. The possibility that Dmitrii might have escaped death in 1591 was supported at the time by other writers besides Margeret, and many rumors about the tsarevich's "escape" circulated throughout Muscovy and Europe by the early seventeenth century. Platonov wrote that while one could not say with absolute certainty the Dmitrii did die in Uglich, it would be extremely difficult to prove that he did not die there. Attempts by Suvorin and Barbour to argue that Dmitrii did in fact survive and later became tsar have encountered little positive response from other scholars. See Thompson, "Legend," pp. 55–56; Platonov, *Stat'i,* p. 276; Koretskii and Stanislavskii, "Amerikanskii istorik," pp. 241–42; Vernadsky, "Death," pp. 12–13; Barbour, *Dimitry,* pp. 317–27.

308. The flight from Muscovy of Otrep'ev and his companion(s) probably took place in the spring of 1602. Two, three, or even four "monks" were involved, depending upon which source is consulted. It is usually assumed that Otrep'ev, who had been in the service of the Romanovs and had even held an important position at the Chudov Monastery in the Kremlin, ran away on his own initiative. Margeret's second-hand version of the story—that someone *sent* Dmitrii (dressed as a monk) out of the country after Boris's election—makes the link between the pretender affair and the Romanovs seem even more likely. In 1598 the Romanovs had been bitterly opposed to Boris becoming tsar, regarding their own family as far more worthy of the throne. By 1600 their connection with the pretender affair is a virtual certainty. See Skrynnikov, *Boris Godunov,* pp. 155–68; Tikhomirov, "Samozvanshchina," p. 118; Pirling, *Iz Smutnago Vremeni,* pp. 20–28; Troitskii, "Samozvantsy," pp. 134–35. Cf. Barbour, *Dimitry,* p. 14; Vernadsky, *Tsardom,* I, p. 223.

309. In 1603 the pretender Dmitrii was apparently employed as a servant in the household of Prince Adam Wiśniowiecki, whose estate at Brahin was located not far from the Muscovite border. Wiśniowiecki belonged to an important Lithuanian family which was related to the extinct Muscovite ruling dynasty. According to tradition, Dmitrii revealed

his "true identity" to Prince Adam, who immediately took up the pretender's cause. Soon thereafter, Dmitrii came to the attention of Prince Konstanty Wiśniowiecki (Adam's cousin and the son-in-law of Jerzy Mniszech), who also took up his cause. Vernadsky claimed that Prince Adam may have heard about the pretender's existence even before this "revelation." See Barbour, *Dimitry*, pp. 7–19; Tikhomirov, "Samozvanshchina," pp. 118–19; Vernadsky, *Tsardom*, I, p. 224.

310. Mniszech was well informed about the pretender Dmitrii before Konstanty Wiśniowiecki brought the young man to his estate in February 1604. Mniszech offered his support, hoping for great financial reward in return for helping Dmitrii to become tsar. See Barbour, *Dimitry*, pp. 19–28.

311. Sigismund III of Poland had been interested in the pretender affair from the time he first heard of Dmitrii's revelation of his "true identity" to Adam Wiśniowiecki. The king even wrote to Adam for more details and commanded him to bring Dmitrii to Krakow. Too cautious to support Dmitrii openly and risk war with Boris Godunov, Sigismund received the pretender at a private audience in March 1604. Apparently, he was favorably impressed by Dmitrii. A few gifts and a small pension were granted to him by the king; but the Polish government avoided any public commitment to Dmitrii's cause and did not provide him with any military assistance. See Barbour, *Dimitry*, pp. 12–14, 28–36; Pierling, *La Russie*, III, pp. 69–70.

312. Otrep'ev was noted for his excellent writing ability, which undoubtedly helps to explain his rapid promotion at the Chudov Monastery where he eventually wrote letters for Patriarch Iov. See Tikhomirov, "Samozvanshchina," pp. 117–18; Skrynnikov, *Boris Godunov*, pp. 157–65, 172.

313. As noted earlier (n.308), the number of runaway "monks" varies. Historians usually mention Varlaam and Misail accompanying Grishka Otrep'ev to Poland-Lithuania. Some sources mention another monk, Leonid, who was supposedly ordered to assume Grishka's identity when the latter declared himself to be Tsarevich Dmitrii. See Tikhomirov, "Samozvanshchina," p. 118; Skrynnikov, *Boris Godunov*, pp. 165–66; Pirling, *Iz Smutnago Vremeni*, p. 162.

314. *Zastava* (plural *zastavy*) means "barrier," or refers to a military unit with defensive or reconnaissance duties. Margeret is again saying that the flight of Otrep'ev and his companion(s) was of immediate concern to Boris, who took strong measures to try to prevent it. Skrynnikov argues that the government of famine-gripped Muscovy was not able to take such measures and that the monks therefore must have escaped unobserved. This is contradicted not only by Margeret's testimony, but also by the very real panic which gripped the Godunov government in response to Otrep'ev's flight and to the circulation of rumors about Tsarevich Dmitrii's survival. See Skrynnikov, *Boris Godunov,* pp. 155–66, 169.

315. Although the year of Otrep'ev's birth is not known, it is doubtful that he was much older than Dmitrii. See Platonov, *Stat'i,* p. 277; Skrynnikov, *Boris Godunov,* p. 161. Cf. Barbour, *Dimitry,* pp. 317–18.

316. This testimony is supported by two Jesuit chaplains (who had accompanied Dmitrii on his campaign to win the Muscovite throne) who claimed in 1605 that Otrep'ev was with Dmitrii in Putivl. Several historians have doubted that Tsar Dmitrii was Otrep'ev because Otrep'ev was well known in Moscow and would have been easily recognized. See Troitskii, "Samozvantsy," p. 135; Barbour, *Dimitry,* pp. 100, 325; Pierling, *La Russie,* III, pp. 420–21; Pirling, *Iz Smutnago Vremeni,* pp. 231–32; Tikhomirov, "Samozvanshchina," p. 118.

317. Otrep'ev's father Bogdan had held lands near Galich, but nothing is known about any other sons he might have had. Grishka's uncle Smirnoi Otrep'ev was sent to Poland by the Godunov government to expose the pretender Dmitrii as his nephew, but Smirnoi's uncertainty about the identity of the pretender instead convinced some at the Polish court that the Godunov government did not know who the pretender really was. Apparently, other members of Grishka's family did not identify him as the pretender Dmitrii. See Skrynnikov, *Boris Godunov,* pp. 156, 161; Palitsyn, *Skazanie,* pp. 111–13; Barbour, *Dimitry,* pp. 67–69; Pierling, *La Russie,* III, pp. 93–95; Pirling, *Iz Smutnago Vremeni,* pp. 30–38.

318. Although much of the legend of the depravity, arrogance, and wayward youth of Grishka Otrep'ev is nothing more than Godunov

and Shuiskii propaganda, he must have been an odd and irritating character. His father was also given to drinking and ended up being killed in a tavern brawl. Grishka Otrep'ev (or someone called by that name) was confined in Putivl for sorcery during Dmitrii's invasion of Muscovy. Margeret's testimony on his confinement in Iaroslavl, which was very near the home of the Otrep'ev family, is unique. See Skrynnikov, *Boris Godunov*, pp. 156–57, 161; Tikhomirov, "Samozvanshchina," pp. 117–18; Massa, *Histoire*, II, p. 84; Troitskii, "Samozvantsy," p. 135; Pirling, *Iz Smutnago Vremeni*, pp. 231–32.

319. The Russia (or Muscovy) Company was established in the 1550s to handle Anglo-Russian trade. Margeret was familiar with the English merchants and knew John Merrick, chief agent of the company, personally. The name of the agent in Iaroslavl is not known. See Purchas, *Hakluytus Posthumus*, XIV, pp. 225–26; Pirling, *Iz Smutnago Vremeni*, pp. 230–31.

320. This is a fascinating story; but, as Pierling pointed out, it is unreliable testimony. Margeret was correct, however, in saying that a great many Russians did believe that Tsar Dmitrii was not Otrep'ev, but rather the true son of Ivan IV. Vasilii Shuiskii faced tremendous difficulties because of this widespread belief. See Pirling, *Iz Smutnago Vremeni*, pp. 230–33.

321. Shuiskii did order the arrest of members of the Otrep'ev family in Galich. Just exactly why he did this is not known. It certainly did not result in more proof that the pretender Dmitrii was actually Grishka Otrep'ev. See Troitskii, "Samozvantsy," pp. 136–37; Tikhomirov, "Samozvanshchina," pp. 117–18.

322. The theory that Dmitrii was a foreigner had several supporters in the seventeenth century (e.g., Konrad Bussow, a German mercenary in Muscovite service) and has been argued by more than one historian in the past. While several people believed Dmitrii to have been Polish, others held that he was Transylvanian, the son of the Transylvanian Prince Stephen Bathory, later king of Poland and chief nemesis of Ivan IV. More than one person has postulated that Dmitrii might have been a Ukrainian Cossack. A variation on this theory (and one acceptable to scholars who do not believe that he was Grishka Otrep'ev) is that Dmitrii came from the petty service people of the

"Ukrainian" part of Muscovy, the province of Severia. Since the pretender did live in Poland for over two years he might well have acquired those "foreign ways" cited by his enemies as evidence that he was an impostor. See Troitskii, "Samozvantsy," pp. 135–36; Massa, *Histoire,* II, pp. 148, 298; Vernadsky, *Tsardom,* I, p. 224; Mérimée, *Épisode,* pp. 293–97, 302–05; Mérimée, "Mémoires," pp. 179–81; Bussov, *Khronika,* pp. 132–33; Tikhomirov, "Samozvanshchina," p. 119; Pirling, *Iz Smutnago Vremeni,* pp. 12–20; Barbour, *Dimitry,* pp. 244, 321–22.

323. Agreeing with Margeret, Platonov and Kliuchevskii have shown that it is indeed useless to search in Poland-Lithuania for a cabal with the initiative to contrive the pretender affair and to train a "tsarevich." See Platonov, *Boris Godunov,* p. 192; Kliuchevskii, *Course,* pp. 30–33.

324. Actually, Sigismund did know about the pretender affair from as early as 1603. Many members of the Polish Senate knew about it also and were convinced that the pretender was a fraud. In order to avoid war with Muscovy and confrontation with the Polish lords, Sigismund did not support Dmitrii publicly. See Barbour, *Dimitry,* pp. 33–38, 47, 98–100, 172–73; Pirling, *Iz Smutnago Vremeni,* pp. 30–38.

325. Although Sigismund was unwilling to commit himself openly to Dmitrii's cause, he did allow men such as Jerzy Mniszech to raise troops for the invasion force as a private venture. The small pension given to Dmitrii by the king was inadequate to pay for such troops, which is one reason why Dmitrii signed a contract with Mniszech offering him very generous rewards *after* the successful completion of the campaign. Mniszech and the Polish mercenaries abandoned Dmitrii after their first encounter with regular Muscovite troops, primarily because he was unable to provide them with more money. See Barbour, *Dimitry,* pp. 89–90.

326. Samples of Dmitrii's handwriting show that he wrote Russian freely but that his Polish was poor. Although almost all scholars agree that he was a Russian, Tikhomirov has pointed out that his handwriting does not necessarily prove that the pretender was actually a "Muscovite." See Skrynnikov, *Boris Godunov,* pp. 171–72; Koretskii and Stanislavskii, "Amerikanskii istorik," p. 244; Tikhomirov, "Samozvanshchina," p. 119.

327. Adam Wiśniowiecki's very sketchy second-hand account of the pretender's story of his past failed to convince several persons at the Polish court of Dmitrii's authenticity, and Dmitrii's faulty recollection of his childhood has been cited by many historians as very significant evidence against him. In fact, Dmitrii was caught in a real dilemma on this point. He had made very good use of the claim that he had escaped Boris Godunov's assassins in 1591. Since Godunov was not actually involved in the Uglich affair, Dmitrii was forced to lie about the incident. See Tikhomirov, "Samozvanshchina," p. 118; Pirling, *Iz Smutnago Vremeni,* pp. 222–23; Barbour, *Dimitry,* pp. 13–14, 28, 34, 326; Skrynnikov, *Boris Godunov,* p. 192.

328. This is a curious statement. The favoritism shown by Dmitrii to Poles and other foreigners was often cited by his enemies as "proof" that he was an impostor. Obviously, Margeret has in mind some specific instances in which Dmitrii did not act like a brother to the Poles. See Platonov, *Moscow and the West,* pp. 34–43.

329. As noted earlier, Mniszech supported Dmitrii's cause primarily for personal gain. And while he probably needed no further inducement, he may have been convinced of Dmitrii's authenticity (although Vernadsky doubted this). See Barbour, *Dimitry,* pp. 25–28; Vernadsky, *Tsardom,* I, p. 226.

330. A variation on the Polish conspiracy theory is that the pretender was part of a Jesuit plot sanctioned by Sigismund. Although no longer accepted by most historians, this theory was quite popular in the seventeenth (and even as late as the nineteenth) century. It gained some support from the Jesuit propaganda campaign in Europe in favor of Dmitrii, especially after Shuiskii's henchmen discovered Dmitrii's secret correspondence with the Jesuits. In fact, Margeret may have been responding to rumors at the French court: Henri IV had been informed about Dmitrii by the great Jesuit Antonio Possevino, who indicated that the Catholic church had great hopes for him. He had secretly converted to Catholicism while in Poland, and the Jesuits (as Sigismund's most trusted advisors) attempted to indoctrinate him. Even the pope was very anxious to use Dmitrii to help bring Orthodox Muscovy into the Catholic faith. However, the Jesuits did not instigate the pretender affair; they merely made use of it, relying

upon Sigismund's word that Dmitrii was authentic. See Treadgold, *West*, I, pp. 48–49; Mérimée, "Mémoires," pp. 179–80; Mérimée, *Épisode*, pp. 297–300; Pierling, *Dimitri et les Jésuites*, pp. 3–10; Pierling, *Dimitri et Possevino*, pp. 4–9; Pierling, *Rome*, pp. 149–50; de Thou, *Histoire*, XIV, pp. 500–03; Howe, *False Dmitri*, pp. 60, 232–35; Massa, *Histoire*, II, p. 185; Pirling, *Iz Smutnago Vremeni*, pp. 190–94.

331. A reference to the long and intermittent Livonian War (1558–83), vigorously prosecuted by Stephen Bathory from 1579 to 1581. The Swedes were also involved in that war and made great gains against the Russians in the period 1581–83. From 1590 to 1595 the Swedes and the Russians were again at war, as the Russians attempted to reverse some of their severe losses.

332. Margeret is implying that Mniszech would have acted quite differently if he thought Dmitrii was an impostor (he expands upon this point below). Cf. Vernadsky, *Tsardom*, I, p. 226.

333. Margeret is quite correct. For example, Tsar Dmitrii wrote his title as "in perator" instead of "imperator." At least one historian (R. N. Bain) rejected the Jesuit plot theory on the basis of Margeret's statement. See Mérimée, *Épisode*, p. 303; Mérimée, "Mémoires," p. 200; Koretskii and Stanislavskii, "Amerikanskii istorik," p. 244; SGGD, II, p. 229; Bain, *Slavonic Europe*, p. 170.

334. Although Margeret was unaware of Dmitrii's secret conversion, it is true that the Jesuits did not enjoy his favor in Moscow. Despite Shuiskii's later claim to the contrary, Dmitrii kept his distance from the Jesuits and made little effort to satisfy their demands. By the time of his assassination, he had lost much of his Catholic support. Indeed, his conversion had been merely a ploy to gain Polish backing. Once on the throne, he showed no inclination to tamper with the Russian Orthodox church or to promote Catholicism in Russia. In reality, Protestants had much greater access to Tsar Dmitrii than did the Jesuits. See Treadgold, *West*, I, pp. 48–49; Platonov, *Time of Troubles*, p. 81; Pierling, *Rome*, p. 150; Barbour, *Dimitry*, pp. 214–15, 272–73; Tikhomirov, "Samozvanshchina," pp. 119–120.

335. All other sources mention only two Jesuits in Dmitrii's retinue, one of them being his confessor. See de Thou, *Histoire*, XIV, p. 455;

Platonov, *Moscow and the West*, pp. 35–36; Vernadsky, *Tsardom*, I, p. 227; Purchas, *Hakluytus Posthumus*, XIV, p. 159; Pierling, *Dimitri et les Jésuites*, p. 3.

336. These were the most common charges leveled against Dmitrii by his enemies. He did make efforts from the beginning of his campaign to demonstrate his own Orthodoxy to the Russian people, but his violations of many Muscovite customs gave his enemies a chance to spread some malicious rumors. See Platonov, *Time of Troubles*, pp. 79–81; Tikhomirov, "Samozvanshchina," pp. 119–20; Troitskii, "Samozvantsy," pp. 135–36; Massa, *Histoire*, II, pp. 151–52, 183–85, 238.

337. This very western, rational point of view overlooks some important characteristics of a traditional society such as Muscovy. Dmitrii can to some extent be compared to Boris as a reformer, but Boris never went so far in adopting western customs. (Of course, some Muscovites regarded any innovation or "Westernization" with horror.) The enemies of Dmitrii often posed as defenders of Orthodoxy against "evil" foreign influences. See Vernadsky, *Tsardom*, I, p. 231; Hellie, *Enserfment*, p. 49; Platonov, *Time of Troubles*, pp. 79–81; Tikhomirov, "Samozvanshchina," pp. 119–20; Troitskii, "Samozvantsy," pp. 135–36.

338. On Postnik Dmitriev, see S. B. Veselovskii, *D'iaki i pod'iachie XV–XVII vv.* (Moscow, 1975), p. 153. More than one member of Dmitrii's court adopted such "enlightened" attitudes. A very similar case is that of Prince I. A. Khvorostinin. On the other hand, there were intelligent Muscovites who were not impressed with western culture. Consider the case of Ivan Nasedka, who also traveled to Denmark but whose reaction to it was quite different than Postnik Dmitriev's. See Platonov, *Moscow and the West*, pp. 61–76; Treadgold, *West*, I, pp. 49–50.

339. This is an interesting and important statement, given Margeret's opportunities to observe Dmitrii's daily activities. Although Dmitrii did not show the devotion to tradition which many at court and in the clergy felt was necessary in an Orthodox tsar, he did generally observe Orthodox ceremonies, and he studied the Bible. No doubt his informality and western ways disturbed many Muscovites and undermined respect for his authority in important circles, but he was not

generally regarded as a blasphemer or a heretic before his assassination. He remained fairly popular with the people even though many Muscovites were deeply shocked by his marriage to a Catholic princess and were indignant about the behavior of the Polish wedding guests. While it may be argued that foreigners such as Margeret could not appreciate Dmitrii's subtle deviations from Orthodoxy which supposedly outraged the Muscovites, it should be remembered that he was not overthrown by a popular rebellion but rather by a group of self-serving conspirators who took advantage of the public hostility toward the Poles to cover their crime. The image of a desperate and unpopular heretic who died unloved and unmourned was, of course, exactly the image Shuiskii wished to project of the murdered tsar. His great difficulty in laying to rest the "ghost" of Tsar Dmitrii shows that many Russians (even in Moscow) had few misgivings about Dmitrii's Orthodoxy, in spite of the long list of horrible and "unholy" crimes which the Shuiskii government leveled against him. This point has been lost on many historians who continue to write the most outrageous charges against Dmitrii, often merely repeating totally unsubstantiated Shuiskii propaganda. See Hellie, *Enserfment*, pp. 42–44, 68–69; Troitskii, "Samozvantsy," pp. 135–36; Tikhomirov, "Samozvanshchina," p. 120; Barbour, *Dimitry*, pp. 142, 158–62, 209, 262; Massa, *Histoire*, II, pp. 148, 175, 298; Pierling, *Rome*, pp. 149–50; Mérimée, *Épisode*, pp. 297–300; Koretskii, *Formirovanie*, pp. 240, 256–57; Platonov, *Moscow and the West*, pp. 34–42; Timofeev, *Vremennik*, p. 83; Palitsyn, *Skazanie*, pp. 114–15; Platonov, *Time of Troubles*, pp. 83–84, 91–92.

340. Although he has been described as one of the few enlightened rulers Russia ever had, Dmitrii was not the first to contemplate establishing a university in Moscow. At the end of the sixteenth century Boris Godunov took great interest in education, sending young Russians to Western Europe to study and, in 1600, considering the establishment of a university in Muscovy staffed by German scholars. He abandoned the project because of opposition from Patriarch Iov and the clergy, who feared trusting young Russian minds to the influence of "heretics." On his campaign to win the Muscovite throne the pretender Dmitrii often discussed the establishment of colleges in Russia

with his Jesuit "advisors." He also intended to follow Godunov's policy of sending young Russians to study abroad. His plans for a university were seriously hampered by the fact that he would need to employ Jesuits as teachers, something even the impulsive Dmitrii knew would encounter serious opposition. Margeret was certainly aware of this problem, which is why he mentions the plans for the university in this passage on Dmitrii's "deviations" from Orthodoxy. As an educated Frenchman of the late Renaissance, Margeret probably assumed that Jesuits would be necessary, at the very least to teach Latin to the Russians. But he also knew that one need hardly embrace the ideology of the Jesuits to employ them. See Paris, *Chronique*, I, p. 402; Hellie, *Enserfment*, p. 49; Mansuy, *Le Monde*, p. 429; Vernadsky, *Tsardom*, I, pp. 215, 231; Pierling, *Dimitri et Possevino*, p. 3; Pierling, *Dimitri et les Jésuites*, p. 4; Treadgold, *West*, I, pp. 48–49; Platonov, *Moscow and the West*, pp. 32–33.

341. Shuiskii was accused of claiming that Dmitrii was an impostor (see n.239). Mniszech was in Poland at the time of Shuiskii's conviction, but Dmitrii and others maintained communications with him. Margeret's point is that Mniszech would have been slow to get further involved with someone he knew was not the true Dmitrii once he had heard that some powerful Muscovite lords suspected Dmitrii to be an impostor. Actually, it appears that Mniszech was convinced to go ahead with the marriage alliance by the Jesuits. See Vernadsky, *Tsardom*, I, pp. 232–33; Barbour, *Dimitry*, pp. 118, 129.

342. This is a very interesting point. The Poles knew that they were regarded as arrogant heretics by many Muscovites. Several ugly incidents between Poles and Muscovites occurred during the festivities associated with the royal marriage. Mniszech was certainly aware of all this as well as of rumors of plots against Dmitrii. If Mniszech had wished to take precautions, he could easily have done so, averting the massacre. However, neither Mniszech nor Dmitrii took the rumors seriously. Margeret's point is that Mniszech would have taken all necessary precautions if he knew (or even suspected) that his son-in-law was actually an impostor. See Platonov, *Moscow and the West*, pp. 40–43; Barbour, *Dimitry*, pp. 262–69, 275–76.

343. See n.317.

344. Boris had indeed resorted to the charge of heresy in an effort to discredit the pretender. The Godunov government wished in part to conceal the political nature of the pretender affair (and the involvement of the Romanovs) by painting a picture of "Grishka Otrep'ev" as an unholy criminal. The charge of heresy was also part of a clumsy effort to prevent other Orthodox Russians from aiding Dmitrii, an effort which proved to be completely ineffective. Dmitrii's response to these charges was to demonstrate his Orthodoxy publicly; Margeret infers that an impostor would have taken even greater care to eliminate any suspicion that Boris Godunov's charges had been true. See Skrynnikov, *Boris Godunov*, pp. 156–65; Troitskii, "Samozvantsy," pp. 135–36; Solov'ev, *Istoriia*, IV, p. 412.

345. Not all of Dmitrii's predecessors had allied themselves with Russian princely families, yet the norm certainly was to marry a Russian princess. One of the major problems of the Godunov clan had been its isolation from the other great Muscovite families, who were (understandably enough) not particularly loyal to the new dynasty. Margeret was not alone in believing Dmitrii could have avoided disaster by marrying a Russian. See Platonov, *Time of Troubles,* p. 64; Howe, *False Dmitri,* p. 60.

346. In fact, the Godunovs were increasingly isolated at court, and many princely clans had suffered from Boris's suspicion. Even so, Boris sat securely upon his throne. Margeret's statement is similar to Dmitrii's own defense of his identity in his speech to the *strel'tsy* in January 1606. See Platonov, *Boris Godunov*, p. 188; Troitskii, "Samozvantsy," p. 136.

347. This is true to a great extent, even though Boris's social policies had stirred up a hornet's nest of opposition in the southern provinces and among the Cossacks. It is worth remembering that Muscovite forces had seriously defeated Dmitrii's army just before Boris's sudden death.

348. The Nagoi clan—the one group anyone claiming to be Dmitrii would have to placate at all costs—must have been deeply involved in the pretender affair. They may have joined from the beginning, although some historians claim that Dmitrii only gained their support through threats and promises once he had invaded Muscovy. When questioned by Tsar Boris in April 1604, however, the nun Marfa did declare that her son

was still alive. See Barbour, *Dimitry*, p. 64; Tikhomirov, "Samo-zvanshchina," p. 121; Troitskii, "Samozvantsy," pp. 135–36.

349. See nn.206–12.

350. Actually, it seems that Dmitrii was in great despair over his defeat at Dobrynichi and contemplated fleeing to Poland. The citizens of Putivl, who had made Dmitrii's cause their own, threatened to turn him over to Tsar Boris themselves unless he stayed and continued his campaign. See Barbour, *Dimitry*, pp. 95–96.

351. Even though Boris never questioned the nun Marfa in public, he and Mariia apparently did so privately in April 1604. They did not like what they heard. See Barbour, *Dimitry*, p. 64; Tikhomirov, "Samozvanshchina," p. 121.

352. In his attempts to discredit Dmitrii, Boris often seemed to admit that he was the true son of Ivan IV. For example, Boris's letter to the Holy Roman Emperor Rudolph II argued that even if the pretender was in fact Dmitrii Ivanovich he would still have no right to the throne because he was illegitimate. This was also the message delivered to the Polish court by Boris's envoy Postnik Ogarev. The subtleties of Orthodox law were lost on many who regarded Boris's "admission" as further evidence that the old Muscovite ruling dynasty was not extinct and that Tsarevich Dmitrii had in fact survived the Uglich affair. See Pirling, *Iz Smutnago Vremeni*, pp. 22–23; Barbour, *Dimitry*, pp. 67–69, 97–99.

353. Ivan IV had been so poorly treated by the boiars in his youth that at age thirteen he ordered Andrei Shuiskii seized and killed. After the death of Ivan, the Shuiskii clan was deeply involved in the power struggle with Boris Godunov. I. P. Shuiskii even stirred up the citizens of Moscow, who revolted unsuccessfully against Fedor's government in 1586; several merchants were executed and the Shuiskiis were banished from the capital, some dying mysteriously in exile. Vasilii I. Shuiskii was apparently involved in attempts to discredit the Godunov government and in the popular revolt which abruptly ended the reign of Fedor Borisovich. For his behavior toward Dmitrii, see nn. 239–41. See Skrynnikov, "Boris Godunov i Dmitrii," pp. 185–88; Vernadsky, *Tsardom*, I, p. 24; Howe, *False Dmitri,* p. 32; Platonov, *Time of Troubles*, p. 90.

Margeret's chronicle reference is probably to PSRL, XIII, pt. 1, pp. 126–27, 140–41, 145. It is not easy to determine just how Margeret knew this, for Western Europeans were not generally familiar with the chronicles. The historian de Thou cannot be the source, as is possible in the case of an earlier reference (see n.20). The best explanation is probably that Margeret heard the Muscovites themselves discussing this chronicle reference to the disloyalty of the Shuiskiis. See Limonov, *Kul'turnye sviazi*, pp. 221–22; Alpatov, *Russkaia mysl'*, p. 30.

354. This is a telling point. Vasilii Shuiskii was apparently reproached by more than one person for not making a public inquiry about Tsar Dmitrii's true identity before killing him. See de Thou, *Histoire*, XIV, pp. 495–96; Howe, *False Dmitri*, p. 60.

355. Immediately after the assassination Vasilii Shuiskii launched a propaganda campaign that included sending long denunciations of Dmitrii to foreign governments. See Howe, *False Dmitri*, pp. 53–59, 221–39; Rudakov, "Razvitie legendy," pp. 256–57; de Thou, *Histoire*, XIV, p. 500; Purchas, *Hakluytus Posthumus*, XIV, pp. 180–91.

356. Shuiskii's men circulated copies of the marriage agreements signed by Dmitrii in the spring of 1604 that granted the towns of Novgorod and Pskov to his future bride Marina and the provinces of Smolensk and Severia to Mniszech, to be shared with Sigismund. However, since Mniszech had abandoned Dmitrii before the campaign was finished, it may be argued that these agreements were null and void. It is certainly clear that, as tsar, Dmitrii made no effort whatsoever to transfer the territories in question to anyone; even before his assassination the Polish government openly complained about his failure to deliver upon his many promises. The agreement was probably as insincere as his conversion to Catholicism. None of this mattered to Shuiskii, however, who was very pleased to make use of these damning documents which showed Dmitrii willing to split up his patrimony. See Platonov, *Time of Troubles*, pp. 81, 88; Barbour, *Dimitry*, pp. 49–50, 190–91; Purchas, *Hakluytus Posthumus*, XIV, p. 174; SGGD, II, pp. 296–324.

357. Although he made large payments to Mniszech (see n.243), Dmitrii certainly had not sent all the treasury to Poland. Yet, armed

with the marriage contract, it was easy for his assassins to exaggerate the financial losses. Shuiskii and other boiars publicly complained about Dmitrii's excessive expenditures, perhaps to cover their own theft. See Koretskii, *Formirovanie,* pp. 252–53; Barbour, *Dimitry,* pp. 177, 185, 253; Massa, *Histoire,* II, pp. 193–94.

358. To prepare for a spectacular entertainment in celebration of his marriage, Tsar Dmitrii had his men assemble the cannon and construct mobile wooden forts outside the city. He planned a mock battle, complete with demonstrations of siege techniques and the accuracy of Muscovite cannon. Dmitrii, who was deeply committed to military reform, had staged similar shows before — sometimes even personally joining in the "battle." On one occasion, in which foreigners were pitted against Muscovites, the Russians were badly beaten and became very resentful. In the ugly atmosphere of Moscow during the tsar's wedding, it is easy to see how Dmitrii's plans could have been misrepresented by the Shuiskii faction. After Dmitrii's death, these charges became public accusations. In fact, Dmitrii may also have been concentrating his military forces near the capital in preparation for an offensive against the Crimean Tatars. See Howe, *False Dmitri,* pp. 33–34, 41; Palitsyn, *Skazanie,* pp. 112–15; Purchas, *Hakluytus Posthumus,* XIV, pp. 189–91; RIB, XIII, col. 165; Zhordaniia, *Ocherki,* I, p. 255; Hellie, *Enserfment,* p. 167; Barbour, *Dimitry,* p. 219; Thompson, "Legend," p. 57; Smirnov, *Vosstanie,* p. 147.

359. This is a good point. What some historians have described as Dmitrii's "frivolousness" may well have been complete (if foolhardy) faith in himself. See Platonov, *Time of Troubles,* p. 81; Tikhomirov, "Samozvanshchina," p. 118; Vernadsky, *Tsardom,* I, pp. 226–27; Kliuchevskii, *Course,* pp. 31–32; Shmurlo, *Kurs,* II, pp. 182–91; Barbour, *Dimitry,* pp. 268, 271, 275; Purchas, *Hakluytus Posthumus,* XIV, p. 149.

360. Cf. n.352. Margeret is only guessing that Boris suspected that Dmitrii was not an impostor. Whatever his belief in the matter was, Boris's reaction to the rumors about Dmitrii certainly made it seem that he felt very threatened by the tsarevich's "ghost." See Pirling, *Iz Smutnago Vremeni,* pp. 22–23; Barbour, *Dimitry,* pp. 67–69, 97–99.

BIBLIOGRAPHY

Adelung, Friedrich von. *Kritisch-literärische Übersicht der Reisenden in Russland bis 1700.* 2 vols. St. Petersburg: Eggers, 1846.

Allen, W. E. D. "The Georgian Marriage Projects of Boris Godunov." *Oxford Slavonic Papers* 12 (1965), 69–79.

_____.*Problems of Turkish Power in the Sixteenth Century.* London: Central Asian Research Centre, 1963.

_____.*Russian Embassies to the Georgian Kings, 1589–1605.* 2 vols. Cambridge: Cambridge University Press, 1970.

_____.*The Ukraine: A History.* Cambridge: Cambridge University Press, 1940.

Alpatov, M. A. *Russkaia istoricheskaia mysl' i zapadnaia Evropa, XVII–pervaia chetvert' XVIII veka.* Moscow: Nauka, 1976.

Anderson, M. S. *Britain's Discovery of Russia, 1553–1815.* London: Macmillan, 1958.

Atkinson, Geoffroy. *The Extraordinary Voyage in French Literature.* Vol. 1. New York: Columbia University Press, 1920.

_____.*Les nouveaux horizons de la renaissance française.* Paris: E. Droz, 1935.

Avity, Pierre d'. *Description générale de l'Europe, quatriesme partie du monde.* 3 vols. Paris, 1637.

Avrich, Paul. *Russian Rebels, 1600–1800.* New York: Shocken Books, 1972.

Avril, Philippe. *Travels into Divers Parts of Europe and Asia.* London: T. Goodwin, 1693.

Bain, R. Nisbet. *Slavonic Europe.* Cambridge: Cambridge University Press, 1908.

Barbour, Philip L. *Dimitry Called the Pretender.* Boston: Houghton Mifflin, 1966.

Barsukov, A. P. *Rod Sheremetevykh.* 8 vols. St. Petersburg, 1881–1904.

BC. See Berry and Crummey.

Berry, Lloyd E., and Crummey, Robert O., eds. *Rude and Barbarous Kingdom.* Madison: University of Wisconsin Press, 1968.

Billington, James H. *The Icon and the Axe: An Interpretative History of Russian Culture.* New York: Knopf, 1966.

Bodin, John (Jean). *Method for the Easy Comprehension of History.* New York: Columbia University Press, 1945.

Bodin, Jean. *The Six Bookes of a Commonwealth.* Cambridge, Mass.: Harvard University Press, 1962.

Boldakov, I. M. *Sbornik materialov po russkoi istorii nachala XVII veka.* St. Petersburg: S. D. Sheremetev, 1896.

Bond, Edward A. *Russia at the Close of the Sixteenth Century.* London: Hakluyt Society, 1856.

Brown, John L. *The "Methodus ad Facilem Historiarum Cognitionem" of Jean Bodin: A Critical Study.* Washington, D.C.: Catholic University Press, 1939.

Bushkovitch, Paul. *The Merchants of Moscow.* Cambridge: Cambridge University Press, 1980.

Bussov (Bussow), Konrad. *Moskovskaia khronika, 1584–1613.* Moscow: Akademiia Nauk SSSR, 1961.

Chaudoir, S. de. *Aperçu sur les monnaies russes et sur les monnaies étrangères qui ont eu cours en Russie.* 3 vols. Paris: F. Bellizard et co., 1836–37.

Cherepnin, L. V. *Zemskie sobory russkogo gosudarstva v XVI–XVII vv.* Moscow: Nauka, 1978.

Cherniavsky, Michael. "Khan or Basileus: An Aspect of Russian Medieval Political Theory." In *The Structure of Russian History,* edited by Michael Cherniavsky, pp. 65–79. New York: Random House, 1970.

Chernov, A. V. *Vooruzhennye sily russkogo gosudarstva v XV–XVII vv.* Moscow: Voen. izd-vo, 1954.

Chistov, K. V. *Russkie narodnye sotsial'no-utopicheskie legendy XVII – XIX vv.* Moscow: Nauka, 1967.

Church, William F. *Constitutional Thought in Sixteenth-Century France.* Cambridge, Mass.: Harvard University Press, 1941.

[Collins, Samuel.] *The Present State of Russia, In a Letter to a Friend at London.* London: J. Winter, 1671.

Cook, John Q. "The Image of Russia in Western European Thought in the Seventeenth Century." Ph.D. dissertation, University of Minnesota, 1959.

Crull, Jodocus. *The Antient and Present State of Muscovy.* 2 vols. London: A. Roper, 1698.

D'iakonov, M. A. *Vlast' moskovskikh gosudarei: Ocherki iz istorii politicheskikh idei drevnei Rusi.* St. Petersburg, 1889.

Dolinin, N. P. "K izucheniiu inostrannykh istochnikov o krest'ianskom vosstanii pod rukovodstvom I. I. Bolotnikova 1606–1607 gg." In *Mezhdunarodnye sviazi Rossii do XVII v.,* pp. 462–90. Moscow: AN SSSR, 1961.

Drevniaia rossiiskaia vivliofika. 20 vols. Edited by N. I. Novikov. Moscow, 1788–91.

Drouot, H., and Gros, L. *Recherches sur la Ligue en Bourgogne.* Dijon: Damidot frères, 1914.

DRV. See *Drevniaia rossiiskaia vivliofika.*

Eaton, Henry LaMar. "Early Russian Censuses and the Population of Muscovy, 1550–1650." Ph.D. dissertation, University of Illinois at Urbana-Champaign, 1970.

Esper, Thomas. "Military Self-Sufficiency and Weapons Technology in Muscovite Russia." *Slavic Review* 28 (1969), 185–208.

Evans, Norman. "Queen Elizabeth I and Tsar Boris: Five Letters, 1597–1603." *Oxford Slavonic Papers* 12 (1965), 49–68.

Fournol, Étienne-Maurice. *Bodin prédécesseur de Montesquieu.* Geneva: Slatkine Reprints, 1970.

Franklin, Julian H. *Jean Bodin and the Rise of Absolutist Theory.* Cambridge: Cambridge University Press, 1973.

Hakluyt, Richard. *The Principal Navigations, Voyages, Traffiques, and Discoveries of the English Nation.* Vols. II–III. Glasgow: MacLehose, 1903.

Haumant, Émile. *La Culture française en Russie, 1700–1900.* Paris: Hachette, 1913.

Hellie, Richard. *Enserfment and Military Change in Muscovy.* Chicago: University of Chicago Press, 1971.

Herberstein, Sigismund von. *Notes Upon Russia.* 2 vols. London: Hakluyt Society, 1851–52.

Howe, Sonia E., ed. *The False Dimitri.* London: Williams and Norgate, 1916.

Hrushevsky, Michael. *A History of Ukraine.* New Haven: Yale University Press, 1941.

Ikonnikov, V. S. *Snosheniia Rossii s Frantsiei, XVI–XVIII vv.: Istoricheskii ocherk.* Moscow, 1893.

Istoriia Moskvy. Vol. I. Moscow, 1952.

Kamentseva, E. I., and Ustiugov, N. V. *Russkaia metrologiia.* Moscow, 1965.

Kappeler, Andreas. *Ivan Groznyi im Spiegel der auslandischen Druckschriften seiner Zeit.* Frankfurt: Peter Lang, 1972.

Kashtanov, S. M. "Diplomatika kak spetsial'naia istoricheskaia distsiplina." *Voprosy istorii* 40, no. 1 (1965), 39–44.

Kavelin, K. D. *Sobranie sochinenii.* 4 vols. St. Petersburg: Tip. M. M. Stasiulevicha, 1897–1900.

Keenan, Edward L. "Muscovy and Kazan: Some Introductory Remarks on the Patterns of Steppe Diplomacy." *Slavic Review* 26 (1967), 548–58.

Kerner, Robert J. *The Urge to the Sea.* Berkeley and Los Angeles: University of California Press, 1946.

Kinser, Samuel. *The Works of Jacques-Auguste de Thou.* The Hague: Martinus Nijhoff, 1966.

Kirchner, Walther. *Commercial Relations Between Russia and Europe: 1400 to 1800.* Bloomington: Indiana University Press, 1966.

_____.*The Rise of the Baltic Question.* Newark: University of Delaware Press, 1954.

Kleimola, A. M. "Up Through Servitude: The Changing Condition of the Muscovite Elite in the Sixteenth and Seventeenth Centuries." *Russian History* 6 (1979), 210–29.

Kliuchevskii, V. O. *Boiarskaia duma drevnei Rusi.* Petrograd, 1919.

_____.*A Course in Russian History: The Seventeenth Century.* Chicago: Quadrangle, 1968.

_____.*Skazaniia inostrantsev o moskovskom gosudarstve.* Petrograd, 1918.

_____.*Sochineniia.* 8 vols. Moscow, 1956–59.

Konovalov, S., ed. "Thomas Chamberlayne's Description of Russia, 1631." *Oxford Slavonic Papers* 5 (1954), 107–16.

Kopanev, A. I., and Man'kov, A. G., eds. *Vosstanie I. Bolotnikova: Dokumenty i materialy.* Moscow: Izd-vo sotsial'no-ekon. lit-ry, 1959.

Korb, Johann Georg. *Diary of an Austrian Secretary of Legation at the Court of Czar Peter the Great.* 2 vols. London: Bradbury & Evans, 1863.

Koretskii, V. I. *Formirovanie krepostnogo prava i pervaia krest'ianskaia voina v Rossii.* Moscow: Nauka, 1975.

_____."Iz istorii krest'ianskoi voiny v Rossii nachala XVII veka." *Voprosy istorii* 15, no. 3 (1959), 118–37.

Koretskii, V. I., and Stanislavskii, A. L. "Amerikanskii istorik o Lzhedmitrii I." *Istoriia SSSR* 14, no. 2 (1969), 238–44.

Kostomarov, N. I. *Smutnoe vremia moskovskago gosudarstva v nachale XVII stoletiia.* Vol. II of *Sobranie sochinenii.* St. Petersburg, 1904.

Kusheva, E. N. *Narody severnogo Kavkaza i ikh sviazi s Rossiei.* Moscow: AN SSSR, 1963.

Lantzeff, George V. *Siberia in the Seventeenth Century.* Berkeley and Los Angeles: University of California Press, 1943.

Lappo-Danilevskii, A. S. *Organizatsiia priamogo oblozheniia v moskovskom gosudarstve so vremen smuty do epokhi preobrazovaniia.* St. Petersburg: Tip. I. N. Skorokhodova, 1890.

Leitsch, Walter. "Herberstein's Impact on the Reports about Muscovy in the Sixteenth and Seventeenth Centuries—Some Observations on the Technique of Borrowing." *Forschungen zur Osteuropäischen Geschichte* 24 (1978), 163–77.

Limonov, Iu. A. *Kul'turnye sviazi Rossii s evropeiskimi stranami v XV–XVII vv.* Leningrad: Nauka, 1978.

McFarlane, I. D. *A Literary History of France: Renaissance France, 1470–1589.* New York: Barnes and Noble, 1974.

Makovskii, D. P. *Razvitie tovarno-denezhnykh otnoshenii v sel'skom khoziaistve russkogo gosudarstva v XVI veke.* Smolensk, 1963.

Mansuy, Abel. *Le Monde slave et les classiques français aux XVIe–XVIIe siècles.* Paris: H. Champion, 1912.

Margeret, Jacques. *Estat de l'Empire de Russie et Grand Duché de Moscovie. Avec ce qui s'y est passé de plus memorable & Tragique, pendant le regne de quatre Empereurs: à sçavoir depuis l'an 1590. iusques en l'an 1606. en Septembre.* Paris: M. Guillemot, 1607.

_____.*Estat de l'Empire de Russie et Grand Duché de Moscovie.* Paris: Langlois, 1669.

_____.*Estat de l'Empire de Russie et Grand Duché de Moscovie.* Edited by Julius Klaproth. Paris, 1821.

_____.*Estat de l'Empire de Russie et Grand Duché de Moscovie.* Edited by Henri Chevreul. Paris: L. Potier, 1860.

_____.*Estat de l'Empire de Russie et Grand Duché de Moscovie.* Paris: Éditions du Genet, 1946.

_____.*Istoricheskiia zapiski.* Moscow: Tip. Lazarevykh instituta vostochnykh iazykov, 1830.

_____.*Sostoianie Rossiiskoi Derzhavy i Velikago Kniazhestva Moskovskago.* Translated and edited by Nikolai Ustrialov. St. Petersburg: Tip. Glavnago Upravleniia Putei Soobshcheniia, 1830.

_____.*Sostoianie Rossiiskoi Derzhavy i Velikago Kniazhestva Moskovskago.* 3rd ed. St Petersburg, [1859?].

_____.*Sostoianie Rossiiskoi Derzhavy i Velikago Kniazhestva Moskovskago.* Moscow: "Pol'za," 1913.

Martino, Pierre. *L'Orient dans la littérature française au XVIIe et au XVIIIe siècles.* Paris: Hachette, 1906.

Massa, Isaac. *Histoire des guerres de la Moscovie.* 2 vols. Brussels: F. J. Olivier, 1866.

_____.*Kratkoe izvestie o Moskovii v nachale XVII veka.* Moscow: Sotsekgiz, 1937.

200 **BIBLIOGRAPHY**

Materialy po istorii SSSR. Vol. II. Moscow, 1955.

Mayerberg, Augustin, Baron de. *Relation d'un voyage en Moscovie.* 2 vols. Paris: Bibliothèque Russe et Polonaise, 1858.

Mercator, Gerard, and Hondius, Henry. *Atlas or a Geographicke Description of the Regions, Countries, and Kingdomes of the World.* Vol. I. Amsterdam, 1636.

Mérimée, Prosper. *Épisode de l'histoire de Russie—les Faux Démétrius.* Paris: C. Lévy, 1897.

Mérimée, Prosper. "Mémoires contemporains relatifs aux faux Démétrius." In *Mémoires historiques (inédits),* pp. 163–206. Paris: F. Bernouard, 1927.

Miege, Guy. *A Relation of Three Embassies from His Sacred Majestie Charles II to the Great Duke of Moscovie.* London: J. Starkey, 1669.

Milton, John. *Milton's Literary Craftsmanship: A Study of "A Brief History of Moscovia."* Princeton: Princeton University Press, 1941.

Mongault, Henri. "Mérimée et l'histoire russe—I." *Le Monde slave.* 1932, no. 8, pp. 192–216.

Montaigne. *The Complete Works of Montaigne.* Stanford: Stanford University Press, 1967.

Morgan, E. D., and Coote, C. H., eds. *Early Voyages and Travels to Russia and Persia by Anthony Jenkinson and Other Englishmen.* 2 vols. London: Hakluyt Society, 1886.

Nechkina, M. V. *Vasilii Osipovich Kliuchevskii.* Moscow: Nauka, 1974.

Ocherki istorii SSSR. Period feodalizma. Konets XV v.–nachalo XVII v. Moscow: AN SSSR, 1955.

Olearius, Adam. *The Travels of Olearius in Seventeenth-Century Russia.* Stanford: Stanford University Press, 1967.

Palitsyn, Avraami. *Skazanie Avraamiia Palitsyna.* Moscow-Leningrad: AN SSSR, 1955.

Paris, Louis, ed. and trans. *La Chronique de Nestor . . . accompagnée de notes et d'un recueil de pièces inédites touchant les anciennes relations de la Russie avec la France.* 2 vols. Paris: Heideloff et Campé, 1834–35.

Pelenski, Jaroslaw. *Russia and Kazan.* The Hague: Mouton, 1974.

Pierling, Paul. *Dimitri dit le Faux et les Jésuites.* Paris: A. Picard, 1913.

————.*Dimitri dit le Faux et Possevino.* Paris: Picard, 1914.

————.*Rome et Démétrius.* Paris: E. Laroux, 1878.

————.*La Russie et le Saint-Siège: Études diplomatiques.* 3 vols. Paris: Plon, Nourrit, 1896–1901.

Pirling, Pavel (Paul Pierling). *Iz Smutnago Vremeni: Stat'i i zametki.* St. Petersburg: A. S. Suvorin, 1902.

Platonov, S. F. *Boris Godunov.* Gulf Breeze, Fla.: Academic International, 1973.

_____.*Moscow and the West.* Hattiesburg, Miss.: Academic International, 1972.

_____.*Ocherki po istorii smuty v moskovskom gosudarstve XVI–XVII vv.* St. Petersburg: Bashmakov, 1910.

_____.*Stat'i po russkoi istorii.* St. Petersburg: Tip. M. A. Aleksandrova, 1912.

_____.*The Time of Troubles.* Lawrence: University Press of Kansas, 1970.

Polnoe sobranie russkikh letopisei. 31 vols. St. Petersburg-Moscow: Arkheograficheskaia Kommissiia, 1841–1968.

Polosin, I. I. *Sotsial'no-politicheskaia istoriia Rossii XVI–nachala XVII v.* Moscow: Akademiia Nauk SSSR, 1963.

Polybius. *The Histories.* 6 vols. Cambridge, Mass.: Harvard University Press, 1975.

Possevino, Antonio. *The Moscovia.* Pittsburgh: University Center for International Studies, University of Pittsburgh, 1977.

Prawdin, Michael. *The Mongol Empire.* New York: Macmillan, 1967.

PSRL. See *Polnoe sobranie russkikh letopisei.*

Purchas, Samuel. *Hakluytus Posthumus, or Purchas His Pilgrimes.* 20 vols. Glasgow: MacLehose, 1905–07.

Pushkarev, Sergei G. *Dictionary of Russian Historical Terms from the Eleventh Century to 1917.* New Haven: Yale University Press, 1970.

Pushkin, A. S. *Boris Godunov.* Chicago: Russian Language Specialties, 1965.

Rambaud, Alfred. *History of Russia.* 3 vols. New York: AMS Press, 1970.

Razin, E. A. *Istoriia voennogo iskusstva.* 3 vols. Moscow: Voenizdat, 1955–61.

RIB. See *Russkaia istoricheskaia biblioteka.*

Rouillard, Clarence Dana. *The Turk in French History, Thought, and Literature, 1520–1660.* Paris: Boivin, 1941.

Rowland, Daniel. "The Problem of Advice in Muscovite Tales about the Time of Troubles." *Russian History* 6 (1979), 259–83.

Rudakov, A. A. "Razvitie legendy o smerti tsarevicha Dimitriia v Ugliche." *Istoricheskie zapiski* 12 (1941), 254–83.

Ruffman, Karl Heinz. *Das Russlandbild im England Shakespeares.* Göttingen, 1952.

Russkaia istoricheskaia biblioteka. 2nd ed. 39 vols. St Petersburg-Leningrad: Arkheograficheskaia Kommissiia, 1872–1927.

Seredonin, S. M. *Sochinenie Dzhil'sa Fletchera "Of The Russe Commonwealth" kak istoricheskii istochnik.* St. Petersburg: I. N. Skorokhodov, 1891.

Sergeevich, V. I. *Russkie iuridicheskie drevnosti.* 3 vols. St. Petersburg: Tip. N. A. Lebedeva, 1890–1903.

SGGD. See *Sobranie gosudarstvennykh gramot i dogovorov.*

Shmurlo, E. F. *Kurs russkoi istorii.* Vol. II, Prague, 1933.

Skrynnikov, R. G. *Boris Godunov.* Moscow: Nauka, 1978.

―――."Boris Godunov i Tsarevich Dmitrii." *Trudy Leningradskogo otdeleniia instituta istorii* 12 (1971), 182–97.

―――."Boris Godunov's Struggle for the Throne." *Canadian-American Slavic Studies* 11 (1977), 325–53.

―――."Politicheskaia bor'ba v nachale pravleniia Borisa Godunova." *Istoriia SSSR* 20, no. 2 (1975), 48–68.

Smirnov, I. I. *Vosstanie Bolotnikova 1606–1607.* Leningrad: AN SSSR, 1951.

Smith, R. E. F. *Peasant Farming in Muscovy.* Cambridge: Cambridge University Press, 1977.

Sobranie gosudarstvennykh gramot i dogovorov. 5 vols. St. Petersburg, 1813–94.

Solov'ev, S. M. *Istoriia Rossii s drevneishikh vremen.* 15 vols. Moscow: AN SSSR, 1959–66.

Staden, Heinrich von. *The Land and Government of Muscovy.* Stanford: Stanford University Press, 1967.

Stashevskii, E. D. "Sluzhiloe soslovie." In *Russkaia istoriia v ocherkakh i stat'iakh,* edited by M. V. Dovnar-Zapol'skii, vol. 3, pp. 1–33. Kiev, 1912.

Struys, Jean. *Les Voyages de Jean Struys en Moscovie, en Tartarie, aux Indes, et en d'autres pays étrangers.* Amsterdam: Veuve de J. van Meurs, 1681.

Szeftel, Marc. "La Monarchie absolue dans l'état moscovite et l'empire Russe." In *Russian Institutions and Culture up to Peter the Great,* pp. 727–57. London: Valorium Reprints, 1975.

―――."The Title of the Muscovite Monarch up to the End of the Seventeenth Century." *Canadian-American Slavic Studies* 13 (1979), pp. 59–81.

Thompson, A. H. "The Legend of Tsarevich Dimitry: Some Evidence of an Oral Tradition." *Slavonic and East European Review* 46 (1968), 48–59.

de Thou, Jacque-Auguste. *Histoire universelle.* 16 vols. London, 1734.

Tikhomirov, M. N. "Monastyr' votchinnik XVI v." *Istoricheskie zapiski* 3 (1938), 159–60.

―――.*Rossiia v XVI stoletii.* Moscow: AN SSSR, 1962.

―――."Samozvanshchina." *Nauka i zhizn'.* 1969, no. 1, pp. 116–21.

Timofeev, Ivan. *Vremennik Ivana Timofeeva.* Moscow-Leningrad: AN SSSR, 1951.

Treadgold, Donald W. *The West in Russia and China.* 2 vols. Cambridge: Cambridge University Press, 1973.

Troitskii, S. M. "Samozvantsy v Rossii XVII–XVIII vekov." *Voprosy istorii* 44, no. 3 (1969), 134–46.

Tsvetaev, D. *Protestantstvo i protestanty v Rossii do epokhi preobrazovanii.* Moscow: Univ. tip., 1890.

Uroff, Benjamin P. "Grigorii Karpovich Kotoshikhin, *On Russia in the Reign of Alexis Mikhailovich.*" Ph.D. dissertation, Columbia University, 1970.

Ustrialov, Nikolai, ed. and trans. *Skazaniia sovremennikov o Dmitrii Samozvantse.* 3rd ed. 2 vols. St. Petersburg, 1859.

Vakar, N. P. "The Name 'White Russia.'" *American Slavic and East European Review* 8 (1949), 201–13.

Vernadsky, George. "The Death of the Tsarevich Dimitry: A Reconsideration of the Case." *Oxford Slavonic Papers* 4 (1954), 1–19.

——.*The Mongols and Russia.* New Haven: Yale University Press, 1953.

——.*Russia at the Dawn of the Modern Age.* New Haven: Yale University Press, 1959.

——.*The Tsardom of Moscow, 1547–1682.* 2 vols. New Haven: Yale University Press, 1969.

Veselovskii, S. B. *Feodal'noe zemlevladenie v severo-vostochnoi Rusi.* Moscow-Leningrad: AN SSSR, 1947.

——.*Soshnoe pis'mo.* 2 vols. Moscow: 1915–16.

Wade, Ira O. *The Intellectual Origins of the French Enlightenment.* Princeton: Princeton University Press, 1971.

Waliszewski, K. *La Crise révolutionnaire, 1584–1614.* Paris: Plon-Nourrit, 1906.

Waugh, Daniel Clarke. *The Great Turkes Defiance.* Columbus, Ohio: Slavica Publishers, 1978.

Zabelin, I. E. *Domashnii byt russkikh tsarei v XVI i XVII st.* 3rd ed. 2 vols. Moscow: Tip. A. I. Mamontova, 1895–1915. [Vol. I, parts 1 and 2, of Zabelin, *Domashnii byt russkogo naroda v XVI i XVII st.*]

Zagorovskii, V. P. *Belgorodskaia cherta.* Voronezh: Izd. Voronezhskogo unta, 1969.

Zagoskin, N. P. *Istoriia prava moskovskogo gosudarstva.* 2 vols. Kazan: Universit. tip., 1877–79.

Zantuan, Konstanty. "The Discovery of Modern Russia: *Tractatus de duabus Sarmatiis.*" *Russian Review* 27 (1968), 327–37.

Zhordaniia, Givi. *Ocherki iz istorii franko-russkikh otnoshenii kontsa XVI i pervoi poloviny XVII v.* 2 vols. Tbilisi: Akademiia Nauk Gruzinskoi SSR, 1959.

——."Les premiers marchands et navigateurs français dans la région maritime de la Russie septentrionale: L'origine des relations commerciales et diplomatiques franco-russes." In *La Russie et l'Europe: XVIe–XXe siècles,* pp. 7–30. Paris: S.E.V.P.E.N., 1970.

Zimin, A. A. "Osnovnye etapy i formy klassovoi bor'by v Rossii kontsa XV–XVI veka." *Voprosy istorii* 40, no. 3 (1965), 38–52.

————.*Reformy Ivana Groznogo.* Moscow: Izd-vo sotsial'no-ekon. lit-ry, 1960.

Zlotnik, Marc D. "Muscovite Fiscal Policy: 1462–1584." *Russian History* 6 (1979), 243–58.

INDEX

Fedor Borisovich (tsar). *See*
Godunov, Fedor
Fedor Ivanovich (tsar): foreign relations of,
xv, 15, 111*n25;* and Boris Godunov,
16, 113*n34;* and Irina Godunova, 16,
18, 114*n35,* 117*n44;* death of, 18,
73, 117*n43;* mentioned, 68, 71, 80,
81, 112*n31*
Feodosia Fedorovna, 16, 114*n35*
First Peasant War, xxx, 168*n259,* 169*n261,*
172*n275,* 176*n290*
Foreigners in Russia, 26; French, xii,
xiii, xv, 76–77, 141*n149,* 175*nn286,*
288; sought by tsars, xiii, xvii, 87;
merchants, xiii, xv, 10, 23, 36, 39–40,
75, 76, 77, 82, 123*n66,* 175*nn286,*
288; English, xv, 10, 75, 82, 141*n149,*
184*n319;* Dutch, xv, 141*n149;*
soldiers, xviii, xix, 26, 42, 47, 63, 65,
97*n20,* 98*n36,* 124*nn72–73,* 141*n149,*
156*n212;* Catholics, 21, 22–23,
122*n57,* 148*nn173, 175,* 170*nn263,*
265, 186*n330,* 187*nn334–35;* Protestants, 22–23, 23–24, 122*n57,*
123*n64;* captives, 23–24, 26,
74–75, 123*n64,* 174*n282;* Livonians,
23–24, 97*n20,* 123*nn64–66;* Tatars
and Turks, 24; Persians, 24; Poles, 26,
47; Italians, 27, 125*n77;* Germans,
47, 156*n212,* 184*n322,* 189*n340;*
Greeks, 47; Swedes, 53–54, 141*n149;*
Danes, 59–60, 141*n149,*
150*nn188–89;* cook, 77, 175*n288. See
also* Margeret, Jacques
France: relations with Russia, xii–xv,
95*n6;* French in Russia, xii, xiii, xv,
76–77, 141*n149,* 175*nn286, 288;*
French interest in Russia, xxviii–xxix,
175*n286,* 179*n302,* 186*n330;* Dmitrii's
interest in, xxix, 75, 174*n283;* mentioned, xvii, xix, xxii, xxiii–xxx
passim, 4, 8, 11, 13, 48, 97*n26. See
also* Henri IV; Margeret, Jacques

French literature: works on Russia, xii,
xxvi, xxvii, xxviii–xxix, xxx, 102*n76;*
influence of, on Margeret, xvi, xxiv,
xxv, xxvi, xxx, 126*n80;* significance of
travel literature on, xxiii–xxvi
French Wars of Religion, xvi–xvii, xxv, 4

Galich, 82, 183*n317,* 184*n321*
Georgians, 48, 51, 52, 144*nn161–63,*
145*nn164–65*
Germany: Margeret in, xxii, xxiii; Germans in Russia, 47, 156*n212,*
184*n322,* 189*n340;* mentioned, 38,
57, 60
Godunov family, 16, 113*n32,* 191*nn345–
46;* overthrown, 66, 67, 159*n224,*
161*nn228–29,* 162*n232*
Godunov, Boris (tsar): Margeret's views
of, discussed, xxxii, 105*n98;* builds
towns and walls, 9, 16–17, 18,
125*n75;* rises to power, 16–20;
aspires to throne, 16, 114*nn35–36;*
and Fedor Ivanovich, 16, 18,
113*nn33–34,* 117*n43,* 135*n123;*
treatment of opponents, 17, 52–53,
60–61, 115*nn38–39,* 146*n169;* treatment of Nagoi family, 17, 60, 80,
81, 89, 113*n34,* 114*n37,* 115*nn38–
40,* 116*nn41–42,* 152*n196,* 191*n348,*
192*n351;* and Uglich affair, 17,
80–81, 115*n40,* 116*n42,* 173*n277,*
174*n280;* struggle for the throne,
18–20, 117*n44–119n49;* crowned tsar,
20, 121*n52;* seeks foreign marriage
alliances, 52, 53, 59–60, 146*n168,*
148*nn173–75,* 150*nn188–89;* treatment of Mstislavskii, 53, 146*n170;*
treatment of Simeon Bekbulatovich,
53, 147*n172;* treatment of Shuiskii
family, 53, 60, 146*n171,* 151*n193,*
192*n353;* illness of, in 1600, 54,
148*n177;* during famine, 58, 59,

28 Days